Brahms's
Choral Compositions and
His Library of Early Music

Studies in Musicology, No. 76

George Buelow, Series Editor

Professor of Music
Indiana University

Other Titles in This Series

Brahms's
Choral Compositions and His Library of Early Music

by
Virginia Hancock

UMI RESEARCH PRESS
Ann Arbor, Michigan

Produced and distributed by
UMI Research Press
an imprint of
University Microfilms International
Ann Arbor, Michigan 48106

Library of Congress Cataloging in Publication Data

Hancock, Virginia.
    Brahms's choral compositions and his library of
early music.

    (Studies in musicology ; no. 76)
    Originally presented as the author's thesis (D.M.A.—
University of Oregon, 1977) under the title: Brahms and
his library of early music : the effects of his study of
Renaissance and Baroque music on his choral writing.
    Bibliography: p.
    Includes index.
    1. Brahms, Johannes, 1833-1897. Choral music.
2. Composers—Germany—Biography. 3. Music—Bibliography—
Catalogs. 4. Gesellschaft der Musikfreunde in Wien—
Catalogs. I. Title. II. Series.

ML410.B8H19 1983   784'.092'4   83-18322
ISBN 0-8357-1496-9

Contents

Acknowledgments

The existence of the Brahms library in the Archiv of the Gesellschaft der Musikfreunde in Vienna made this book possible, and the help and friendly encouragement I received from Drs. Hedwig Mitringer and Otto Biba of the Archiv in 1975-76 made my investigation of the primary material a pleasure. Many of the secondary sources were located in the British Library, London, and the Musiksammlung of the Oesterreichische Nationalbibliothek, Vienna.

Christfriede Caesar-Larson patiently answered my questions about the German language and helped with several difficult translations; and without the alphabet provided by Helga Rilling, I would have had even more trouble deciphering Brahms's German script. Hans Michael Beuerle loaned me an advance copy of his dissertation, and provided me with several stimulating ideas. An opportunity to learn much of the Brahms a cappella choral repertoire was given me by Helmuth Rilling and the Gächinger Kantorei.

Professor Peter Bergquist of the University of Oregon was of inestimable help throughout the project, and an impetus in the early stages was provided by the singers of the Reed Collegium Musicum, who in 1975 illustrated a lecture-recital which helped to define the topic. My parents, Clark and Ardis Oglesby, provided constant encouragement; and John Hancock's steady support, interest, and patience—together with his skill as copyist of the music examples—were invaluable assets through the years we spent with Brahms.

1

Early Music Study and Performance in the Life of Brahms

Johannes Brahms was born in 1833, four years after Mendelssohn's revival of the *St. Matthew Passion*. He died in 1897, shortly before the close of the nineteenth century. Thus he lived and worked throughout the period of the great nineteenth-century revival of interest in early music, and he himself contributed substantially to that revival.

As a child in Hamburg, he was given a thorough classical piano and theory training by his teachers, Friedrich Cossel and Eduard Marxsen, and his first solo concert contained a Bach fugue—an unusual choice in that period of virtuoso performances.[1] Nothing is known about the repertoire of his first choir, a small men's chorus which he conducted in Winsen in the summer of 1847, except that he wrote two pieces for it, one of which showed "a feeling for independent part-writing."[2] However, it is certain that his interest in early polyphonic music had already begun to develop before April 1853, when he left Hamburg with Eduard Reményi on the concert tour which resulted in Brahms's friendships with Joseph Joachim and the Schumanns. By this time he had already copied out works by Palestrina, Corsi, Durante, and Lotti which he kept in his library all his life.

Robert and Clara Schumann and their friends encouraged Brahms not only in his composing and playing, but also in his interest in early music.[3] Schumann had carefully studied the keyboard works of Bach, and also had a high regard for Palestrina and his Italian followers which had developed during his days as a student in Heidelberg, when Anton Thibaut, the author of *Über Reinheit der Tonkunst,* had been one of his law professors. He had rehearsed works by Palestrina, Lasso, Lotti, and Bach with his chorus in Düsseldorf, and had a good-sized collection of early music in his personal library, including a number of the important earlier nineteenth-century collections.[4] After Schumann's breakdown and hospitalization in February 1854, Brahms moved to Düsseldorf to be with

Clara and to stay with the children when she was away on tour. He spent a large part of his time in Schumann's library, first organizing it,[5] and then studying and copying material from it. By early 1855 he was systematically studying counterpoint on his own, reporting progress in writing "all possible sorts of canons" to Clara;[6] and in February 1856 he embarked on a cooperative program of contrapuntal study with Joachim, who was never as enthusiastic about the project as Brahms, but who faithfully evaluated the large amount of material that Brahms sent to him, and cheerfully paid his fines when he failed to produce his own share of music.[7] Brahms later destroyed most of his counterpoint exercises along with a mass of sketches and other unpublished material, but his earliest surviving choral works belong to this period.[8]

The exchange of counterpoint studies was broken off by Schumann's death in July 1856 and never really revived, though Brahms and Joachim discussed the possibility occasionally for another several years. However, Brahms continued his own investigation of early music. During a trip to Switzerland made with Clara Schumann, two of her children, and Brahms's sister Elise shortly after Schumann's death, he spent some time in the monastery library at Einsiedeln, where he copied out a number of keyboard works by Frescobaldi. Once he had returned to live in Hamburg, he made considerable use of the city library, patronized the second-hand bookshops, and renewed his friendships with members of the city's musical establishment who shared his interests and encouraged him to use their private libraries as well as helping him add to his own.[9]

In 1857, Brahms's appointment as choral conductor to the small court at Detmold provided him with a practical reason for the diligent study and accumulation of choral repertoire. He held the position for three consecutive autumn seasons, each time earning enough in a few months to support himself for the rest of the year and enable him to devote his time to further study and composition. During the 1857 season, he concentrated on a cappella works (see Appendix 1), while in his second season he tackled two Bach cantatas. In Hamburg, meanwhile, he had begun to direct a ladies' choir, for which he composed a number of pieces and also arranged works by other composers (see Appendix 1). Throughout the years in Detmold and Hamburg, with the help and advice of such friends as Joachim, Clara, and Julius Otto Grimm added to his own experience, Brahms was acquiring practical knowledge in all areas of choral music—repertoire, directing, and composing for voices.

One of the reasons Brahms stayed on in Hamburg until 1862 was that he hoped to be chosen as the new director of the Philharmonic concerts there. When, in the middle of his first visit to Vienna for the 1862-63 winter season, he learned that his friend Julius Stockhausen had been chosen instead, his disappointment was severe. However, he had had a considerable artistic success in Vienna, had made a number of good friends, and had enjoyed the opportunities the city had to offer, including the two excellent music libraries, the Hofbibliothek (now the Nationalbibliothek) and the Archiv of the Gesellschaft der Musikfreunde (also known as the Musikverein). Therefore, when he was offered the position of director of the Wiener Singakademie for the 1863-64 season, he accepted enthusiastically and returned to Vienna with high hopes.

Although Brahms was happy in Vienna and eventually settled there permanently, the Singakademie proved to be a disappointment, since his attempt to put into practice his ideas of what an ideal choral society should be met with resistance on the part of both the members of the society and the public. His first performance, which included the first Viennese performance of Bach's Cantata 21, "Ich hatte viel Bekümmernis," as well as works by Beethoven and Schumann (see Appendix 1), was a musical and critical success. By the second, however, the charm of novelty had worn off; and a largely a cappella program consisting of early music by the composers Schütz, Gabrieli, Rovetta, and Eccard, with works by Beethoven and Mendelssohn as the only more up-to-date offerings, inadequately prepared by the chorus and badly performed by the poor instrumentalists who were all that the Singakademie could afford to hire, was altogether too dismal for press and public alike, especially at the beginning of the carnival season. Clara Schumann wrote to Brahms urging him to attempt a more gradual transformation of Viennese musical taste:

> Unfortunately I have heard that your second concert didn't go well, that the chorus wasn't enough prepared—why didn't you put it off? Then I heard that you had done the sort of old sacred pieces that people in Vienna don't like—is that true? Surely you did other things as well, and then one or two such old pieces could perhaps be pleasing![10]

The situation was made worse by the rivalry of the Singverein of the Gesellschaft der Musikfreunde, a larger, more competent, and far better financed group, which moreover had a large orchestra available for its concerts. Thus when the Singakademie performed sections of Bach's *Christmas Oratorio* as its third concert under Brahms within a few days of the Singverein's *St. John Passion,* the contrast was not at all flattering to Brahms. He improved his standing slightly with his last concert of the season, which he was persuaded to make up entirely of his own works; but although he was offered a three-year renewal of his contract, he decided to give up the position, and in future to undertake such a responsibility only on his own terms.

During the next several years, Brahms traveled a great deal, but he always returned to Vienna, where he became more and more settled. He continued his studies in the Hofbibliothek and the Archiv of the Musik-verein, where the librarian, C. F. Pohl, became a close friend. The great success of the *Deutsches Requiem* meant that, from about 1869 onwards, Brahms could support himself entirely by composing, and no longer needed to appear as a performer—either pianist or conductor—unless he chose to. He was briefly tempted in 1870 to become the director of the Or-chesterverein of the Gesellschaft der Musikfreunde, but decided not to on the grounds that he really wanted a choir to direct as well.[11] In 1872, however, he was persuaded to accept the position of musical director of the Gesellschaft, with responsibility for both the chorus (the Singverein) and the orchestra. He held this position for three years.

As had been the case when he conducted the Singakademie (and probably also the Detmold choir, although for that period we have far less information), Brahms was only a qualified success in this new position. His musical taste was too severe for the bulk of the Vienna concert-going public of the 1870s, and he was firmly opposed to the practice of per-forming new works simply for their novelty value.[12] He demanded too much work from his amateur singers: almost his first official act was to double the number of rehearsals and to institute section rehearsals. He also found the political and organizational responsibilities of such a post uncongenial. His performances were, nevertheless, generally well re-ceived, and he successfully introduced a number of Bach and Handel works to Vienna, along with occasional smaller pieces of early music and several of his own choral works (see Appendix 1).

In 1875 he gave up the position at the Musikverein, and from then on he only directed other conductors' choirs and orchestras, almost al-ways in performances of his own compositions. In this later part of his career, he took more of a scholar's (or a pedagogue's) than a performer's interest in early music, although in 1879 he devoted a large amount of time to realization of the figured basses of the Italian duets and trios for Chrysander's edition of the complete works of Handel.[13] He continued to greet each new volume of the Bach collected edition with enthusiasm, reading through it carefully; and when Philipp Spitta's edition of the com-plete works of Schütz began to appear in 1885 he was equally delighted,[14] studied and marked the volumes with his usual thoroughness, and copied out a number of passages of particular interest (A130, 21-24). He also copied one of these Schütz fragments into the collection of counterpoint examples which he himself entitled "Oktaven and Quinten" (A132). This collection, which illustrates Brahms's long-continuing interest in the study of counterpoint, particularly in cases where the strict rules might be considered to have been broken, contains examples by composers ranging from Victoria through Bach and Beethoven to Bizet.

Brahms's last compositions for chorus were the three motets Op. 110, probably written in the summer of 1889.[15] He participated in the establishment of both *Denkmäler deutscher Tonkunst* (1892) and *Denkmäler der Tonkunst in Oesterreich* (1894), but did not live long enough to receive many of their volumes. His last compositions, the eleven chorale preludes for organ Op. 122, were completed in 1896 and published in 1902, several years after his death. They show clearly that his long involvement with early music continued to bear fruit to the end of his life.

What is meant by the phrase "early music" in the context of Brahms's life and career? For him, as for most of his contemporaries, the earliest music of real interest was that by composers of the middle and late Renaissance in Italy and Germany—men such as Isaac, Senfl, Palestrina, Lasso, Eccard, and Praetorius. Although work on still earlier periods of music was going on throughout Brahms's life, his library shows no evidence of any concern with it. "Early music" was considered to end with the music of Bach and Handel, whose more up-to-date German contemporaries such as Mattheson and C. P. E. Bach would be included only insofar as their writings helped to illuminate the older tradition.[16]

Brahms's interest in early music seems to have been considered at least unusual, if not actually eccentric, by most of his contemporaries. It is true that his strong historical bias is also shown by the character of his interest in the music of Haydn, Mozart, Beethoven, and Schubert; the scholars Pohl, Nottebohm, and Mandyczewski were among his best friends in Vienna, and he came into contact with Otto Jahn in Bonn during the 1850s while Schumann was hospitalized there. However, the music of these composers was part of the living Classic-Romantic tradition, and was accepted by performers and audiences alike. The value of early music was still a matter for debate;[17] and in order to hear such works, enthusiasts had first in many instances to prepare their own editions, next to convince performers to try them, and then to drum up audiences prepared to listen to and perhaps even appreciate their esoteric efforts.

One of the outgrowths of Romanticism was the awakening and subsequent development of historical consciousness in music as in other areas. At first, old things had a purely antiquarian appeal, but the simple collector's instinct deepened into a further urge toward study and classification, and finally toward actual revival, either for re-creation in performance or for assimilation and eventual use in the process of new creation. We can see this sequence at work in the young Brahms of the 1850s: at first he bought old books and copied pieces of old music mainly

because they *were* old; then, encouraged by Schumann but also com-
pelled by his own instincts, he undertook a more systematic collection
and study; and finally he put his new knowledge into practice in contrapuntal exercises and compositions. Although these works may have originated as attempts to duplicate an antique style, they persistently show
the composer's individuality.[18]

By the early 1850s, the period of Brahms's developing awareness of
pre-Classical vocal music, the revival of Bach's oratorios and cantatas
was well under way, although performances were still fairly rare events.
Handel's oratorios hardly needed reviving, since they had been maintained in the English choral repertoire, and by this time had found their
way back into active German musical life. Composers of earlier periods
were also receiving an increasing amount of attention: the publication of
sacred works by Palestrina and his Italian contemporaries and followers
was accelerating under the sponsorship of the Catholic church; and the
composers of the German Renaissance and of early Baroque Italy and
Germany were beginning to be known, largely through the enormous
efforts of Carl von Winterfeld.[19]

Most composers of choral music in the first half of the nineteenth
century were not especially affected by these developments. Those such
as Schubert who wrote fugal sections in their masses at the traditional
places were participating in the unbroken *prima prattica* tradition trans-
mitted through the Viennese codifiers of counterpoint, Fux and his successors, rather than receiving ideas directly from Palestrina and other
composers of the late Renaissance. E. T. A. Hoffmann, on the other
hand, did feel himself to be inspired by Palestrina as the exemplar of the
pure a cappella ideal of religious music;[20] his passionate, mystical enthusiasm is far removed from the Cecilian movement's later adoption of Palestrina as the model of unsullied, unsecularized Catholic music. From
neither viewpoint were composers able to write successful imitations of
Palestrina. Opera and oratorio composers occasionally used techniques
consciously derived from early music to establish an archaic or religious
atmosphere for a scene—for example, Schumann included a canonic chorus in the death scene of *Manfred*—but such uses for dramatic effect
were by no means new.

Mendelssohn was the only composer of this period who made an
important effort to write choral music which belonged to the earlier tradition in both genre and style,[21] and is thus the only one up to mid-
century whose choral works could not have been produced without the
influence of the early music revival. Like the others, however, he apparently felt that techniques from the older style were suitable for use only
in serious music; he helped to meet the needs of the proliferating amateur

choral societies for lighter music by writing simple, tuneful pieces in homophonic style. Thus the old distinction between *prima* and *secunda prattica,* developed through the Classic period into a contrast between contrapuntal (often sacred) and homophonic choral styles, was perpetuated in the contrast between serious works, which could contain learned devices adopted from the old music, and light pieces which taxed the abilities of neither composers nor singers, and which were produced in great quantity. Under the circumstances, it is not surprising that one of the principal reasons a substantial amount of early vocal music was in circulation in handwritten copies, and an increasing number of such works was being published, was that good amateur choirs were hard pressed to find music that was really satisfying to sing.[22]

Brahms's career as a composer, while it came after the initial rediscovery of Bach and Palestrina, coincided with the further spread of interest in their music and the widening of that interest to include the study, publication, and performance of works by other Renaissance and Baroque composers. During the second half of the nineteenth century, this tendency, in combination with nationalistic fervor and enthusiasm for folk music in Brahms and a number of his fellow German musicians, resulted in a particular interest in specifically German early music like the polyphonic Lieder of the Renaissance and the compositions of Heinrich Schütz.

Brahms was unique among the important composers of his time in his interest in early music and in his expert knowledge of the developing area of music history. He was also, for his time, a uniquely prolific and successful composer of choral music which has continued to hold an important place in the repertoire in almost all of the main categories of choral composition—large and small, sacred and secular, a cappella and accompanied. Only in the areas of liturgical music and compositions for male chorus is his contribution to the repertoire of no special significance. It seems reasonable to conclude that there must be some causal connection between these phenomena; and, indeed, this conclusion is reached by nearly all writers on Brahms who have given any serious thought to his choral writing, among them Spitta, Hohenemser, Evans, Kalbeck, Niemann, Geiringer, Kross, James, and Beuerle.[23]

The thesis of the present work is that some aspects of the Renaissance and Baroque attitudes to choral music, together with actual techniques of composition, had an influence on Brahms's thinking that helps to account for the high quality and success of his choral writing. An attempt will be made to demonstrate the existence of this connection and illustrate some of its effects by examining first the works of early music which Brahms himself knew and studied, and then his own choral compositions.

It is clearly of great importance to such a study to establish with reasonable confidence *which* works Brahms gave his attention to. In addition to his efforts in the field of early music performance, he amassed a considerable collection of Renaissance and Baroque music, much of which he copied himself, and also a number of books and journals on the subject. It is certain, of course, that he was acquainted with any piece which he himself copied or performed, and it can usually be assumed that it was of some musical value to him for it to be worth the effort. There is also the evidence of the many marks that he made in his books and printed music; sometimes these annotations are cryptic or illegible, but often it is possible to learn his opinion of a particular statement or musical idea. These kinds of evidence are particularly important in the case of a composer like Brahms, who was as a rule reticent about what he considered significant in music.[24] It is therefore fortunate that his library survives, essentially intact, in the Archiv of the Gesellschaft der Musikfreunde. The examination of Brahms's collection in the field of early music forms the core of the present study.

2

Early Music in Brahms's Library

The Collection in the Archiv of the Gesellschaft der Musikfreunde

Beginning in his youth in Hamburg, Brahms was a passionate collector of books and music. When he had money, he spent it to add to his library, and when he did not, he copied music out by hand and thus continued to increase the size of his collection. As he grew older and more successful, he was able to buy the things he wanted, including a number of important manuscripts; he had no further need to copy music himself, unless it was available only in libraries or he wanted to make brief extracts for some reason. As a successful composer, he was also often presented with gifts for his library by grateful enthusiasts or by ambitious authors or fellow musicians. After his death, his very large collection was eventually left to the Gesellschaft der Musikfreunde in Vienna, according to his wishes.[1]

Brahms's library has been described by various writers,[2] but only the non-musical part of the collection has been carefully catalogued.[3] He himself kept a catalog for more than thirty years;[4] and although the information it contains is far from complete, as a private record of the accumulation of his library it is an exceedingly interesting document. Brahms kept his catalog in a large notebook; unfortunately it was carelessly rebound in the library at some time, and the pages were trimmed so that some words at the edges are cut off. Starting from one end of the book, the reader finds nonmusical books arranged by author on pages headed by letters of the alphabet. If one turns the volume over and starts from the other end, he finds music and books about music arranged in a similar way, except that some composers receive their own pages before the general entries under their letters of the alphabet—Joh. Seb. Bach and Beethoven, for example. A number of entries were clearly made at the time the catalog was first laid out, since they are in the same ink and the same handwriting as the letters which head the pages;[5] later entries appear below and between the original ones, and often spill over onto empty pages that face less-used letters of the alphabet. After the main alphabetical section, there are further pages of lists of autographs (both musical and nonmusical, including a number of letters), other handwritten music, and dedications. Finally, after several blank pages follows a twelve-page pencil list of loans of books and music to Brahms's friends, begun in January 1879, with each item crossed out as it was returned. Brahms seems to have stopped making entries in this volume in 1888, which is the last date of any newly published work that appears in it.

Brahms later revised and recopied this catalog.[6] Like the earlier version, the new one is laid out so that music and nonmusical material can be approached from opposite ends of the volume. However, autographs and other handwritten materials are included in the main alphabetical list instead of being separated, and there are no lists of dedications or loans. Works published up to 1897, the year of Brahms's death, are included. The musical portion of this revised catalog was published by Alfred Orel in the 1930s[7] with an introduction but no further information on the items in the list beyond that supplied by Brahms himself. In this version of the catalog there is often even less bibliographic detail than Brahms provided in his original list.[8]

The compilation of an adequate catalog of Brahms's complete holdings of music and of books on music is beyond the scope of this investigation. Such an undertaking would be complicated by the fact that his music collection is not separated from the general holdings in music in the Archiv, nor is there a separate section of the card catalog which lists this material. (In the book collection of the Archiv, there is a separate shelf area for the material from Brahms's library; furthermore, his books about music are shelved apart from the nonmusic books which have been catalogued by Hofmann.) However, the present writer did attempt to locate and examine all of the items listed in Orel's catalog (Brahms's revised catalog) that might have relevance to the subject of early music. They are described in later sections of this chapter.

A few items from the Orel catalog are missing from the Archiv, and at this time it is not known whether they have perhaps been mislaid, or whether Brahms himself might have given some of them away.[9] Also, Brahms in his informal will said that after his death his friends should be allowed to choose items from his library for themselves, with certain exceptions and in consultation with Simrock and Mandyczewski.[10] This provision may account for the absence of all four of the collections of early music edited by Franz Wüllner which Brahms certainly owned.[11] If such requests were made and honored, no record of actual removals from the collection is now available. In at least one case it seems that a request was denied: Chrysander asked for a work by Reinhard Keiser published in 1713[12] which is still in the Archiv, presumably because Mandyczewski was reluctant to let it go.

Handwritten copies (*Abschriften*) form a special part of Brahms's library, especially in early music. Those made by Brahms himself are kept with his other autographs in the Archiv, as are a number of the copies made for him by his friends. Other Abschriften are part of the general music collection, and only a notation on the catalog card and a stamp on the manuscript signify that they once belonged to Brahms. Until now, no catalog of any of this material has been made, although a few incomplete and to some extent inaccurate lists have been compiled. The Abschriften are the subject of the next sections of this chapter.

Brahms Abschriften

Brahms made manuscript copies of works of early music for a variety of reasons which can often be deduced from the manuscripts themselves. Some works he wanted to add to his library were not available in convenient modern editions.[13] Also, the young Brahms may not have had the money to buy published versions. In addition, he used copying as an aid in the study of early music techniques. Some pieces he may have rewritten in order to simplify their study, as in the cases where double choir works which he owned in full score published versions appear in the Abschriften in reduced score. His studies in notation include a number of transcriptions from lute and organ tablature; he also prepared several scores or portions of scores from partbooks. Sometimes, especially later in his career, when he could afford to buy all the newly published music he wanted, in addition to marking the printed versions he copied short extracts to add to his collection of counterpoint examples ("Oktaven und Quinten," A132); there are also several sheets of fragments from the complete works of Schütz.

Knowing of his interest in early music, several of Brahms's friends provided him with handwritten copies. Clara Schumann volunteered to write out pieces that interested him;[14] and several of her copies are bound into one of the collections (A134, 29-34) along with a professional copy of a W. F. Bach work ordered for Brahms as a gift by Joachim. Julius Allgeyer copied the entire contents of two sixteenth-century Catholic songbooks for him;[15] and the grateful Philharmonic Society of Karlsruhe presented him with beautifully copied scores of all five volumes of Georg Forster's *Ein aussbund schöner Teutscher Liedlein* to commemorate the first performance of the *Deutsches Requiem* in that city.[16] Copies of early music made by Robert Schumann and by Gustav Nottebohm, which presumably came to Brahms after their deaths, are also found in his collection. In addition to the Abschriften Brahms made himself and those made by identifiable friends of his, there are a number by unknown copyists.

After Brahms's death, when the bulk of his library eventually reached the Archiv of the Gesellschaft der Musikfreunde, it was catalogued by Eusebius Mandyczewski, Pohl's successor as Archivar and a close personal friend of Brahms.[17] A number of items which had been in the care of the Wiener Stadtbibliothek were transferred to the Archiv during the 1930s and added to the collection.[18] At present, all the Abschriften which are classified as Brahms manuscripts are as follows: they are in Brahms's hand unless otherwise stated. The last two items do not appear in Mandyczewski's catalog.

A128. Collection of folk songs from different countries.
        (25 sheets, unbound)
A129. Folk songs from the Siebengebirge, collected by Friedrich Wilhelm Arnold. Not in Brahms's hand.
        (29 sheets, bound)
A130. Copies of works from the sixteenth to eighteenth centuries.
        (46 sheets, unbound)
A131. Copies of canons.
        (13 sheets)
A132. "Octaven u. Quinten u. A.," the counterpoint examples.
        (7 sheets, unbound)
A133. Works by Schubert.
        (35 sheets)
A134. Palestrina's *Missa Papae Marcelli* and other Renaissance and Baroque works. Also contains copies made by Clara Schumann, and the W. F. Bach work ordered by Joachim.
        (62 sheets, bound)
A135. Johann Bertram, "O wy arme Sünders," sixteenth-century setting of a Plattdeutsch text by Hermann Bonn.
        (3 MS sheets plus 2 sixteenth-century printed sheets, bound)
A136. Gallus [Handl], "Ecce quomodo moritur justus," in Brahms's hand, plus additional works in a copyist's hand.
        (5 sheets, bound)
A137. Arcadelt [attributed], "Ave Maria."
        (one sheet, bound)

In the following discussion of these Abschriften, the most detailed consideration is given to the italicized items, which contain complete pieces of polyphonic music from the Renaissance and Baroque periods—that is, catalog numbers A130, 134, 135, 136, and 137. Each piece is listed, the source from which it was copied is identified (if it can be ascertained),[19] and an attempt is made to learn the approximate date when it was copied. Copies which are of special importance to the subject of this investigation are described as fully as possible. A list of the works contained in these Abschriften, arranged alphabetically by composer, with some information about modern editions, is given in Appendix 2.

The remaining Abschriften from the list above are discussed only insofar as they bear on the present topic. Of the two folk-song collections, A128 assumes some importance in the discussion of Brahms's own folk-song settings but has little connection with his early music studies; and A129 is irrelevant to Brahms's choral music and is therefore listed only for the sake of completeness. The Schubert copies in A133 help to date two pieces in A130 but are otherwise unimportant to this study. Since A132 has been published in facsimile, it is unnecessary to describe it completely, but a list of the pre-Bach fragments contained in it, along with their sources, is provided.

These "Brahms" manuscripts (even those not copied by Brahms) are discussed in the order of their Archiv catalog numbers. Descriptions then follow of the other early music Abschriften which Brahms owned but did not make himself.[20]

A few general remarks should be made before the examination of the Abschriften is begun. Brahms wrote in a German script which is no longer in common use, except when he was copying texts or titles in languages other than German; these he wrote in Latin script. As a child he could, when he wanted, produce a very clear and careful pointed script.[21] As he grew older, however, his handwriting deteriorated and is often extremely difficult or even impossible to read; fortunately his music copying, though often hurried, is nearly always quite clear. He tended to write fairly carefully, in a style closer to his youthful handwriting, at the beginning of a piece he was copying, and then to get sloppier as he went along.

With practice, and by comparing his handwriting and style of music copying with dated examples, one can attempt to assign approximate dates to the Abschriften. The paper on which copies were made can also occasionally be helpful in estimating dates, although a number of qualifications should be kept in mind. This is by no means a scientific study of the low-quality paper Brahms generally used, and so comparisons are based merely on measurements of overall size of the sheets and number and spacing of the staves, along with occasional stamps or watermarks. Also, Brahms kept blank sheets of paper for a very long time, and often used empty lines on a sheet many years after he had begun writing on it. No doubt a much more complete collection of information about dates of handwriting styles and paper types could have been obtained by making use of the manuscripts of Brahms's own compositions, and of his letters;[22] however, for this project the material used was limited to that contained in the Abschriften themselves. Information gathered from Brahms's published correspondence or from reminiscences and biographies can also sometimes be used to help determine chronology, although with the reservation that a number of obviously incorrect statements about dates have been made by writers on Brahms who did not have access to his library themselves, and therefore any remarks made without supporting primary evidence should be treated with caution.

In the following discussion of the Abschriften, complete explanations of the processes used in assigning approximate dates to undated items are given in the cases of the italicized catalog numbers only (see the list on p. 12 above).

A128.   Collection of Folk Songs from Different Countries

> Archiv title: Grosse Sammlung deutscher, schwedischer, böhmischer u.a. Volkslieder aus verschiedenen Quellen. 25 sheets, unbound, unnumbered.

Brahms accumulated these copies over a long period of time: the earliest is dated Düsseldorf, April 1854 (he used the abbreviation 'Ddf'' in such cases); and the latest, on paper from Eberle in Vienna, contains material taken from an 1877 publication. It seems strange that this collection of copies has only recently begun to be thoroughly investigated by students of Brahms's folk-song settings, since answers to several remaining questions about his sources can be found here.

For this discussion, the sheets are taken up in chronological order (insofar as it can be determined), and they have been assigned numbers as an aid to identification and cross reference. Blank sheets are not numbered.

All of the copies are of tunes and/or texts only; there are no copies of polyphonic settings, although a few drafts or sketches of four-part settings by Brahms himself are found in the Corner sheets, nos. 14-21. Brahms labeled many of the tunes and texts with their sources at the time of copying, and also added a number of later references; this practice of providing cross references and accounting for variants is characteristic of his printed library of folk-song material as well.

1-2.   The earliest bifolio, dated "Ddf. April 54," contains, along with Bohemian songs and dances and other German songs, what is apparently Brahms's first copy of Hans Leo Hassler's "Mein G'müth ist mir verwirret," with the title "An Maria" and the source identified as C. F. Becker's *Lieder und Weisen vergangener Jahrhunderte.* Becker's version of the barring is used, and his own reference to his source is given.[23]

3. A single sheet containing Swedish and German folk tunes is dated Düsseldorf, May 1854. The paper, ink, and copying style are identical to those found in A134, sheets 37 and 38.

4. The same copying style is found in another single sheet, this time on N. D. D. Köster paper from Hamburg.[24] It contains tunes from Kretzschmer and Zuccalmaglio's *Deutsche Volkslieder mit ihren Original-Weisen,* including their version of "Ich stund an einem Morgen" (I: no. 73), which they labeled "Aus dem 16. Jahrhundert," though it was written by Nicolai in the eighteenth century.[25] Brahms copied this citation, and set this version of the tune for voice and piano; he later learned three genuine sixteenth-century melodies (see below, in the discussion of sheets 5-12). He acquired his own copy of the Kretzschmer & Zuccalmaglio collection in August 1856, from his friend Grädener in Hamburg, and so this Abschrift was probably made from Schumann's copy.[26] The sheet also contains incipits of a number of Hungarian tunes whose style of copying apparently is that of a later time.[27]

5-12. The next four bifolios have been carefully examined by George Bozarth, who concludes that two (Bozarth's source F1) were copied in 1855 or soon thereafter, and the remaining two (F2) in the early 1860s.[28] Most of the material contained in them was obtained by Brahms from the folk-song collector and publisher Friedrich Wilhelm Arnold (1810-64), as Brahms's own note "Aus der Sammlung des Hrn. Arnold" on one of the earlier bifolios clearly shows.[29] This same bifolio contains the tune and one verse of text of "In stiller Nacht," under the title "Todtenklage." The source of this tune has been the subject of much discussion and controversy among the writers on Brahms and folk song, some of whom concluded that he had written at least part of it himself;[30] however, although Arnold's ultimate source remains unknown, it is now clear that Brahms did not compose any part of the melody. Another version of "Mein G'müth ist mir verwirret" also appears here, under the title "Liebesklage," with a more rational barring than in Becker's version and a few changed note values which remove the hemiolas in the 6/4 measures.

    The two later bifolios in this group contain some more material which Brahms presumably obtained from Arnold, although the only references to him are later pencil references to his multi-volume collection of settings for voice and piano published during the 1860s, and to his edition of the

Lochaimer Liederbuch, the source of "All' mein Gedanken." Bozarth
suggests that an additional group of early tunes may have no connection
with Arnold:[31] it includes "Es steht ein Lind in jenem Thal," with a
reference to Berg and Neuber's *68 Lieder* of 1550 and two versions of
barring, one copied in ink and the other added later in pencil; and three
more tunes for "Ich stund an einem Morgen," all with references. One
is the tenor of the Senfl setting which Brahms copied complete in A130,
7-9; it appears here with a note "ohne Taktstriche" (without bar lines)
and more than one attempt by Brahms to add them satisfactorily. Another,
labeled "Satz von H. Fink. (Taktstriche ungenau)," has irregular barring,
copied in ink. Additional attempts by Brahms to add bar lines to a tune
without them appear in "Nach Willen dein," from a setting by Hofheimer.[32]

13.   This is a text sheet only, and was presumably compiled in about
1861. The sheet was originally headed "Variationen über ein Thema von
Robert Schumann" and "Joh. Brahms," and two treble clefs were written
for the beginning of the Primo part. All this was smeared out, and the
empty space on the sheet used for folk-song texts. Brahms wrote the
Schumann variations for piano, four hands, Op. 23, in November 1861.

14-21, the Corner sheets.   This group of four bifolios contains material
identified by Brahms as coming from David Gregor Corner's *Gross' Catolisch Gesangbuch,* published in Nürnberg in 1631, which he found in
the Hofbibliothek in Vienna in the winter of 1863-64.[33] This collection,
as Brahms said in a letter to Hermann Deiters,[34] was the source of most
of the sacred folk songs in his 1864 group of four-part settings: these are
numbers 4, "Komm Mainz, komm Bayrn"; 5, "Es flog ein Täublein"; 7,
"Tröst die Bedrängten"; and 12, "Wach auf, mein Kind" (which appears
in Corner as "Auff auff mein Kind"). Corner is also the source of the
text of no. 14, "Es wollt gut Jäger jagen," but Brahms used a version of
the tune which he found in Meister's *Das katholische deutsche Kirchenlied*
(1862), p. 160;[35] this same process also took place in connection with the
text and tune of the motet "O Heiland, reiss die Himmel auf" (Op. 74/2).[36]
      The Corner sheets also contain one bifolio with a number of tunes
copied in ink as soprano lines with a single verse of text written above
and a second staff below, with a bass clef, left blank, ready for a setting.
Three of these have been completely or partially filled in; they are the
only ones of this group of tunes that Brahms ever set chorally, as far as
we know. "Sankt Raphael" has alto, tenor, and bass parts and dynamics
completely filled in in ink; this setting is identical to that published as
no. 7 in the 1864 collection (text "Tröst die Bedrängten").[37] The sketches
of "Sankt Emmerano" (no. 4, text "Komm Mainz, komm Bayrn") and

"Morgenlied" (no. 12, text "Wach auf, mein Kind"—the title is "Morgengesang" in the published version) are particularly interesting because they show Brahms deciding how to deal with these genuinely old melodies in order to write satisfactory settings. These sketches are described in connection with the discussion of the 1864 folk-song settings in chapter 3.

22.   This sheet is similar to the Corner material in copying style. It contains one monophonic Lied in Bar form, headed "Im langen Thon Regenbogens," with a reference to the complete works of Lessing.

23-24.   A bifolio of No. 33 paper from Eberle in Vienna contains material from Ditfurth's collection of 1877, "50 ungedrukt Balladen u. Lieder," according to Brahms's own citation. The copying style is similar to that found in the Schütz copies of about 1890 in A 130, 21-24.

Although all the music included in A 128 is monophonic except for the three four-part settings sketched in the Corner sheets, and thus seems to have little connection with Brahms's choral music, these copies have been discussed in some detail not merely to document his already well-known interest in folk music. Rather, the intent has been to demonstrate the strong connection in his mind between folk music and early music, especially in the area of the sixteenth-century polyphonic Lied, and to illustrate some of the ways in which he observed these old melodies. In particular, his approach to their often irregular rhythms is relevant to his methods in some of his own music.

A 129.   Folk Songs from the Siebengebirge

29 sheets, bound. Not in Brahms's hand.

On the first sheet is a title written by Brahms:

Volkslieder
aus dem Siebengebirge
gesammelt von
Prof. Grimm u. Dr. Arnold.
(nach Dr. A's Handschrift copirt)

To this title someone else has added in pencil: "von Hlavacek im Auftrag von Brahms." Presumably, therefore, Brahms requested the Viennese copyist Hlavacek to make the copies for him, probably in the late 1870s.[38]

The collection contains 135 songs—melodies only and sometimes one verse of text. Brahms occasionally wrote in additional text verses, and he also added many pencil corrections and cross references to other

collections of folk songs. One song he set for mixed chorus appears—
"Erlaube mir, fein's Mädchen"—as well as a few others that he arranged
for women's voices or for solo voice and piano.[39] A setting of "Maria im
Dornenwald" for voice and piano, with all the verses given, has been
inserted; it is in a different hand from the rest of the collection, and could
conceivably be one of Arnold's arrangements.

> A 130.   Copies of Works from the Sixteenth to the Eighteenth
>   Centuries
>   Archiv title: Abschriften hervorragender Meisterstücke des 16-18. Jahrhun-
>   derts zu Studienzwecken. Zusammengestellt von Edith Kern. 45 sheets,
>   unbound.

This is the largest and most varied of the collections of Brahms Abschriften. It comprises works or parts of works by composers ranging in date
from Isaac to Cherubini (who provides the single example here of a nineteenth-century piece and is disregarded in the title of the collection). The
loose sheets were assembled, arranged, and numbered for the Archiv by
Edith Kern (no date given), who also prepared a list of the contents which
is found in the front of the collection. Her list gives the composer of each
piece when the name is provided by Brahms, the title or beginning of the
text, and in some cases the source of the copy if Brahms noted it. A new
catalog, prepared in April 1976 by the present writer, has also been inserted in the collection.

The sheets are not arranged in any systematic order, except that
copies on identical paper are placed together, and pieces by the same
composer are usually found together. However, since this arrangement is
in use in the Archiv, the sheets will be discussed in the order fixed by
Edith Kern, and her numbers will be used. (A list of the contents of the
Abschriften by composer, together with information about recent editions
of the music, is given in Appendix 2.) For each piece or group of pieces,
a summary of the catalog information, which identifies the music and as
far as possible gives its source and places it in Brahms's career, is given
first; "Brahms Nachlass" means that a published version of the source
was also left by Brahms in his library. A description of the copy and the
process used in the attempt to learn more about it follows, together with
any information which seems to give it special importance.

1-2.

> Palestrina, "Surge illuminare Hierusalem" a 6 (Winterfeld example
> no. I.A.10, pp. 46-50)
> G. Gabrieli, "Beata es, virgo Maria" a 6 (I.A.7, pp. 29-31)

3-4.

    G. Gabrieli, "Jubilate Deo" a 8 (I.A. 8, pp. 32-41)

5-6.

    G. Gabrieli, "Benedictus" a 12 (I.A.9, pp. 42-45). Performed by the
    Singakademie, 6 January 1864
    G. Gabrieli, "O quam suavis" a 8 (II.A.2, pp. 58-61)
        Source: Carl von Winterfeld, *Johannes Gabrieli und sein Zeitalter* III: 1834. Brahms
        Nachlass. Example and page numbers are given above (see Table 4 for contents).
        These five pieces are also among eleven from Winterfeld's volume of musical ex-
        amples that were reprinted in February 1856 by Schlesinger in the second volume
        of their collection *Musica Sacra*. (For more information on this latter collection,
        see the discussion of A130, 27-29.) Date: probably 1856-58

These three bifolios of 16-stave, horizontal format Köster paper from
Hamburg contain five complete pieces taken from Winterfeld's important
collection. Bifolios 1-2 and 5-6 each have one work copied on the front
and back covers and one on the two inside pages. Brahms copied "O
quam suavis" without naming the composer, and it is not included in
Edith Kern's list. He also did not identify the source of the copies. At
some time after making them in ink, he added German translations of the
texts of the second, third, and fifth pieces in pencil; these translations
come from the discussion in volumes I and II of Winterfeld.

    In the published versions, each piece is printed in full score, and
treble, soprano, alto, tenor, and bass clefs (denoted Tr, S, A, T, and B
respectively) are all used. Brahms reduced each to half the original number of staves, probably to save paper, and used only Tr, A, and B clefs.
In the case of "Jubilate Deo," he also rearranged the eight parts into two
choirs, and in doing so presumably became more aware of Gabrieli's
methods of writing for many voices.

    Brahms's Hamburg friend Theodor Avé-Lallemant gave him Winter-
feld's work in 1858. If Brahms made the Abschriften from his own copy,
presumably he did so in order to facilitate study of the pieces. He could,
of course, have made the copies earlier in one of his friends' libraries; for
example, he wrote excitedly to Clara Schumann as early as December
1854 about the collections of Avé-Lallemant and G. D. Otten.[40] Winterfeld's *Gabrieli* was well known and widely available, and Schumann may
also have had a copy, although the Köster paper suggests that the Abschriften were probably made in Hamburg.

    A further piece of evidence supports the possibility that these copies
may have been made before 1858. The second volume of *Musica Sacra*
was published by Schlesinger in early 1856 and included reprints of eleven

of the twenty-three complete pieces contained in Winterfeld's volume of examples. The fact that all five of the pieces Brahms chose to copy are among these eleven may be more than a coincidence; it suggests that *Musica Sacra* might have been his source, and that he made these Abschriften before he had access to Winterfeld. The pencil translations could have come from a later study of the pieces, perhaps when Brahms copied a fragment of one, Gabrieli's "Beata es," onto page 5 of "Octaven und Quinten" (A132). (In the counterpoint collection he wrongly identified the composer as Palestrina, but added the citation "nach Winterfeld Gabrieli.")

Brahms made only a few pencil marks apart from the German translations. In "Surge illuminare" and "Beata es," the beginnings of important new phrases are shown by brackets, and in "O quam suavis" several possible wrong notes are marked. The "Benedictus" contains blue pencil brackets which point out imitation between the tenor of choir 1 and first tenor of choir 3. More interesting annotations, including performance dynamics for the "Benedictus," some revisions of voice leading to avoid parallels, analytic observations, and a few additions of bass figures in places of particular harmonic interest, are found in Brahms's printed copy of Winterfeld; see the discussion below (p. 101). The fact that these markings are found in the printed volume rather than in the Abschriften supports the idea that Brahms made these copies before 1858 in his first study of this music, and that he later studied it again from the published copy, recording his new observations there.

7-8.

Stephan Zirler, "Die Sonn' die ist verblichen" (Forster III: no. 42)
Thomas Stoltzer, "Entlaubet ist uns der Walde" (Forster I: no. 61)
Matthias Greitter, "Es wollt ein Jäger jagen" (Forster II: no. 17)
Ludwig Senfl, "Ich stund an einem Morgen" (Ott, 1534, no. 22).
The end of this Senfl setting is on sheet 9.

Source: manuscript "Deutsche vierstimmige Volkslieder aus dem 16ten Jahrhunderte," compiled by Nottebohm. Brahms Nachlass[41]
Date: after 1862

Although this bifolio and the next are both on Köster paper from Hamburg, their contents cannot have been copied before 1862, because the source of the four Tenorlieder is a manuscript in the hand of Gustav Nottebohm, whom Brahms met on his first visit to Vienna. It seems likely that Brahms made these Abschriften within a year or two of his arrival in Vienna, perhaps while he was thinking about repertoire for the Singakademie. His ink copies are almost identical to Nottebohm's, except that he changed some of the clefs and drew bar lines through the staves only and not through the spaces in between. His headings are exactly the same, and for the first two pieces he also added later pencil references to Forster. These additions were apparently made after he was given his own copy of the five volumes of Forster in 1869, and show that he had not lost interest in these Abschriften some years after he had made them.

For "Die Sonn' die ist verblichen," Brahms copied the heading "Satz von S. Zirler" from the source, and then added "aus Forster (Bd. III) Nr. 42" in pencil. He changed the clefs from the original treble, mezzo-soprano, alto changing to tenor, and bass to SATB, without noting his alterations. All editorial accidentals he copied exactly as given, usually above the staff but once in a while on it; he also copied one suggested correction in the alto.[42] The only important change is that Brahms wrote the text in the tenor part, whereas Nottebohm had placed it in the so-prano. This is the only one of the four pieces where the text is given in a voice other than the tenor (it appears in all four partbooks of the 1549 edition). Brahms, realizing that the tenor was the cantus firmus, could quite easily have simply transferred the text to that part, since there are no repetitions or other problems.

The Abschrift of "Entlaubet ist uns der Walde" is headed "Satz von Th. Stoltzer," and then in pencil the heading is enlarged to "Thomas" and "Forster I, 61 (1560)" is added.[43] In his copy Brahms showed how he had changed the clefs from S, A, A, and baritone to SATB; originally he intended to use the baritone clef and copied several bars, but he changed his mind, crossed out what he had already written, and rewrote it in the bass clef. He also altered the first word of the repeated section from a second "Entlaubet" (which appears in his source) to "Beraubet." This melody is also found in another of the Abschriften, A134, 41-42, where Brahms copied an Eccard setting with the sacred text "Ich dank' dir lieber Herre," and made a note of the relationship. In other editions of this work, the text of the first phrase is "Entlaubet ist der Walde"; here the word "uns" must be accommodated by contracting the first word to "Entlaub't."

"Es wollt ein Jäger jagen" is identified only by "Satz v. M. Greitter"; there is no added reference to Forster II.[44] In the source this piece is also labeled "Ionisch," but Brahms left the comment out of his copy. He indicated a change from alto to tenor clef in the tenor part, and did not write out the repeat of the second part of the piece; otherwise his Ab-schrift is identical with Nottebohm's.

As we have already seen in the description of A128, Brahms knew several melodies for "Ich stund an einem Morgen"; and in fact, by the time this copy was made, he had already written his setting for voice and piano of the tune by Nicolai. There are no fewer than five settings of this Lied, four of them by Senfl, in Nottebohm's collection; perhaps this one appealed to him especially because it is identified as being in the Phrygian mode—the only one of the five settings so identified. He copied "Phrygisch" at the beginning, and added "Satz von Senfl" at the end, on the first side of the next bifolio. His copy is identical to the source except for the change of clefs from TrAABar to SATB, which Brahms indicated only for the lower two voices.

9.

[Senfl, "Ich stund an einem Morgen" (end of piece)]
Lassus, "Aus meiner Sünden Tiefe" (*Newe deutsche Lieder,* 1583, no. 14)
Scandellus, "Schein uns du liebe Sonne" (*Nawe und lustige Weltliche Deudsche Liedlein,* 1578, no. 16)

> Source: unknown. Probably copied from someone else's transcription
> Date: after 1862

The first four staves of this sheet are taken up by the end of the Senfl Tenorlied begun on 7-8; the other two pieces were added at a later time. The paper is identical to bifolio 7-8, and the sheet is the first half of a bifolio which was at one time completed by sheet 10.

There seems to be no possible published nineteenth-century source for either of these two pieces. The Scandellus setting is not listed in Eitner's *Verzeichniss* at all;[45] and the Lassus piece appears only in Commer's *Musica Sacra* 8 (1863), where the information given about its origin does not include the correct number 14 cited by Brahms. Although he could in theory have copied both pieces from partbooks, it is far more likely that he used transcriptions by Nottebohm or some other collector, complete with all the information on their origins. This suggestion is supported by the tidiness of the copies: there is no trace of the difficulties Brahms had with the Gallus "Ecce quomodo" (A130, 18-19) or his other direct transcriptions from partbooks.

"Aus meiner Sünden Tiefe" is labeled at the end "No. 14 / Orl. Lassus /Newe deutsche Lied 1583." It is also provided with pencil performance dynamics and red pencil Roman numerals V (crossed out) and III. It is impossible to know whether Brahms added these dynamic markings while he was conducting the Singakademie, or whether he put them in for the first time when he was preparing for his second season as director of the Musikverein concerts. There is no record of his ever having performed this piece, but it appears in the set of performance copies from which three works were sung on 7 December 1873 (see A136 and the score and parts prepared from it). The dynamics which appear here in A130 for the first time are later reproduced in the performance copies, and the red pencil numerals refer to the work's place in the later collections. Here it is copied in SATB clefs and barred in 4/2. In order to fit the last three measures into the two staves remaining at the bottom of the page, Brahms reduced the four staves to piano score. When he was adding dynamics, he forgot about these three measures, and consequently had to add markings to them later, to the copyist's version in A136.

"Schein uns du liebe Sonne" is on the reverse side of the sheet. At the bottom left, at the same time the Abschrift was made, Brahms wrote "Vers 2-7 in Ambraser Liederbuch 66." I have been unable to trace this reference. Since Brahms copied no additional verses of text and had no "Ambraser Liederbuch" in his possession, it seems likely that he obtained this information also from his source. At the bottom right, he wrote the complete citation "Antonius Scandellus / Nawe u. lustige Welt. /deudsche Liedlein / 1567. No. 16."

10.

Hassler, "Ach Schatz, ich sing' und lache" (*Lustgarten,* 1601)

> Source: Neue Ausgabe. Vol. XV (1887), edited by Friedrich Zelle, of *Älterer praktischer und theoretischer Musikwerke* (general editor Robert Eitner), p. 5
> Date: after 1887

Jacob Regnart, "Wer wirdet trösten mich" (*Tricinia,* 1584)
Christoph Demant, "Wer wirdet trösten mich" (*Neue deutsche weltliche Lieder,* 1595)

> Source: Reinhard Kade, "Christoph Demant. 1567-1643," in *Vierteljahrsschrift für Musikwissenschaft,* 6 (1890), 469-534. Both pieces are in the Musik-Beilagen, pp. 535-36. Brahms Nachlass
> Date: after 1890

This sheet demonstrates the futility of relying only on information about paper in the determination of dates of Brahms manuscripts. Although it is Hamburg Köster paper, the second sheet of a bifolio (only recently separated) whose first sheet, 9, contains copies probably made in the early 1860s in Vienna, the Abschriften sheet 10 contains were made late in Brahms's career.

He identified his sources: the Hassler piece on one side of the sheet is headed "Hans Leo Hassler. (Ausgab Eitner) Nr. V. S. 5." On the other side, at the bottom, is "Vierteljahrsschrift 1890. IV." (This citation is incorrect; it is volume VI.) All three pieces were copied complete, but it appears that Brahms's main interest in them may have been the usefulness of two of the pieces as counterpoint examples: fragments of the Regnart and Hassler works appear in "Octaven und Quinten" (A132, p. 6), the former for its series of parallel fifths, and the latter for its avoidance of parallel octaves. In Brahms's Abschrift of the Demant piece, a five-part reworking of Regnart's original for three voices, he marked imitative entries.

11-12.

> Calvisius, "Josef, lieber Josef mein" [incomplete]
>
> > Source: Bodenschatz, *Florilegium*, 1603, partbooks, in the Musikverein
>
> Schütz, Psalm 23: "Der Herr ist mein Hirt" [incomplete], SWV 398
>
> > Source: *Symphoniae Sacrae* III, 1650, partbooks, probably in the Musikverein
> > Date: after 1862
>
> Brahms, pencil sketches for duet "Die Schwestern," Op. 61/1[46]
>
> > Date: later than the transcriptions, since the sketches are written, upside down, in the blank space left on the back page of the bifolio after the Calvisius piece breaks off

Along with the Gallus "Ecce quomodo" (A130, 18-19) and Bertram's "O wy armen Sünders" (A135), these are the only surviving Abschriften of early vocal music which Brahms certainly compiled himself from separate parts.[47] Since neither piece is complete, he may have made the copies more as an exercise in scoring from old partbooks than from a desire to study the works for their musical content or for possible performances.

Brahms was interested in the tune "Josef, lieber Josef mein" for many years. In April 1863 he sent part of it to Joachim in the letter congratulating him on his engagement, and he also used the melody in the viola part of the song "Geistliches Wiegenlied" (Op. 91/2).[48] Therefore it is not surprising he chose a setting of the tune for an exercise in transcription. He labeled it "Sethus Calvisius aus Bodenschatz Florilegium 1603 (Musik-Verein)," and copied about two-thirds of it on the front and back pages of the bifolio, including the text of only the first phrase. The transcription evidently gave him some difficulty, since there are occasional false starts and corrections. The six parts are copied in SSATTB clefs, with note values in the triple meter section reduced by a factor of two and barred in 6/2.

For the Schütz piece, copied on the two inside pages of the bifolio, Brahms gave no composer's name; it therefore appears in Edith Kern's catalog simply as "23 Psalm: 'Der Herr ist mein Hirt'." It is the first work in the third set of *Symphoniae Sacrae*; perhaps Brahms chose it for transcription because he came to it first in the partbooks. Both the Archiv and the Nationalbibliothek have complete sets of partbooks, but it seems probable that Brahms used the Archiv set for this piece as well as for the Calvisius.[49] The original is scored for soprano, alto, and tenor solos, two violins, basso continuo, and SATB complementum parts. Brahms left out the complementum parts altogether, and copied the two violin parts only through the introductory Symphonia. He added bar lines to these violin parts (in 4/4), and a few irregular bar lines to the vocal parts at places where they occur in the original bass. Otherwise, apart from leaving out a few words and making some minor errors, he copied the original parts exactly. He broke off when the two pages were nearly filled, and at some later time used the rest of the second page for scratch paper; it contains red pencil numbers that look like calculations about the numbers of voices in the sections of a large chorus.

13-14.

> Clemens non Papa, Psalm 65, "Vrolick en bly loeft god," with tenor "Ick seg adieu" (*Souter Liedekens*)
>
> Source: Franz Commer, *Collectio Operum Musicorum Batavorum Saeculi XVI*, Tom. XI (1857): 30. Brahms Nachlass
>
> Vreedman, "Ich segge adieu"
>
> Source: lute tablature in *Nova longeque . . . carmina*, 1568. Nationalbibliothek
>
> Ammerbach, "Wer das Töchterlein haben will" [incomplete]
> Ammerbach, "Ich sage ade" (no. 34)
> Ammerbach, "Ganz sehr betrübt ist mir mein Herz" (no. 10)
> Wolff Heintz, "Gar hoch auff einem Berge" (no. 9 of last section, "Gecolorirten Stücklein")
>
> Source: tablature in Ammerbach's *Orgel- oder Instrument-Tablatur,* 1571. Archiv
>
> Judenkönig, "Mag ich Unglück nicht widerstan" (tenor and bass)
> Judenkönig, "Mag ich Unglück nicht widerstan" (for lute)
>
> Source: lute tablature in Judenkünig [sic], *Ein schone kunstliche underweisung . . . ,* 1523, pp. 12v and 23v. Nationalbibliothek
> Date: after 1862

This bifolio contains a series of exercises in the transcription of tablature from original sources. That it was intended as a study sheet is clearly shown by the inclusion of the first piece (another setting of a tune which appears twice later), and by the complete citations of sources, cross references, and information about the music. The copies must have been made after 1862 in Vienna, since all of the sources can be found in the two main music libraries there, and the paper is the same as that used for A130, 30-37, which can only have been copied in Vienna, very probably under the guidance of Nottebohm.

These transcriptions illustrate one aspect of Brahms's study of early music—details of instrumental notation. The only vocal piece is the Clemens non Papa setting, which Brahms identified completely as " 'Ick seg adieu' aus 'Souter Liedekens' II (Antwerpen, 1556).[50] Der 65 Psalm Jubilate Deo. Der Tenor van der wyse, 'Ick seg adieu, wy twoo wy mooten scheiden." At the end of the piece he gave his source: "Aus: Franz Commer 'Collectium Operum musicorum bavatorum'[sic], Berlin, Trautwein Tom. XI." He provided similarly complete information for the instrumental works in this bifolio.

15.

Michael Praetorius [?], "Maria zart von edler Art"

> Source: Winterfeld, *Der evangelische Kirchengesang* I, no. 89
> Date: probably 1857-60

This four-part setting, said to be by Michael Praetorius,[51] is one of a number of copies Brahms made from Winterfeld's great three-volume study of Protestant church music in the sixteenth, seventeenth, and eighteenth centuries, published between 1843 and 1847. In addition to hundreds of pages of text, each volume contains an appendix with many complete musical examples. Brahms did not own these volumes, but he must have studied them, because he made Abschriften from all three. The earliest copies are those he made in 1854 (A134, 37-40), almost certainly in Schumann's library.[52] The other Winterfeld Abschriften in A130 (sheets 15, 16, and 18-19) and A134 (43-44) appear to have been made several years later, judging from the copying style, perhaps on the 1858 visit to Clara in Berlin (when the Lotti copies in A134, 17-24, which are on the same type of paper, were probably made), or perhaps earlier from a set in some Hamburg library.[53] The proposed final date of copying is suggested by the inclusion in the same group of sheets (see 16 and 18-19 below) of the Gallus "Ecce quomodo" transcription.

Brahms labeled his Abschrift of "Maria zart" with the information given by Winterfeld: at the beginning is "Mel. aus dem 15ten Jahrh. der Tonsatz 1610," and at the end "Mich. Prätorius aus 1610." The piece is copied exactly from Winterfeld's version except that Brahms wrote one wrong note in the tenor part.

16.

Johann Rudolf Ahle, "Es ist genug"

> Source: Winterfeld, *Der evangelische Kirchengesang* II, no. 123
> Date: probably the same as 15 above

Gallus, "Ecce quomodo moritur justus" [incomplete; see 18-19 below]

This sheet is the same paper as 15; the two were probably a bifolio at one time, and the copies on them were probably made all at once.

Brahms copied Winterfeld's heading for the chorale setting exactly: "Joh. Rud. Ahle (1662) Ueber die Sehnworte des Elias: Es ist genug." He also identified his source many years later, in 1885, in a letter to Julius Spengel.[54] A large red-pencil Roman number IV refers to the position of the piece in the performance copies, A136 and the score and parts subsequently prepared from it.

This six-part chorale setting, along with the Bach setting of the same chorale (17 below) and the Gallus "Ecce quomodo," were performed in a concert by the Singverein under Brahms's direction on 7 December 1873. It seems likely, however, that this Abschrift may have been made when Brahms was accumulating material for the Detmold choir.

The copy is identical to Winterfeld's original, but Brahms also supplied two missing accidentals in pencil, and provided performance dynamics in ink, apparently at the same time he made the Abschrift.[55]

17.

Bach, "Es ist genug" (from Cantata 60, "O Ewigkeit, du Donnerwort")

> Source: *Bach Gesammt-Ausgabe* 12 (1862): 190
> Date: probably 1863

The copy of Schubert's "Lazarus" in A133, dated "Wien März 63," is on identical paper, and in the same copying style, as this sheet. Therefore, although Brahms did not perform the Bach chorale during his one season with the Singakademie, he probably copied it as soon as it appeared in the complete works for possible use in conjunction with the Ahle setting.

As we have already seen, he did finally perform both settings with the Singverein in 1873; the red pencil IV (crossed out) and V here refer again to A136 and subsequent performance copies which were made at that later time.

Brahms added dynamics to this chorale in ink, apparently when he made his original copy. Later he made some additions and changes in these performance instructions, probably in three stages, since they appear in pencil, blue pencil, and ink. Several more small changes also appear in A136 and the later score and parts.[56]

18-19.

> Daniel Vetter, "Liebster Gott, wann werd' ich sterben?"
> Bach, "Herrscher über Tod und Leben," from Cantata 8
>
>   Source: Winterfeld, *Der evangelische Kirchengesang* III: nos. 97a & b
>
> Jacobus Gallus [Jakob Handl], "Ecce quomodo moritur justus"
>
>   Source: Bodenschatz, *Florilegium,* 1618, partbooks, perhaps in Hamburg
>   Date: probably 1857-60, the same as 15 and 16 above

Brahms gave his source for the Vetter setting as "Daniel Vetter, 1695. (Winterfeld III.)" but labeled the Bach only "J. S. Bach." The two pieces appear together in Winterfeld's volume to show how Bach used the earlier version as the basis for his very similar setting of the last verse of the chorale. Brahms performed the Bach chorale with the Singakademie in January 1864.[57]

The Gallus piece was clearly of great interest to Brahms; he arranged it for the women of the Hamburg Frauenchor,[58] and performed it with the Singverein.[59] This first copy may have been made when he was directing the Detmold choir. Unfortunately there is no complete record of the choir's repertoire under Brahms, so we do not know whether he worked on it with them. He began an identical transcription on sheet 15 (see above), but evidently did not have room to finish it; his first complete copy is the one found here.

The Abschrift is headed "Jac. Gallus. (aus Bodenschatz Florilegium, 1618)." It is a direct transcription from the separate partbooks, although the piece was also available in a number of nineteenth-century editions. The copy may have been made in Hamburg, where a complete set of the 1618 partbooks was available, according to Eitner's *Quellenlexikon.*[60] Brahms copied the parts exactly as he found them in the separate books into his score, except for changing the clefs of the two middle voices from S and A to A and T, as he himself indicated. He chose to copy the bass part from the *Bassi generali* book instead of the vocal *Bassus,* including its rather primitive figures, which are given mainly as accidentals in front of the affected notes, with numbers appearing only at the first cadence. The only other markings are several NB's, which point out errors and corrections.

20.

> Gregorian hymn, "Veni creator spiritus," first verse
> Martin Luther, "Komm Gott, Schöpfer, heiliger Geist," two versions
> Praetorius, "Vom Himmel hoch"
>
> Source and date: unknown

Brahms, pencil sketch for a song in C minor, crossed out[61]

This single sheet contains no clue to when or where the copies on it were made. The three hymn tunes and the chorale setting on one side look as if they were all copied at the same time, and at some different time Brahms used a small portion of the reverse side for the three measures of song sketch.

It seems that he was interested in the relation between the Gregorian tune "Veni creator spiritus," the hymn for Pentecost, and Luther's two versions of its German translation. These, which are given as melodies only, are both clearly derived from the Gregorian tune, but are different from it and from each other. They are identified only as "Luther I" and "II."

"Vom Himmel hoch" appears here in a simple four-part chordal setting in C major, in piano score. It occupies only two staves. Brahms labeled it "18 (in d)" at the beginning and "(Prätorius in d)" at the end. It does not appear in Michael Praetorius's *Werke.*

21-22.[62]

> Schütz, fragments from *Il primo Libro de Madrigale,* 1611
>
> Source: *Sämmtliche Werke,* edited by Philipp Spitta, Vol. IX (1890). Brahms Nachlass
> Date: 1890 or later

Brahms copied four fragments from the volume of Italian madrigals onto this sheet, which he headed "Schütz IX (Madrigale)." Each fragment is identified by its page number. The first two appear exactly as they are found in the printed volume, in SSATB clefs: they are four and a half bars of "Selve beate"[63] and just over two bars of "Quella damma son io."[64] The other two fragments both come from "Dunque addio";[65] Brahms copied the first seven and the last ten bars of the piece, transposing it down a minor third in such a way that the positions of the notes on the staff remain unchanged from the source—from Spitta's two treble, mezzosoprano, alto, and baritone clefs with one flat to Brahms's SSATB clefs with two sharps.[66]

Each of these passages is also marked in pencil in Brahms's copy of the printed edition, but unfortunately there is no indication of why he chose them for special attention. The first demonstrates a large-scale motion in parallel fifths which he might have considered including in "Octaven und Quinten." In the others the outstanding characteristic seems to be the expressive use of chromaticism.

23-24.

Schütz, fragments from the Passions and the *Psalmen Davids* (1619)

Source: *Sämmtliche Werke* I (1885), *Die evangelischen Historien und die Sieben Worte Jesu Christi*; and II (1886), *Psalmen Davids*, first part. Brahms Nachlass
Date: 1886 or later

This bifolio of Eberle No. 6 paper (Vienna) contains seventeen fragments, each identified by its page number, copied from the first two volumes of Spitta's Schütz edition. Table 1 shows, for each fragment in the Abschrift, the volume and page number in Spitta's edition, the text of the fragment, and the volume, page, and measure numbers in the new Schütz edition (Bärenreiter), except for the one which is not included.

Table 1.   Fragments Copied from Spitta's Schütz Edition

Vol./p. no. Spitta edition	Work	Text of Fragment	Vol./p. and measure no. New Schütz edition
I: 60	Matthäus-Passion SWV 479 (1666)	"denn es ist Blutgeld"	2:125
I: 67	Matthäus-Passion	"Halt, halt, lasst sehen" [repeated]	2: 136
I: 93	Markus-Passion[67]	"Ist er Christus und König in Israel" [repeated]	not included
I: 70	Matthäus-Passion	"Darum befiehle, dass man das Grab verwahre"	2: 140
I: 70	Matthäus-Passion	"ärger, denn der erste"	2: 141

I: 144	Johannes-Passion SWV 481 (1666)	"deinen Tod und sein Ursach" [repeated]	2: 103
II: 11	Psalm 110 SWV 22	Chor 2: "Deine Kinder werden dir geboren, wie der Thau aus der Morgenröthe"	23: 708, mm. 36-43
II: 25	Psalm 22 SWV 23	Chor 3: "Aber der im Himmel wohnet, lachet ihr, lachet ihr"	23: 29-31, mm. 31-38
II: 40	Psalm 6[68] SWV 24	Tutti: "denn ich bin schwach [repeated], heile mich, Herr"	23: 57, mm. 25-29
II: 42	Psalm 6	Chor 1: "Ich bin so müde von Seufzen"	23: 61, mm. 60-65
II: 43	Psalm 6	Tutti: "denn der Herr hört mein Weinen, der Herr hört mein Flehen"	23: 64, mm. 88-92
II: 47	Psalm 130 SWV 25	"Aus der Tiefe ruf ich, Herr, zu dir"	23: 73, mm. 1-8
II: 86	Psalm 8[69] SWV 27	Chor 2: "und auch dem heilgen Geiste"	23: 129-30, mm. 107-16
II: 104	Psalm 84 SWV 29	"Wie lieblich sind deine Wohnunge"[70]	23: 155, mm. 1-8
II: 112	Psalm 84	Chor: "Die durch das Jammerthal gehen und graben daselbst Brunnen"	23: 167-68, mm. 101-14
II: 116	Psalm 84	Chor 1: "Ich will lieber der Thür hüten in meines Gottes Hause, denn lange wohnen in der Gottlosen Hütten"	23: 173-74, mm. 146-64
II: 162	Psalm 136 SWV 32	Chor 4: "denn er gedacht an uns"	24: 51-52, mm. 124-28

Many of these fragments contain examples of the sort of disguised parallel motion that Brahms was collecting for "Octaven und Quinten"; in fact, the last two bars of the Abschrift from II: 25 also appear there, on page 10. A note in the fragment he copied from I: 93 clearly shows his intent: he marked the 5th-to-diminished-5th motion in the first phrase with the parallel lines he often used to denote parallel motion; and then at the corresponding place in the second phrase, where true parallel fifths occur as a result of sequential imitation, he marked the parallel again and labeled it "consequent" (see Ex. 1).

Example 1

Another attraction for Brahms seems to have been clever uses of imitation. In the case of I: 144, he added the comment "schöne Nachahmung" to his copy (Ex. 2).

Example 2

In II: 47, which is cited in the discussion of the motets Op. 110 in chapter 3 (Example 22), Brahms's characteristic brackets point out a series of entrances.

Striking or unexpected chromaticism, especially that which arises as a consequence of imitation, may have caused him to choose particular fragments to copy. Specifically, the interval of the diminished fourth or its complement the augmented fifth, either melodic or harmonic, occurs several times, as do conspicuous cross relations; an example is the second fragment from I: 70 (Ex. 3; the annotations are mine).

Example 3

Stepwise chromatic motion, either up or down, also appears in several of the fragments.

Brahms's own copy of volume I of Spitta's edition contains no markings which correspond to the Abschriften. In volume II, however, there are several pencil notations in Psalm 6, "Ach Herr, straf mich nicht in deinem Zorn," including underlining of the text "denn ich bin schwach" and a line in the margin next to "Ich bin so müde von Seufzen" (see the description of these volumes, pp. 91-93).

Unfortunately, his copy of Wüllner's 1878 edition of three of the *Psalmen Davids*, Psalms 6 (SWV 24), 130 (SWV 25), and 98 (SWV 35), has disappeared from the Archiv. Since two of the same psalms are represented in the Abschriften, it would have been especially interesting to see whether Brahms made written comments in Wüllner's heavily edited performance versions, which he had owned for a number of years before Spitta's scholarly edition appeared.

25-26.

Frescobaldi, works from *Toccate d'intavolatura*, 1637
  Libro I: Toccata duodecima; Partita sopra l'Aria dei la Romanesca [first part only]; Toccata quarta per l'Organo da sonarsi alla levatione [incomplete]
  Libro II: Aria detta la Frescobalda [first part only]

Source: original edition, in the Klosterbibliothek, Einsiedeln.
Date: September 1856

Soon after Robert Schumann's death, Brahms took Clara, two of her children, and his own sister Elise on a recuperative trip to Switzerland. They spent two weeks at Gersau on the Vierwaldstättersee, and during that time he worked in the library of the Benedictine abbey at Einsiedeln.[71] This bifolio contains several keyboard works by Frescobaldi for which Brahms provided an unusually complete accounting of his source, writing "Toccate d'intavolatura di Cemb. et Org. / Partite div: etc. di Girolamo Frescobaldi / libro 1° / Roma M.D.C.XXXVII" at the head of the bifolio, along with "Kloster Bibliothek / Einsiedeln." He also gave the title of each piece, and for the last one added "aus libro II / Roma 1637. (Toccate, Canzoni etc.)"

Brahms's NB appears a few times in these copies. With one he called attention to his own comment, "Druckfehler " (printing error), and in another place he decided that a possible error was, after all, "richtig" (correct).

27.

> Durante, "Misericordias Domini" (*Musica Sacra,* no. 1)

28-29.

> Lotti, "Vere languores" ("Alle die tiefen Qualen," no. 5)
> G. Corsi,[72] "Adoramus te Christe" (no. 6)
> Palestrina, "Crucifixus" from *Missa Papae Marcelli* (no. 20)
>
>> Source: *Musica Sacra* I (Schlesinger, 1852)
>> Date: on or before 17 January 1853

> Two Hungarian melodies. The first is the theme Brahms used for the piano variations Op. 21/2
>
>> Source: unknown. Possibly Eduard Reményi
>> Date: 17 January 1853

The polyphonic works which are found here on a sheet and a bifolio of identical Köster paper were all copied at the same time. At some time after Brahms had finished them, he added the two Hungarian melodies to a few empty staves at the bottom of the page which contains the Lotti piece, and dated them "17te Jan. 1853." Thus the pieces copied on or before that date are the earliest surviving Brahms Abschriften of early music.[73]

The date of copying is particularly important to us in this case because it proves that Brahms was already sufficiently interested in early music to have made these copies *before* he encountered Robert Schumann. The often-stated assumption that Schumann was responsible not only for encouraging Brahms's interest in Renaissance polyphony, but for awakening it in the first place, is, therefore, mistaken.[74]

The source of these Abschriften is the first volume of a collection entitled *Musica Sacra* published by Schlesinger of Berlin.[75] This two-volume *Musica Sacra* should not be confused with several other collections of the same title, especially the other German publications, which are now much more widely available than the Schlesinger *Musica Sacra.* The history of these other collections begins with a series edited by Franz Commer and published by Bote & Bock (Berlin) starting in 1839. After four volumes, Commer continued to edit additional volumes under the same general title, but these contained only music by Lasso and were published by Trautwein (Berlin). Bote & Bock also continued their series under the direction of various editors.[76] Brahms was probably acquainted with these other *Musica Sacra* collections in addition to the Schlesinger one; but none was his source for Abschriften, although they do contain several pieces which he copied.[77]

Schlesinger's *Musica Sacra* I was published both as a complete volume of scores, and as separate numbers, which were available in parts as well as in score. For the convenience of singers, the individual parts were printed using only treble and bass clefs, while the scores all used SATB clefs and sometimes others as well. Brahms's copies from this source are all in treble and bass clefs only, so he may have been making his own scores from sets of individual parts, or he may have changed the clefs from the score version for greater ease in reading his copies.[78] The eight-voice Durante piece he reduced to four staves in two choirs from the original eight staves in two choirs. He copied the headings of all four pieces exactly as they appear in *Musica Sacra*:

Misericordias Domini etc. von Francesco Durante. N. 1. 4 stimmig in 2 Coro

Vere languores—Alle die tiefen Qualen 3 stimmig comp. von. <u>Ant. Lotti</u>

Adoramus te Christe. componirt von G. Corsi. 4 stimmig

Crucifixus aus der Missa Papae Marcelli 4 stimmig comp. von Palestrina (Nach der römischen Ausgabe vom J. 1598)

A singing translation into German is provided for "Vere languores";[79] Brahms wrote only the first three words of the Latin text, and then crossed it out and copied the entire German translation instead. Performance dynamics are given in the source for Corsi's "Adoramus te," and he copied them exactly.[80]

30-37.

Cesti, *Serenata fatta in Firenze . . . 1662* [incomplete]

Source: autograph, in the Nationalbibliothek, Vienna [Signatur 16890]
Date: after 1862

These four bifolios are the same kind of paper as that used for the transcriptions from tablature, A 130, 13-14. The Abschriften were probably all made at about the same time, as part of a study project in the Viennese libraries.

Brahms's heading is "Aus 'Serenata fatta in Firenze etc.' / 1662 /di <u>Ant. Chesti</u> [sic]." The only source for this piece, according to Eitner's *Quellenlexikon,* is the autograph, which is still in the manuscript collection of the Musiksammlung of the Nationalbibliothek (then the Hofbibliothek). The complete title is "Serenata fatta in Firenze p. la Sera della Nascita del Ser^{mo} Principe Sposo Cosmo di Toscana il di 14 Agusto 1662," and the composer is identified in a pencil note as A. Cesti.

Brahms copied about the last third of the "Serenata" complete.[81] On two interleaved bifolios are an ink copy of a soprano recitative, "Raffrenate l'ardir Ninfe," with figured bass, followed by a strophic aria with instrumental ritornelli in four parts. Verbal instructions show that the ritornello is to be repeated at the midpoint of each verse as well as between verses. After the third strophe, the direction "Segue il Coro" appears, followed by three blank pages where Brahms evidently intended to recopy the chorus.

The two remaining bifolios contain rough draft pencil copies of the recitative and the final chorus, which is headed "Coro (d' Instrumenti Servono Come p. Coro di ripieno)," and begins with the text "Ceda de fior la reggia" in twelve parts, SATB, SSSAATBB. Brahms copied the irregular barring and archaic notation exactly as they appear in the manuscript.

38-39.

Mattheson, "Chor der Juden" from *Das Lied des Lammes*

Source: autograph, Hamburg Stadtbibliothek
Date: summer 1859, or perhaps earlier

Brahms identified his source for this copy carefully: the heading is "Chor der Juden aus 'Das Lied des Lammes' von Joh. Mattheson. 1727. (Handschriftlich aus der Hamburger Stadtbibliothek.)" It is not surprising that the piece should have attracted his attention, since he was very much occupied with canons for several years; and this is an example where the same musical material is used with two different arrangements of the time intervals between the voices. The text is from St. John, and after the evangelist's recitative "Die Juden aber schrieen und sprachen," the chorus sings "Lässest du diesen los, so bist du des Kaisers Freund nicht" as a "Canon perpetuus in Hyperdiapente, 4 vocum (Fuga in Consequenza)." Then, at the double bar, the heading is "Idem Canon, alio modo, et aliis verbis," as the text goes on, "Denn wer sich zum Könige machet, der ist wider den Kaiser." Brahms copied the Latin explanations as well as the instructions showing which instruments double the chorus parts.

Kalbeck (I: 357) mentions this Abschrift, and says that it was made during the summer of 1859, when Brahms was working in Hamburg on material for the Frauenchor. The final double bar of this copy is decorated with a flourish signature identical to those found at the end of the Rovetta and Lotti copies in A134, made in 1857 and 1858. It is perhaps more likely that Brahms copied the Mattheson chorus in 1856 or 1857, when he was working intensively on canonic writing and preparing for his job with the Detmold choir.

40.

> Handel, Largo, from Trio in B minor
> Eisenstädter Nachtwächter
> Haydn [attributed], excerpt from *Pastorelle de Noele*[82]
>
>> Source: the Archiv, and its librarian, C. F. Pohl
>> Date: 1863

The Handel movement appeared some years later in the *Werke* 27 (1879): 102.

Brahms identified the excerpt from the *Pastorelle* by writing at the end "Aus eine Pastorelle de Noele für Chor u. Instr. angeblich von Jos. Haydn (nach alten Stimmen in Musik-Verein zu Wien.)" It has the text of a night watchman's song. Presumably Brahms made these copies in the Archiv under the aegis of Pohl, who dictated the traditional tune as a comparison; Brahms labeled it "Eisenstädter Nachtwächter nach C. F. Pohl 1863."

41.

> Bach, Prelude quasi Fantasia [incomplete]
>
>> Source and date: unknown, but see 42 below

This copy is a sketchy and incomplete version of the middle section of the Fantasia in G major for organ, BWV 572. No source is given, and the paper is different, but the content and copying style suggest that this sheet is part of the same copying project as 42 below.[83]

42.

> Bach, Fuga [F major, BWV 901]
> Bach, Fuga [G major, BWV 902, incomplete]
>
>> Source: autograph owned by Franz Hauser, Munich
>> Date: perhaps 1869

At the bottom of the page containing the F major fugue, Brahms wrote "Nach Bach'schen Autografen, (Hauser in München)." Brahms visited

Munich for the first time in 1864,[84] but there is no mention in the literature of any contact with Franz Hauser, the eminent Bach collector and scholar, who moved to Karlsruhe after his retirement in 1864 and lived there and in Freiburg until his death in 1870.[85] Hauser's son was a singer in Karlsruhe and performed in the *Deutsches Requiem* in 1869; Brahms could have made these copies (presumably also including sheet 41) then or on some other visit.[86]

The copies on both sheets 41 and 42 are rather fragmentary, and look as though they were made quickly and carelessly. Some sections are missing, and others are enclosed in parentheses without explanation. Brahms wrote an NB next to one gap in the F major fugue, but it may not refer to the gap at all.

43-44.

Haydn, Andante from Symphony no. 16 in B-flat major
Haydn [attributed[87]], "Chorale St. Antoni"

Source: parts in the Archiv
Date: November 1870, for the Andante only

This is the famous bifolio which contains Brahms's first copy of the theme of the Haydn Variations, Op. 56. The first three pages are occupied by the symphony movement, which is headed "Aus einer Sinfonie in B von Haydn für 2 Ob. 2 Viol. Viola u. B." At the end of the movement Brahms wrote "Nov. 70 (copiert)." He made another copy in September 1871 to give to Joachim; it is now in the Wiener Stadtbibliothek (catalog number MH 4033/C).

The "Chorale St. Antoni," which was shown to Brahms by Pohl, is identified as "2ter Satz aus einem Divertimento für Blasinstr. von Haydn." At the end Brahms wrote "das Div. ist Nr. 1 von Sechzehn u. fängt an:" with a quotation of the first two unison bars of the first movement. As McCorkle says, Kalbeck had no evidence to back up his assertion that the Chorale was copied at the same time as the symphony movement.

45.

Cherubini, "Ora pro nobis," from *Litanies de la Sainte Vierge* (1810)

Source: *Oeuvres posthumes*, Vol. I
Date: probably 1854

This piece is not early music, but it does illustrate Cherubini's late, sacred contrapuntal style. Brahms copied the first thirty-two bars, with SATB vocal parts and a piano reduction of the orchestral parts. His copying style here is identical to that found in Abschriften made in 1854. He identified the music fully: "Aus: <u>Litanies de la Sainte Vierge</u> par L. Cherubini (1810). (Oeuvres posthumes 1ᵉʳ Volume)."

A131.   Copies of Canons

> Archiv title: Abschriften klassischer Kanons von Caldara, Cherubini, Haydn, Mozart u.a. 13 sheets, unbound, unnumbered.

The earliest copies in this collection are on a bifolio of the same kind of Hannover paper as A134, 35-36, which is dated April 1854. The canons by Bach, Mozart, and Beethoven come from a collection by André,[88] according to a note by Brahms, along with a table of illustrations of various kinds of canons: augmentation, diminution, inversion, retrograde, and retrograde inversion. The one example of a pre-Bach piece found in the entire collection is also in this first bifolio: Byrd's "Non nobis Domine," which also appears in the Hamburg Stimmenhefte.[89]

The remainder of the collection seems to have been accumulated over a long period, much later in Brahms's career. Some of it is on Eberle no. 16 paper from Vienna. Material identified as coming from the Musikverein includes a number of canons from a collection by Caldara and the "Ten Commandments" of Haydn; the remaining canons include a few more by Haydn, and works by Mozart, Cherubini, Moritz Hauptmann, W. F. Bach, and Kirnberger.

Some additional material is also kept with this collection. It consists of copyist's versions of three of Brahms's own canons, with corrections in his hand;[90] Julius Stockhausen's handwritten copies of some Cherubini canons and Brahms's "Töne, lindernder Klang"; and Franz Böhme's published solution to Brahms's puzzle canon "Mir lächelt kein Frühling."

A132.   "Octaven u. Quinten u. A." Fragments (counterpoint examples)

> Archiv title: Sammlung interessanter Stellen aus grossen Meistern. 7 sheets, unbound, with pages to 11 numbered by Brahms.

This collection was published in facsimile in 1933 by Universal-Edition of Vienna with three pages of explanatory notes by Heinrich Schenker. The notes contain transcriptions of most of Brahms's written remarks, as well as explanations and classifications of the various types of "forbidden" motion found in the collection, together with the reasons many are permissible under the circumstances. A new facsimile, transcription, translation, and discussion of both Brahms's and Schenker's comments has been published by Paul Mast in *Music Forum.*

The examples Brahms copied include parallel octaves and fifths separated by rests or phrase endings, avoided by voice crossing, or disguised by intervening sixths, tenths, or octaves; and parallel octaves and fifths which arise as a consequence of decoration of the essential melodic-contrapuntal lines, although the lines themselves do not produce the parallel motion. Some conventional uses of rows of parallels, such as those found in the Marenzio *Villanelle,* also appear.

The first bifolio is Köster paper, and the second is identical to that used for Brahms's Einsiedeln copies of Frescobaldi (A130, 25-26). This information might suggest that Brahms began his collection of examples during the 1856-57 period when he was assiduously studying counterpoint. However, Mast (pp. 162-63) dates the beginning of the collection at about 1863 on the basis of the 1862 publication of a concerto by Hiller which appears on the first page, and the presence of pieces Brahms performed with the Singakademie. Late in his life he added a large amount of new material to the collection, citing his sources, many recently published. (The last bifolio, which has music copied on only one page, is Eberle no. 17 paper from Vienna.)

It looks as though Brahms may have been considering publishing a monograph or an article of some kind from this material. The collection is full of notes he wrote for himself: cross references, remarks about the various kinds of motion, including a number of quotations from counterpoint books by Ambros and Hauptmann, and many blue pencil markings which seem intended to help organize the material. His unusual care in giving exact sources of the examples supports this idea.

The music ranges in date from two fragments by Clemens non Papa to examples from Bizet's *Carmen.* Composers represented are (in alphabetical order) Bach, Beethoven, Bizet, Caldara, Cherubini, Chopin, Clemens non Papa, Eccard, G. Gabrieli, Gluck, Handel, Hassler, Haydn, Hiller, Kittl, Lasso, Marenzio, Méhul, Mendelssohn, Mozart, Palestrina, Praetorius, Regnart, D. Scarlatti (in an edition by Czerny), Schroeter, Schubert, Schütz, Schumann, Victoria, and Vivaldi (as transcribed by Bach). The one fragment for which no composer is given has a citation to Meister's collection in Brahms's library, and is identified there as being from a *Catechismus* of 1625 by G. Vogler.

Most of the examples by composers who lived before Bach come from various nineteenth-century collections.[91] While the music in each example may be easily read in the facsimiles, the sources are sometimes difficult to decipher; the pieces from which the pre-Bach fragments come, and the sources from which Brahms copied them, are shown in Table 2, in the order in which they appear in the collection. See the list of Brahms's printed music and books (Appendix 3) or the bibliography for information on these nineteenth-century collections. (A letter [N] signifies that the published work is part of the Brahms Nachlass; and numbers such as [A 130] are Abschriften.)

Table 2.   Pre-Bach Fragments Copied by Brahms in A 132

Composer	Piece	Source
Caldara	Salve Regina	Rochlitz II/1: 58
Gabrieli	Benedictus a 12	Winterfeld III: 45 [A 130, 1-6]
Eccard	Am Tage d. heil. Dreifaltigkeit	Teschner II: no. 13 [N]
Praetorius	Puer nobis nascitur	Tucher, no. 128 [N]
Praetorius	text "Wer wird Wohnungen han" (end of piece)	not given
"Palestrina" [really Gabrieli]	Beata es virgo	Winterfeld III [A 130, 1-6]
Gabrieli	Hodie Christus natus est	Becker, *Drei Gesänge von Gabrieli*
Schroeter	Weihnachtsliedlein no. 1	*Musica Sacra* I: no. 11 (Schlesinger)
Clemens non Papa	Souterliedekens (Psalms 20, 22, 13)	Commer, pp. 13, 15, 9 [N]
[G. Vogler]	Jesus der ging den Berg hinan	Meister, Anhang II, no. 19 [N]
Hassler	Nun hat ein end mein Klagen; Ihr musici, frisch auff; Gleich wie ein Hirsch; Ach Schatz, ich sing' und lache	*Lustgarten*, pp. 40, 49, 51, 5 [A 130, 10]
Regnart	Wer wirdet trösten mich	*Vierteljahrsschrift* [A 130, 10]
Marenzio	Villanelle I: nos. 1, 5, 6, 7, 13, 28; II: nos. 5, 11, 14, 18; III: nos. 1, 9	*Villanelle* [92] ("Musikverein")
Victoria	Ave Maria	Wüllner III: 38 [93]
Schütz	Psalm 22	*Werke* II: 25 [A 130, 23-24]
Palestrina	O crux ave	Wüllner III: 25
Palestrina	O vos omnes [two fragments]	Wüllner III: 24, 25

Palestrina	Christus factus est	Wüllner III: 20
Lassus	Ave Regina	Wüllner III: 29
Victoria	Ave Maria	Wüllner III: 32
Lassus	Annelein	Wüllner III: 80

A 133.   Works by Schubert

> Contains beginning and end of Act I from the Easter cantata *Lazarus* (D. 689), the Lieder "Der Strom" (D. 565) and "Herbst" (D. 945), and two fragments of piano pieces. 35 sheets.

The sections from *Lazarus* are copied in full score on the same kind of paper as that used for Bach's "Es ist genug" (A 130, 17); Brahms dated the Schubert copy "Wien März 63," and subsequently sent it both to Grimm and to Clara Schumann.[94] The work was performed under Herbeck on 27 March 1863 for the first time. According to Kalbeck (II: 78), Brahms made his copy while Schubert's autograph score was still at Spina's publishing house, and it was the source of the performing version; however, in view of Brahms's own date in his Abschrift, and its incomplete state, Kalbeck must have been mistaken.

The two songs were copied at different times on different sorts of paper. The second is a hasty copy made on Eberle no. 17 paper like that found in the last part of "Octaven und Quinten." On the back of this sheet is Brahms's incomplete copy of a primitive double-choir setting of the German Te Deum ("Herr Gott, dich loben wir").

The piano pieces are on paper like that used for A 130, 41, the Bach fugues. No dates or other information appear on these or on the song copies.

A 134.   Palestrina's *Missa Papae Marcelli* and Other Renaissance and Baroque Works.

> Also contains copies made by Clara Schumann, and the W. F. Bach work ordered by Joachim. 62 sheets, bound (40 Brahms, 6 Clara Schumann, 16 copyist).

The Abschriften in this volume all appear to have been made between 1854 and about 1858. Some of them are dated, and for all the others the available evidence suggests this early period of Brahms's career, the time when he was most directly under the influence of Robert and Clara Schumann. Brahms himself must have arranged these copies and had them bound, since his signature appears on the extra sheet bound inside the front cover; there is no record of when he placed them together, however. He numbered the pages of the Palestrina mass, the two Lotti pieces, and the Rovetta separately, but the rest of the collection has no page numbers. The sheet numbers used in this discussion are mine, and have been assigned for convenience only.

There are four main sections in the collection. The first part, sheets 1-28, contains Brahms's own Abschriften of large pieces of Italian sacred music on fourteen bifolios of paper which is like that found in A130, 15-16. Although there is no direct evidence, it seems quite likely that the four pieces in this section were copied at various times in Schumann's library, both in Düsseldorf and in Berlin. Clara's copies of pieces by Palestrina and Eccard occupy sheets 29-34. Sheets 35-46 are Brahms copies again, an assortment of short sacred pieces, on different sorts of paper. The last section, sheets 47-62, is a professional copy of a Wilhelm Friedemann Bach work from the Berlin library, ordered by Joachim as a gift for Brahms.

The Abschriften are described here in the order in which they appear in the bound volume.

1-16

Palestrina, *Missa Papae Marcelli*

> Source: unknown. Possibly a handwritten copy in Schumann's library, Düsseldorf
> Date: June 1856 (dated by Brahms)

The title page of the Abschrift reads as follows:

Missa.
dicta
Papae Marcelli,
VI vocum.
auctore
Joanne Petro Aloysio Praenestino.
B [Brahms's flourish initial]

Johannes Brahms
Juni 1856

At the very end of the copy, on page 32, there is just a flourish initial attached to the final double bar. We do not know how long it took Brahms to copy the entire mass, but it appears to have been done within a fairly short period of time. He was working on this project in Düsseldorf during the sad and confused time just before Robert Schumann's death on 29 July 1856.[95]

The *Missa Papae Marcelli* was the work of Renaissance music best known to nineteenth-century musicians, and it was available in several published editions by the time Brahms's copy was made. I have, however, been unable to find a published version that could have been his source, and therefore feel that his most likely source was someone else's manuscript copy in Schumann's library.[96] Brahms's version is transposed down a whole tone from the original, and the note values are reduced by half.[97] It is barred in common time, with bar lines that run all the way through the systems. Brahms began to copy the alto part in treble clef, but after seven bars he changed his mind and decided to use alto clef instead; he then went back to the beginning and scratched out what he had already copied. He finally used TrATB clefs throughout. The seven-voice second Agnus Dei, which did not appear in published editions until later in the century, is not included.[98]

The Abschrift is in ink. At some later time, Brahms added a number of performance markings to the score. Dynamic markings, found throughout the piece, are in pencil; and phrase marks, in the Kyrie and Benedictus only, are in red pencil.[99] There is no record of his having ever performed any part of the piece with any of his choirs, and no indication of when or why these performance markings were added, although the writing style suggests they could have been added during the Detmold years.

17-19, 20-24.

Lotti, "Crucifixus a 8 voci" and "Crucifixus für 10 Stimmen"

Source: unknown. Perhaps a handwritten copy in Schumann's library, Berlin
Date: May 1858 (dated by Brahms)

Schumann owned copies of both these pieces; he also studied a "Crucifixus von Lotti (Bibliothek)" with the Düsseldorf Chorgesangsverein in the winter of 1851-52.[100] After his death, when Clara was preparing to move to Berlin, Brahms wrote her in October 1857 about the way he had packed some of the music, and mentioned a "Crucifixus von Lotti" specifically.[101] He might then have taken the opportunity during his visit to Clara in Berlin in April and early May 1858 to make his own Abschriften from Schumann's copies.

The two pieces were clearly copied at the same time, and Brahms himself numbered the pages from 2 to 15. At the last double bar, he signed his name with a flourish and added the date "1858 Mai." Each piece is copied in TrATB clefs with an Organo part at the bottom.

While both these works were well known in the nineteenth century, the eight-voice Crucifixus in particular was available in a large number of contemporary editions, including Rochlitz's collection and the *Musica Sacra* series published by Schlesinger and also by Bote and Bock.[102] All of these have important differences from Brahms's versions, however, especially in the treatment of the Organo part. A separate Schlesinger publication containing both pieces, edited by A. B. Marx, was published in 1825 or 1826; if this was not Brahms's source, he must have used a handwritten copy.[103]

25-28.

Giovanni Rovetta, "Salve Regina"

Source: *Allgemeine musikalische Zeitung* 15 (1813): Beilage no. 1
Date: before autumn 1857

Rovetta does not appear in Eitner's *Verzeichniss* at all.[104] The British Library catalog of printed music contains an entry for this 1813 edition, however, and it is unquestionably Brahms's source, since the heading and the editorial dynamics are identical to those in his ink copy. He signed the end of his copy with the flourish "Brahms" he also used in the Lotti copies, but did not date it; it seems certain, though, that he made the copy before the autumn of 1857, when he worked on the piece with the choir at Detmold and mentioned it in letters to both Clara Schumann and Joachim.[105] He later performed it in his second concert with the Singakademie, on 6 January 1864. Perhaps it was for this performance that he made some pencil alterations in the dynamics in his Abschrift.[106]

Brahms's title is taken directly from the source: "Salve Regina di Giov. Rovetta. (vice-Maestro di Capella a Venezia, 1640.)" The piece is copied in SATTB clefs, with a figured bass labeled "Organo."[107] Brahms did not write the Latin text into all the voices, but it is clear what the underlay should be in the missing sections. In two places the exact spelling and placement of the text have been clarified by another person; the handwriting looks like that of the copyist who prepared the parts for the Singakademie. Brahms wrote a German translation in pencil along the bottom.

The published version was printed in the *Allgemeine musikalische Zeitung* as supplement to a news report from Breslau (cols. 12-16) on the establishment of a Sing-Institut on the model of the Fasch-Zelter group in Berlin. The director was a Herr Bierey, who had himself provided much of the group's repertoire by making scores of works by seventeenth-century Italian composers from old partbooks in the library of the Elisabethian Gymnasium. The editors of the journal included the score of Rovetta's "Salve Regina" as an example of Herr Bierey's work, saying that they had chosen it because of its "characteristic, simple, and still artistic melodies, especially towards the end, which make it so exalted, devout, and moving.''

In spite of this editorial evaluation, the attraction of the piece for Brahms is something of a mystery. After the dramatic chromaticism of the opening phrases, the pedestrian quality of the remainder of the setting, which has the added disadvantage of being too long because of much unnecessary repetition, is a disappointment; the initial flavor is recaptured only in the last few measures. Also, in spite of Brahms's assertion that the work is relatively easy, the present writer's opinion is that the reward would not be worth the effort of getting the innumerable tricky entrances in the right places. It seems likely that because Brahms came into contact with the piece at an early and still impressionable age, and associated it with the largely enjoyable initial experience of directing the Detmold choir, he retained a fondness for it that made him want to work on it again with the Singakademie in spite of its deficiencies.

29-34. Clara Schumann's copies

Palestrina, "Gloria Patri"
Palestrina, "Pleni sunt coeli"
Palestrina [attributed], "O bone Jesu"[108]
Palestrina, *Improperia*: "Popule meus"

> Source: Rochlitz, *Sammlung vorzüglicher Gesangstücke* I (1835), Abtheilung 2: 2-7.
> In Schumann's library (another copy is in the Brahms Nachlass)

Eccard, "Übers Gebirg Maria geht"

> Source: unknown
> Date: unknown, but perhaps summer 1858

In the summer of 1858, Clara Schumann offered to make Brahms copies of works which interested him.[109] It may be that these few Abschriften are all that remain of her efforts, or they may be all that she finally made for him. It is also, of course, possible that these copies were made several years earlier, when both Schumanns were encouraging Brahms to pursue the study of early music; in that case, Clara may very well have copied pieces from her husband's library which she wished to recommend to Brahms. At one time the three bifolios were tied together with string.

The Palestrina copies are the first four pieces in the second part of volume I of Rochlitz's important collection; Schumann had the volume in his library.[110] Clara copied them precisely as they occur in the published version, with all editorial clefs, dynamics, and tempo indications.

Eccard and Schütz are the two composers Brahms mentioned specifically in the 1858 correspondence. If Clara had made these copies earlier, so that he already knew "Übers Gebirg," he may have wanted to learn more music by a composer who could write in the sixteenth century such a remarkably lush and beautiful work, full of seventh chords, secondary dominants, and Romantic-sounding suspensions.[111] It certainly remained one of his favorites: he arranged it for the Frauenchor,[112] and performed it in his first concert with the Musikverein in November 1872.

The only nineteenth-century printed sources listed by Eitner for this piece which would have been available to Clara are Winterfeld's *Der evangelische Kirchengesang* I, and Teschner's 1858 edition.[113] Neither could have been her source, since there are too many differences, not the least of which is the text of the first verse; this text is different in every nineteenth-century version of this piece I have seen.[114] Clara's copy is in F major (the original key, according to Winterfeld, who like Teschner transposes it down to D major) and TrTrATB clefs, with a number of added dynamics. Brahms made a few minor alterations in the dynamics, added several accent marks, and corrected several wrong notes as well as the text underlay of the second verse in one spot.

Hübbe and Kalbeck both state that "Übers Gebirg" was the inspiration for Brahms's *Marienlieder*.[115] Kalbeck also says that the copy was made in Düsseldorf in 1854, and implies that Brahms made it; it seems likely that he confused this Abschrift with the Responsoria which follow it in the bound collection.

35-36.

   Palestrina [attributed; actually Ingegneri], *Responsoria*
   I. "Velum templi scissum est"
   II. "Tenebrae factae sunt"

   Source: unknown, but probably in Schumann's library
   Date: April 1854 (dated by Brahms)

These are two of the twenty-seven Responsoria which were generally thought to be by Palestrina until 1897, when a copy of the original 1588 edition turned up in a sale.[116] "Velum templi" was available in a number of nineteenth-century editions, but none that I have seen is Brahms's source. Eitner does not list "Tenebrae," although it was printed singly in at least one version which is also not a source for Brahms.[117]

It seems most likely that a printed or manuscript copy in Schumann's library was the source for these pieces. In 1852 Schumann had prepared "Responsorien von Palestrina" for performance with his choir.[118] Brahms dated his copy "Ddf. April '54"; this is in the period shortly after Schumann's breakdown, when Brahms moved to Düsseldorf and occupied himself by arranging Schumann's library.[119] The copies are on paper which bears a printed stamp "Adolph Nagel in Hannover"; it is the same as that used for the earliest copies of canons in A131, and was no doubt acquired by Brahms when he was staying with Joachim in Hannover. The pages of the bifolio are numbered 1 through 4 in red pencil.

37-38.

Nine sacred continuo Lieder (1690-1714)
Krüger, "Herzliebster Jesus"

Source, Winterfeld, *Der evangelische Kirchengesang*[120]
Date: probably May 1854

These continuo Lieder, taken from various songbooks of the period, appear in Winterfeld's third volume as illustrations to the chapter (text pp. 21-26) on Freilinghausen's songbooks published in Halle. The melodies are in soprano clef, and each has a figured bass; Winterfeld also gives information on the songbooks and their dates, and the names of the authors of the texts. No composers are identified.

Brahms chose to copy only nine of the thirteen songs given by Winterfeld as examples nos. 1-12 (no. 9 appears with two different melodies). He changed the soprano clef to treble and copied only parts of the explanatory notes, but otherwise his copies are identical to the original. The following list shows Brahms's own numbering of the songs, together with the notes he copied from Winterfeld; then, in square brackets, Winterfeld's numbers are given, along with the beginning of the text and any additional information provided about each piece in the source.

1. Das Lied, wie die folg. bis No. 11, von Johann Angelus; die Mel. 1698 im Züehlenschen [sic] Gesangbuch (aus Winterfeld). [1. "Jesu wie süss ist deine Liebe"]

2. Die Mel. 1704. [2. "Ach, sagt mir nichts von Geld und Schätzen." From the first part of the Freilinghausen Gesangbuch]

3. Die Mel. 1714. [3. "Dein' eigne Liebe zwinget mich." From the second part of the Freilinghausen Gesangbuch]

4. [4. "Du zuckersüsses Himmelsbrot." Melody 1705, from the second edition of Freilinghausen's first book]

5. Die Mel. 1704. [5. "Hochheilige Dreieinigkeit"]

6. Die Mel. 1704. [7. "Komm, Liebster, komm in deinen Garten"]

7. Die Mel. 1690. [8. "Meine Seele willt du ruhn." From the appendix to Feuerlein's songbook from Nürnberg]

8. Die Mel. 1698. [10. "Wo ist der Schönste den ich liebe"]

9. Die Mel. 1698. Das Lied von Christian Friedr. Richter. [12. "Die lieblichen Blicke die Jesus mir giebt"]

There is no written clue to why Brahms chose to copy the particular pieces he did. The texts express a personal, pietistic feeling toward religion; and the music ranges from stern chorale melodies to saccharine dance tunes. The four he left out are perhaps of lower quality than the others, but there is no way to be sure that he left them out for that reason; and of course it is a temptation to conclude that they are of lower quality simply because he *did* leave them out.

The space left on the back page of the bifolio after the songs end is occupied by a four-part chorale setting headed " 'Herzliebster Jesus' von Johannes Krüger. 1640." Just above the first notes Brahms wrote again "Joh. Crüger." His source was the second volume of Winterfeld, example 76 (p. 58). He copied the chorale exactly, including all original and editorial accidentals, but did rather a careless job, so that he had to make several corrections.

At the bottom of this last page is a heading "Romance, Attribué à Henry IV, Roi de France" followed by a treble clef; it has all been crossed out.

The paper of this bifolio is identical to sheet 3 of A128, which contains Swedish and German folk tunes and is dated May 1854 in Düsseldorf; the copying style is also identical. These Abschriften are, therefore, several years earlier than most of the others which come from *Der evangelische Kirchengesang*.

39-40.

Attaignant, "Il me suffit" [melody and text only]
Praetorius, [Hieronymus], "Was mein Gott will"

Source: Winterfeld, *Der ev. Kirchengesang* I: nos. 138a and 66

Erythräus, "In dich hab' ich gehoffet, Herr" [first melody, Strassburg 1560; in Tucher, no. 146, notes p. 356]
Praetorius, M., "In dich hab' ich gehoffet, Herr" [second melody, by Calvisius, 1594; no. 184, notes p. 373]
"Herzlich thut mich verlangen," two rhythmic versions[121] [melody and text only; no. 315]
Gesius, "O Welt ich muss dich lassen" [no. 181]
Isaak, "Insbruck ich muss dich lassen" [melody and text only; perhaps copied from Winterfeld][122]

Praetorius, M., "In dulci jubilo" [text "Lobt Gott, du Christenheit";
no. 363, notes p. 408]

Source: Tucher, *Schatz des evangelischen Kirchengesangs* II (Melodienbuch), 1848.
Brahms Nachlass
Date: probably 1854

The style of copying here is the same as that in sheets 37-38, and therefore
the date is probably 1854 also. Brahms was evidently using Winterfeld
and Tucher to investigate the origins and development of various well-
known chorale melodies. He copied not only the music as it was given
in his sources, but also enough information from their notes to show that
he had tried to track down all the available information.

In the copy of "Was mein Gott will," Brahms identified the composer
of the four-part setting as "M. Praetorius, 1604." The date is correct, but
the composer named by Winterfeld is Hieronymus Praetorius. The Attaignant tune is identified as the original version of the chorale melody
by Winterfeld. For "In dich hab' ich gehoffet" Brahms copied all the
information given about the origins of the tunes, but did not give the
composers of the settings; they may be found in Tucher's notes.

Above the two versions of "Herzlich thut mich verlangen" is the title
"Ursprüngliche Melodie des Liedes: O Haupt voll Blut u. Wunden."
These, along with the copies of "Mein G'müth ist mir verwirret" that
have been mentioned in A128 (1-2 and 5-12), as well as the complete
version in A134, 43-44 (see below), serve to illustrate Brahms's continuing
interest in the history of the Passion chorale. His concern with finding a
satisfactory solution to the tune's rhythmic problems is shown here. The
second example is labeled "Von Tucher theilt die Melodie, wie nach steht
rythmisch [sic] ab," and is barred in an unchanging 4/2. The first example,
with its irregular barring in a mixture of 6/4 and 4/4, may have been
copied from Winterfeld's version of "Mein G'müth ist mir verwirret,"
and the sacred text, slightly different from Tucher's, inserted from another source.[123]

"Insbruck" is another tune which appears several times in the Abschriften. Here Brahms copied the four-part setting by Gesius of the
sacred text and then added a note "Siehe umstehend—Original Melodie." On the other side of the sheet is the secular text and tune, copied
in treble clef and barred in unchanging 4/2; Brahms probably obtained
this version from Winterfeld (see A134, 43-44 below).

At the end of the bifolio, after the setting of "In dulci jubilo," Brahms
wrote "Eingerichtet von Freiherr von Tucher," and added his initials. He
owned a copy of Tucher's collection and may have used it as his source
for all these Abschriften (there is no record of when he acquired it), or

he may have used a copy belonging to Schumann or one of his other friends. If his intent in making these Abschriften was study and comparison rather than performance, it is probably just as well: Eitner, in his *Verzeichniss,* says that in Tucher's collection "the settings are so willfully changed that one obtains only a mutilated version of the compositions."

41-42.

> Arthophius, "Die Brünnlein die da fliessen"
> Steurlein, "Der Gnadenbrunn thut fliessen"
> Eccard, "Ich dank dir lieber Herre"
>
> Source: Winterfeld, *Der ev. Kirchengesang* I: nos. 108a, 108, 137
> Date: probably 1857-60

The copying style of these Abschriften is later than that of the preceding bifolio, and they may have been made at the same time as the Winterfeld copies of A 130, 15-19 and bifolio 43-44 below. They continue the story of Brahms's interest in chorale settings.

The pieces and their headings come directly from Winterfeld. The first is labeled with the name of the tune and "Tonsatz von Balthasar Arthophius 1537." For the second Brahms wrote only "Dieselbe Mel. umgewandelte der Tonsatz 1588," and did not give the composer of the setting, Johann Steurlein, who is identified by Winterfeld only in the table of contents to the appendix of musical examples. The third appears to be included because of its origin as a well-known secular tune; Brahms copied the complete citation, and included a reference to the source: "Die Mel. zuerst m. d. weltl. Lied. 'Entlaubt ist uns der Walde' 1539. . . . Der Tonsatz 1597. (von Eccard.) Winterfeld Bd. I. (evang. Kirchenges.)"[124]

43-44.

> Isaac, "Insbruck ich muss dich lassen"
> Hassler, "An Maria" ["Mein G'müth ist mir verwirret"]
>
> Source: music from Winterfeld, *Der ev. Kirchengesang* I, nos. 110a and 80; texts from C. F. Becker, *Lieder und Weisen vergangener Jahrhunderte,* pp. 9 and 21-22, in the Brahms Nachlass
> Date: probably 1857-60

The paper of this bifolio is the same as 41-42 above, and the copies seem to have been made at about the same time. Brahms may have made them originally for the mixed choir in Detmold; both pieces also appear in arrangements for women's voices in the Hamburg Stimmenhefte.[125]

In both cases the music and the first verse of text are copied directly from Winterfeld, and the text of all other verses comes from Becker's collection, which contains texts and tunes only. For "Insbruck," Brahms supplied a note from Winterfeld: "Die Mel. 1539 der Tonsatz von Heinr. Isaac ebenfalls." Where the music of the first section is repeated, he left out all but the soprano part and text. He barred the ink copy in the regular 4/2 which comes from Winterfeld, but added short red pencil strokes in the soprano part to show the true meter, which changes between 6/2 and 4/2; this metric problem is discussed further in chapter 3, below (p. 161). The additional verses of text appear on a different page from the music, and are copied with modernized spelling and capitalization.

The few pencil markings in "Insbruck" include a large "No. 1" and some words from the end of the second verse, showing the correct underlay according to a revision Brahms had made in the text. These additions were probably made so that the copyist of the Musikverein could use this Abschrift as his model for the parts prepared for performances in November 1872. These parts also contain dynamics; but no intermediate version, such as model copies of the parts with additional markings in Brahm's hand, has survived.

For the second piece in this bifolio, the title "An Maria" comes from Becker. At the end of the music, Brahms identified both his sources and included some information from Winterfeld: "Zuerst gedruckt 1601. (v. Leo Hassler)/(Texte in Becker)" appears in ink; and "(Aus Winterfeld Ex. 79)" was added in pencil. The other pencil markings include a large "2" at the beginning and a number of notations which show how to fit in the text after the first verse. Brahms originally decided to perform verses 1, 2, 4, and 5, and wrote in a note to that effect at the end of the extra verses of text, but he later changed his mind and crossed out the number 4. In spite of all these plans, however, there is no record of a performance of "Mein G'müth ist mir verwirret" by any of his mixed choirs. The barring in this version is the mixture of 6/4 and 4/4 which best fits the rhythm of the text.

45-46.

Luther, "Jesus Christus, unser Heiland"
Schein, "Veni redemptor gentium"
Praetorius, "Nun komm der Heiden Heiland"
Calvisius, "Allein Gott in der Höh' sei Ehr"
Walther, "Mitten wir in Leben sind"
Isaac, "Insbruck ich muss dich lassen"

Source: unknown
Date: 1856-58?

The copying style of this bifolio (which is ruled for piano music) is similar to that of the Palestrina, Lotti, and Rovetta copies (A134, 1-28) which were made during the period 1856-58. The Abschriften found here, clearly made as part of Brahms's investigation of chorales, were done rapidly and carelessly. The Luther and Walther pieces appear as melody and figured bass only; the others are all in four parts, reduced to two staves. When one piece ends, another is begun immediately on the same staves.

The appearance of these copies suggests that the pieces were all obtained at once from a single source—but Eitner's *Verzeichniss* shows no such source, and, indeed, does not list several of the works at all. We can only speculate that Brahms found them in a hymnal or a history of Protestant church music and copied them, each with its explanatory notes. These notes are as follows, in the order in which the pieces appear in the bifolio:

Mel. Wittenberg 1543. Ges. M. Luther 1543.

Mel. u. Text von Ambrosius †397. (Tonsatz v. Schein 1627.)

Aus dem Lateinischen u. Umbildung die Mel. M. Luther 1524. Harm. M. Praetorius 1607.

Die Mel. 1540 nach d. altkirchl. Gloria in excelsis Deo. Tonsatz v. Calvisius 1597. Ges. v. Decius 1529.

Mel. aus der 15tn Jahrh. (bei Walther 1524 / Luther.)

Mel. u. Harm. v. Hein. Isaac / 1440 geb./
   Mel. zu: "In allen meinen Thaten" v. Flemming
      "Nun ruhen alle Wälder" v. Gerhardt
      "O Welt ich muss dich lassen" Joh. Hesse
      "Der Mond ist untergangen" v. Claudius

47-62. Made by a professional copyist.

Wilhelm Friedemann Bach, Kyrie & Gloria [*Deutsche Messe*]

Source: "aus der Berliner Bibliothek copiert" [autograph]
Date: "6/9 1856."

This work, for SATB, 2 violins, viola, and basso continuo, was copied as a gift for Brahms from Joachim, according to a note in the front of A134. Brahms sent his thanks on 19 October 1856,[126] but said no more about the piece in letters, and made no marks in the score. The piece is described in *MGG* as "teilweise Parodie."

A135. Chorale "O wy arme Sünders," Set by Johannes Bertram (1569)

Plattdeutsch text by Hermann Bonn.
Archiv title: Bonno: Choral "O wy arme Sünders" in Partitur gesetzt. Autograph Brahms.
3 sheets, bound; plus two sixteenth-century sheets.

At some unknown time, Brahms acquired two sheets, numbered 79 and 80, from a sixteenth-century book, containing a chorale setting in choirbook format. He transcribed the music and investigated the tenor melody; but he never succeeded in tracking down the source of his two sheets, or he would surely have added a note to his copies.[127]

A reference work published near the end of Brahms's life, Johannes Zahn's *Die Melodien der deutschen evangelischen Kirchenlieder,*[128] would have made it possible, oddly enough, for him to find the source of his two sheets on the shelves of the Archiv itself. They come from Lucas Lossius's *Psalmodia,* published in Wittenberg in 1569 by Joh. Schwertelius. In the Musikverein copy, sheets 79 and 80 are identical to Brahms's two isolated sheets, right down to the printing errors;[129] whereas another copy of the 1569 edition, in the British Library, has a number of small differences.[130]

Psalmodia contains a very large quantity of plainchant with Latin texts, and all of the introductory material and commentary is also in Latin; however, six chorales, the Te Deum, a litany, and a Credo are found in Plattdeutsch versions, together with an order of service used in the Lüneburg church in the early days of the Reformation. The only four-part setting is "O wy arme Sünders"; two of the other German chorales have two-part settings. "O wy arme Sünders" also has a long title, which Brahms copied in full in his final ink Abschrift, along with the heading at the top of the pages which places the chorale in the church year:

In die
Parasceves.
Canticum de Peccato
& Passione Christi, germanicum,
Autore Hermanno Bonno,
ad melodiam cantici veteris:
"O du arme Judas,"
Quatuor vocibus compositum
per Jo. Bert. C.

To this title Brahms added the note

('O wy arme Sünders')
plattdeutsch

and the references[131]

Liliencron N. 1.
Meister   131
Böhme   539

   This title, with the name of the author of the text appearing in the
ablative form "Bonno," has led not only to the misleading Archiv title of
this Abschrift, but to the presence of the nonexistent Bonno in Geiringer's
list of composers whose works were copied by Brahms.[132] The actual
composer of the setting, as the title makes clear, was "Jo. Bert. C."; he
also appears in *Psalmodia* as the author of a poetic elegy to Lossius, and
is there identified as Johannes Bertram, Cantor of Lüneburg. The author
of the text, on the other hand, or at least the man who "corrected" it
into this Plattdeutsch version, which was first published in the Magde-
burger Gesangbuch of 1543, was Hermann Bonn (or Bonnus), Superin-
tendent at Lübeck.[133]

   Brahms copied the chorale setting twice. The earlier copy is a piano
reduction in pencil, a direct transcription from the sixteenth-century parts.
This is a correct copy, and shows the voice crossing in the phrase "Christe
eleison." It also has added blue pencil references to the three folk-song
collections, and a single blue pencil stroke down the middle of the page,
presumably meant to cross it out once the later ink copy was made.

   The ink copy is headed by the complete title given above, along with
the references. The music is laid out in score, with the original names and
clefs of the four parts given as "Discantus," "Tenor," "Altus," and
"Bassus," in S, A, A, and baritone clefs respectively. Brahms then indicated his changes to SATB clefs. After giving all this information from
the original parts, he seems to have copied the music from his own piano
reduction, since he made an error in the Bassus at "Christe eleison"
which results from the voice crossing with the Altus; this error would be
impossible to make from the single part, but is very easy from the reduction. He later queried this error in a pencil note, since it results in a
series of parallel unisons.

   The earliest date the ink copy could have been made is 1877, the year
of publication of Böhme's collection. There is no information on how
much earlier Brahms made the pencil transcription. The two original
pages probably attracted his attention because of the Plattdeutsch text,
which recalled his north German youth. The setting as a whole is remarkable to modern ears for the uncompromising simplicity with which
the Mixolydian tune is harmonized.

   A transcription of the setting, prepared by the present writer from

the parts in *Psalmodia,* is given as Example 4; parallels and other faulty
voice leading are in the original.

Example 4

"O wy arme Sünders"

Setting by Johannes Bertram
Text by Hermann Bonn

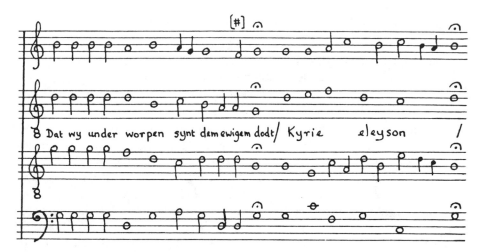

Dat wy under worpen synt dem ewigem dodt/ Kyrie eleyson

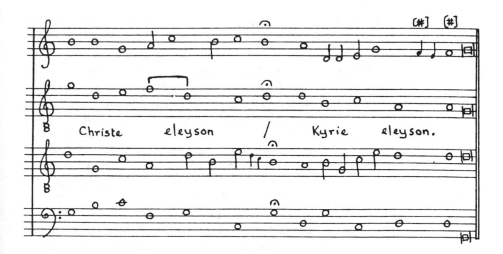

Christe eleyson / Kyrie eleyson.

A136.   Gallus [Handl], "Ecce quomodo moritur justus," in Brahms's hand

In a copyist's hand: Palestrina, "Haec dies" a 6
                      Lasso, "Aus meiner Sünden Tiefe"
                      Ahle, "Es ist genug"
                      Bach, "Es ist genug"

This group of Abschriften represents the intermediate stage in preparation for Brahms's concert with the Singverein of the Gesellschaft der Musikfreunde on 7 December 1873, when the Gallus, Bach, and Ahle works were performed. There is no record of any performance of the other two pieces under Brahms. All of the works except the Palestrina appear in earlier Brahms copies in A130; and all five are also found in the copyist's final versions of the score and parts.[134] The five sheets bound together here are the same kind of paper as that which the copyist used for his final version of the score; therefore all of these copies were probably made within a fairly short space of time before the rehearsals for this performance began.

Brahms prepared this performance edition of the Gallus piece from his own transcription from the partbooks (see A130, 18-19) by transposing it down a minor third from F to D and adding regular barring in 4/2 and bar numbers. He used SATB clefs, and added dynamics in red pencil. He clearly made this copy as a model for the professional copyist to work from in preparing the parts; thus we find Brahms's instruction "ausschreiben" at the end, to tell the copyist to write out the repetition of the last section.

The Lasso, Ahle, and Bach works were taken by the copyist directly from Brahms's earlier versions in A130 (sheets 9, 16, and 17 respectively), to which he had added dynamics, or in some cases altered previous dynamics. In all three pieces, the copyist used only treble and bass clefs. In the Lasso piece, Brahms had to supply dynamic markings in the last few bars, since they had been inadvertently left out of the earlier copy (see above, p. 23). In the Ahle chorale setting he made two corrections, but left his original dynamics unchanged; and in the Bach, which is a copy of the version he finally arrived at in A130 (see p. 28), he deleted three fermatas and added one "p."[135]

Palestrina's "Haec dies" appears here for the first time in the Abschriften. Probably Brahms instructed the copyist to prepare his own transposed version from the source, S. W. Dehn's *Sammlung älterer Musik aus dem 16ten und 17ten Jahrhundert* (Berlin: Crantz), Vol. 11, pp. 7-9, the only published version of the six-voice setting listed by Eitner. In the copy the piece is transposed up a half step, from D to E flat major.[136] After it was made, Brahms added performance markings in red pencil and corrected errors in the transposition. He later made a few changes, and then transferred his instructions to sample copies of the individual parts.

A137.   Brahms's Title: " 'Ave Maria' von Arcadelt. c. 1530-75."

One sheet, bound

The paper on which Brahms made this Abschrift is vertical format, with spacing and size of the staves identical to those found in the horizontal format sheets 1-28 of A134. A similar copying style also suggests that this copy was made in the period 1856-58, when Brahms was collecting repertoire for the Detmold choir.

His source was H. Kästner's collection *Chor-Gesänge ohne Instrumenten Begleitung* (Hannover, 1851). His own copy of this collection, catalogued under "Verschiedene" in the Archiv (Signatur H27302), is lacking the title page; but Brahms wrote "NB. Kästner in Hannover" in it. There is nothing to show when he acquired it. His Abschrift is identical in every respect to the source, including the addition of dynamics and a German singing translation, except that he did not include Kästner's piano reduction.

Brahms did not know that the piece was not really by Arcadelt. Eitner mentions the misattribution in his 1871 *Verzeichniss,* and Reese says,

> The famous "Ave Maria," attributed to Arcadelt and apparently first published in 1845, is in reality a modern adaptation of his lively three-part chanson, "Nous voyons que les hommes font tous vertu d'aimer," whose text is scarcely suggestive of religious contemplation.[137]

Other Abschriften

The early music Abschriften which are part of the Brahms Nachlass in the Archiv, but which he did not make himself, are discussed here in a arbitrary order which is roughly chronological by their musical contents:

1.   Forster's *Ein aussbund schöner Teutscher Liedlein,* 5 vols., scored from the partbooks by Carl Dreher in 1867 and recopied by Hof-Musicus Dorsihel, Karlsruhe, 1869
2.   "Deutsche vierstimmige Volkslieder aus dem 16ten Jahrhunderte" [Archiv title]. Copied by Gustav Nottebohm
3.   Melodies from the sixteenth-century Catholic songbooks of Leisentrit and Canisius. Copied by Julius Allgeyer, 1856

4. Sacred works by Palestrina, Anerio, and Victoria. Copied by Robert Schumann
5. Palestrina, "Princeps gloriosissime" and "Gaude Barbara beata." Copyist unknown
6. Schütz, "Wer will uns scheiden" [SWV 330]. Copyist unknown
7. "Alte Instrumentalcompositionen" [Nottebohm's title]. 6 vols., mostly copied and all assembled by Gustav Nottebohm. Contains only a few vocal pieces
8. "Composizioni di differenti Maestri": sacred works by Italian Baroque composers. Copyist unknown
9. Durante, *XII Cantate a due.* Copyist unknown (18th century?)
10. Bach, Cantata 150, "Nach dir, Herr" [in the Stadtbibliothek, Vienna]. Copyist unknown; discarded by Brahms

1. [Georg Forster: the title of volume I is as follows:]

Ein aussbund schöner Teutscher Liedlein zu singen, und / auff allerley Instrumenten, zugebrauchen, / sonderlich ausser lesen. . . . Nürnberg: Johann vom Berg, 1560. . . . Aus der Gymnasialbibliothek zu Heilbronn spartirt. Carl Dreher.
Five volumes, copied by Hof-Musicus Dorsihel.
[Archiv Signatur II/30130. Listed in both Brahms catalogs.[138]]

A dedication page in the first volume, containing the following statement, is signed by a number of people, including Hermann Levi and Carl Dreher.

Johannes Brahms
zur Erinnerung
an die
Aufführung des
deutschen Requiem
am 10ten März 1869.[139]
Vom
Philharmonischen Verein
Carlsruhe.
Der Vorstand.

At the end of this volume, complete explanatory information about the copies is supplied. There is a signature from the copyist: "geschrieben von Hof-Musicus Dorsihel zu Carlsruhe"; and a statement written by Carl Dreher, a teacher at the Lyceum there, dated 16 October 1869. He explains that he had borrowed the partbooks from the Gymnasium library in Heilbronn in 1867 and had prepared his own score from them, that many printing errors had been corrected with the help of a Munich music librarian, and that this new copy of the score has been prepared from his transcription.

At the beginning of each volume, the title page and introductory material from the tenor partbook are all copied; the title pages of the other partbooks and the Register for that volume are found at the end. As we have already seen, volume I is a transcription of the 1560 edition. Volume II is from 1553, III from 1552, IV from 1556, and V from 1556.[140]

In the copy, all variations from the original partbooks—clef changes, transpositions, and corrections or errors—are shown. Note values are unreduced, with duple meter barred in 4/2 and triple meter in 3/1. Almost no editorial accidentals are added. Texts appear only in the tenor and soprano parts, and any verses after the first are copied at the end of each piece.

Brahms studied all five of these volumes with considerable care. He turned down the corners of a number of pages, including several where melodies which he himself had set are found. He also wrote in many cross references to different settings of the same tune and to other collections where the settings had been published. In some pieces he added accidentals, mainly in order to provide cadential leading tones. In two works where verbal instructions for filling in missing parts are provided, he wrote them in: one of these is a canon for four equal voices (IV, pp. 76-77; he marked a place where parallel fifths occur in the solution); and the other is a piece for two five-voice choirs, where the second imitates the first exactly (V, no. 52). Often he made corrections or questioned possible errors. The three pieces from Forster which appear in A130, 7-8 do not contain an unusual number of annotations.

The various kinds of quodlibets found in volume II seem to have attracted Brahms's particular attention. He identified four pieces as quodlibets and apparently studied them with extra care, since they are marked with added accidentals, square brackets which denote the entrances of the various tunes and texts, and additional texts where they had sometimes been left out of the tenor. An especially interesting example is no. 60, by Leon. Heydhammer (whose name is spelled in several ways in the collection), with a text which begins "Der Winter kalt ist vor dem Haus." This piece is an example of the third type of quodlibet described by Walther,[141] in which a number of well-known tunes follow one another in quick succession. Brahms marked all the entrances of new tunes throughout both sections of this long piece; they are usually in the tenor but occasionally appear in other voices as well. He also added a number of accidentals, most (but not all; see chapter 3, p. 157) to raise cadential leading tones. Two rhythmic features are clearly marked: a cadential hemiola which occupies two 3/1 measures is identified by square brackets above the staff; and a short section where the soprano breaks into sesquialtera triplets against duple meter in the tenor and bass is pointed out by NBs and numbers. These rhythmic markings are discussed further and illustrated below, in chapter 3 (pp. 159-60).

In volume IV, three four-voice settings of "Mein selbs bin ich nicht gwaltig mehr" by Stephanus Zirlerus (Nos. 37, 38, and 39) are marked not only by cross references, but by a note "NB die Cadenzen." Each cadence then has its own NB in the voice that carries the cantus firmus— the tenor, bass, and soprano respectively in the three settings. Brahms may have been interested here in the way the outline of the tune is changed in each case in order to make it fit the standard cadential pattern, which is almost identical regardless of which part ostensibly has the melody.

By the time Brahms acquired these five volumes, he was no longer making an attempt to imitate the style of the Renaissance Lied in any of his choral works. Nonetheless, he was interested in this music for its own sake, as his markings clearly show. He also used the collection as an important source of material for his continuing study of German folk songs.

2.   "Deutsche vierstimmige Volkslieder aus dem 16ten Jahrhunderte"

> [Archiv title]. 30 sheets, unbound, copied by Gustav Nottebohm. [Signatur V/45373. Not listed in either Brahms catalog.] A collection of melodies, 10 sheets also copied by Nottebohm, has the Signatur V/45373a.[142]

This collection of twenty-six four-part settings is the source of the four Tenorlieder Brahms copied, probably soon after he arrived in Vienna (A 130, 7-8). It and the companion collection of melodies were presumably added to his library after Nottebohm's death in 1882.[143]

Nottebohm had studied in Berlin and Leipzig for a number of years before moving to Vienna, and could certainly have transcribed these Lieder, which come from a variety of sixteenth-century sources, from partbooks in north German libraries. Originally he gave each transcription an ink number. After he had made a separate copy of the melodies (V/45373a), he assigned new pencil numbers to them; he then crossed out the original ink numbers of the four-part settings, and replaced them in pencil with the numbers corresponding to the melodies. The unbound settings (V/45373) are now arranged in order of the pencil numbers, which are repeated for different settings of the same tune; some transcriptions have evidently been lost, because the numbers are not consecutive.[144]

Table 3 shows the surviving contents of the collection V/45373, arranged in order of the pencil numbers (the ink numbers are given in

parentheses). Any additional information Nottebohm added to his transcription, such as the mode of the melody or the source of the setting, is
also provided; and original spellings are used. The four Lieder marked
with asterisks are those Brahms copied into A130.

Table 3.   Contents of Nottebohm's Collection

Pencil No.	Ink No.	Composer	Melody
1.	(2)	[Walter[145]]	Ach Gott vom Himmel sieh darein (Dorisch plagalisch)
7.*	(31)	Zirler	Die Sonn' die ist verblichen
9.	(1)	Walther	Ein newes Lied wir heben an (Dorisch)
10.*	(25)	Stoltzer	Entlaubet ist uns der Walde
12.*	(26)	Greitter	Es wolt ein Jeger jagen (Ionisch)
13.	(39)	Zirler	Ach Gretlein (Dorisch)
14.	(32)	Brant	Frisch auf in Gottes Namen (Mixolydisch)
15.	(12)	Senfl	Ich stund an einem Morgen
15.*	(11)	Senfl	Ich stund an einem Morgen (Phrygisch)
15.	(20)	Finck	Ich stund an einem Morgen
15.	(13)	Senfl	Ich stund an einem Morgen
15.	(15)	Senfl	Ich stund an einem Morgen
17B.	(35)	Brand	Ach Gott, ich muss verzagen (Sopran ist Tenor-melodie von "Innsbruck." Forster IV, 14)
20.	(44)	Senfl	Mag ich Unglück nit widerstan
22.	(21)	Senfl	Nun wölt ir hören newe mer [Title: "Vom Buchsbaum und Felbinger"]
24.	(28)	Grefinger	Schwer langweilig ist mir mein Zeit
28.	(16)	Senfl	Von erst so wöll wir loben
29.	(8, 27)	Greitter	Von üppiglichen Dingen (Dorisch plagalisch)
30.	(47)	Senfl	Was wird es doch des Wunders noch
30.	(41)	Senfl	Was wird es doch des wunders noch (a 7)
30.	(36)	Brant	Was wird es doch des Krankens noch (a 8)
33.	(37)	Brant	Wer das ellend bauen wil (Dorisch)
34.	(29)	(Forster II, 67)	Ich armes Megdlein (Phrygisch, plagalisch, aber mit dem Ambitus a-a)
35.	(30)	(Forster III, 25)	Nur wider glück mit freuden (Mixolydisch, plagalisch)
37.	(33)	Dietrich	Nur nerrisch sein ist mein manier
38.	(43)	Forster	Von Gottes Gnad ward in den Tod (Phrygisch)

Nottebohm transcribed all the pieces in score, using original clefs.
He first drew evenly spaced bar lines, and then filled in notes to make
4/2 measures. He added accidentals and corrections in red or blue pencil;
some of these he changed or queried. Brahms made no additional annotations in these copies. In his Abschriften from this source, he left out
Nottebohm's question marks, but otherwise made only minor changes.[146]

3.   Melodies from the Sixteenth-Century Catholic Songbooks of Leisentrit and Canisius.

> 9 sheets, copied by Julius Allgeyer in 1856. [Signatur VI/42288. Listed in Brahms's
> earlier catalog under "Melodien"; not listed in the later catalog.]

Brahms's friend Julius Allgeyer wrote to him in May 1856 from Überlin-
gen on the Bodensee, saying

> I have also been working for you, but won't boast prematurely since I don't know
> what value they may have for you. I've written out about 200 old melodies from old
> Catholic songbooks that I tracked down in the library here. Also a few polyphonic
> ones among them in clefs I don't recognize. . . .
>
> The songbooks date mostly from the 16th century. The text, which I have mostly
> left out, is wretched monastery poetry, the kind that was in full swing then. Still, the
> tunes, which are older in any case, may contain much that is interesting.[147]

Several weeks later, Allgeyer sent the copies to Düsseldorf, along with an
invitation to come down and stay with him on the Bodensee, but Brahms
was involved in the events surrounding the death of Schumann, and nothing ever came of the invitation.

It appears that Brahms did not study these copies with any particular
care. His only markings are page numbers, a note at the bottom of the
first page which says "Abschrift von Julius Allgeyer," and an addition to
Allgeyer's first-page title to say where the copy was made.

Allgeyer's title of the first section is "Melodien / aus Jos. Leisentrits
(von Olmütz, Domdechant zu Budissen) Christkath. Gesangbuch. 1566."
Brahms added "(in der Bibliothek zu Ueberlingen am Bodensee)." What
looks like the entire contents of the songbook follows: 138 monophonic
melodies copied in square notation, with "Finis" at the end. The tunes
are partly chant melodies and partly Latin or German sacred songs for
the entire church year. Tunes and titles only are given.

On page 14, a new title is given: "Melodien aus d. katholischen Gesangbuch des Peter Canisius, geb. 1524, gest. 1597. / Gedruckt zu Ror-
schach am Bodensee bei Bartholomäus Schnell." This book is also
apparently copied complete; a few texts are included along with the music. There are fifty-four mostly monophonic pieces in all. The last two,
one in four parts and one in three, are copied out in choirbook format.

4.   Sacred Works by Palestrina, Anerio, and Victoria

> 4 sheets, copied by Robert Schumann from Tucher's *Kirchengesänge der berühmtesten
> älteren italiänischen Meister.*
> [Archiv number A295, part of the Schumann manuscript collection. Listed in both
> Brahms catalogs.]

There is no record of when Schumann copied these pieces, or when or how they came into Brahms's possession. They presumably formed a part of Schumann's own study of Renaissance polyphony. His source in this case was most of the first volume of Gottlieb Freyherr von Tucher's *Kirchengesänge der berühmtesten älteren italiänischen Meister,* published in 1827 with a dedication to Beethoven. Schumann left out only no. 5, Palestrina's "Loquebantur variis."[148]

The contents of the manuscript are as follows (composers and numbers are given as they appear in the source):

Palestrina	1) Adoramus te Christe[149]
	2) O bone Jesu[150]
	3) Hosanna in excelsis (a 4)
	4) Pueri Hebraeorum
Felice Anerio	6) Christus factus est
	7) Christus factus est
	8) [O sacrum convivium]
Vittoria	9) [O vos omnes]
	10) Jesu dulcis memoria[151]

Part of Schumann's study of these pieces consisted of writing in bass figures through the first two pieces and the beginning of the third. He copied complete texts only in the first three, and thereafter wrote in words only for the first few bars in all except nos. 8 and 9, which were identified for the list above from Tucher's collection.

5. Palestrina, "Princeps gloriosissime" and "Gaude Barbara beata"

   6 sheets by an unknown copyist.
   [Signatur H27588. Not listed in either Brahms catalog.]

These two pieces are both beautifully copied, possibly from some other manuscript source. Eitner lists only Alfieri's *Raccolta di Musica Sacra* VII (1846) as a source for both; but although the first piece could have come from this collection, the second differs both in the choice of clefs and in the order of the voices.

Brahms may have been given these copies, or may have bought them in this form. When he went home to Hamburg for a visit in November 1855, he wrote to Clara Schumann[152] that he was spending half his time in the second-hand bookshops, and had bought a handwritten copy of a two-piano sonata by W. Friedemann Bach, along with other things.

Brahms wrote his name on the title page of these three interleaved bifolios, and certainly worked on both pieces with the Frauenchor.[153]

This copy is probably the one from which the singers copied their own parts into their Stimmbücher, because Brahms went through it and added rehearsal letters in blue pencil. He also corrected wrong notes, clarified the text underlay in several places, and at a number of entrances where the parts are in soprano, mezzosoprano, or alto clefs wrote in pencil treble clefs and a few of the first notes, apparently to get the singers started correctly copying their own parts.[154]

6. Schütz, "Wer will uns scheiden" [SWV 330: *Kleine geistliche Konzerte* II, no. 25].

> 4 sheets by an unknown hand.
> [Signatur Q2569. Not listed in either Brahms catalog.]

There is no way of knowing where or when Brahms acquired this copy. He wrote his initials in blue pencil on the first page, but otherwise made no marks at all in it.[155] According to Eitner, the only nineteenth-century published source for the work before 1871 is the third volume of Commer's *Musica Sacra* (Bote & Bock, 1843). In that edition, the continuo part is labeled "Continuo," whereas here it is "Organum."

7. "Alte Instrumentalcompositionen" [Nottebohm's title]

> 6 volumes, bound, mostly copied by Gustav Nottebohm.
> [Signatur XVII/52891. Brahms's earlier catalog says there are 6 volumes and leaves a page to fill in the contents (he left it blank); the later catalog says there are 5 volumes.]

These six volumes contain the results of Nottebohm's years of study and transcription of early instrumental music; there are only a few vocal pieces in the collection. A complete description of the very large amount of material will have to await a student of Nottebohm's life and work. It is certainly clear from a cursory examination of these volumes and of the collection of Tenorlieder (see pp. 62-63 above) that in addition to his important studies of Beethoven, he put a great deal of scholarly effort into the investigation of early music.

The volumes contain many pieces transcribed from parts and from tablature. In many cases Nottebohm copied the original, often with lengthy verbal instructions and commentary, and then provided his own transcriptions. He also added comments, including queries (often about the notation of rhythm), corrections, and the remark "richtig." The fourth and fifth volumes have some printed material and Abschriften by other unidentified people bound in along with Nottebohm's own copies. Volume VI consists of what looks like rough drafts, which have been crossed out as they were recopied elsewhere; many of the pieces found here appear in the other volumes of the collection.

The only identifiable Brahms annotations are a note on the title page of the first volume giving Nottebohm's name and his own, and tables of contents for volumes IV and V. Nottebohm had provided them for the first three volumes, and volume VI contains a list which seems to have been compiled by Edith Kern, who listed Brahms's Abschriften in A130. A few square brackets which point out entrances of the various voices in keyboard pieces may also have been added by Brahms; but it seems unlikely that he studied the collection carefully, since it contains none of his characteristic NBs, question marks, marks of parallels, or underlinings.

8. "Composizioni di differenti Maestri": Sacred Works by Italian Baroque composers

41 sheets by an unknown hand.
[Catalogued under "Verschiedene," Signatur Q512. Listed in Orel's catalog, but not in Brahms's earlier one.]

This collection contains nineteen pieces with sacred Latin texts by Perti, G. Corsi, Carpani, Casali, Bencini, Casciolini, Terziani, and Marcello, for from one to four voices, with continuo in all but four of the pieces. Brahms may have acquired it after 1888, since it appears in his later catalog but not in the earlier one. He wrote his name on the table of contents page, and also provided dates for the composers he could find in the eighteenth-century music lexicons of Walther and Gerber, both of which he owned. In the music he wrote only a few queries and corrections.

The contents of the collection are listed here, together with the setting used for each piece.

1.	Giacomo Perti	Beatus vir	SATB, cont.
2.	Giacomo Perti	Adoramus te	SATB, cont.
3.	Giacomo Perti	O vos omnes	SATB
4.	Perti or Corsi[156]	Caligaverunt oculi mei	SATB
5.	Perti	Adoramus te	SATB
6.	Perti	Adoramus te	SATB
7.	Gaetano Carpani	Miserere mihi Domine	ST, cont.
8.	Gio. Battista Casali	Benedictus	AA, cont.
9.	Antonio Bencini	Benedictus	BB, cont.
10.	Claudio Casciolini	Benedictus	SB, cont.
11.	Casali	Benedictus	SAB, cont.
12.	Casali	Benedictus	AB, cont.
13.	Casali	Benedictus	ATB, cont.
14.	Pietro Terziani	Benedictus	SAT, cont.

15. Benedetto Marcello	Benedictus	S, cont.
16. Benedetto Marcello	Benedictus	S, cont.
17. Casali	Benedictus	SATB, cont.
18. Marcello	Benedictus	SS, cont.
19. Pietro Paolo Bencini	Benedictus	SATB, cont.

9. Durante, *XII Cantate a due*

115 pages by an unknown (eighteenth-century?) hand. [Signatur Q10524. Listed in both catalogs.]

On the flyleaf, someone (not Brahms) has written a note to say that the Breitkopf and Härtel edition of these pieces appeared with a realized bass. Brahms wrote his signature on the title page, but made no other marks in the collection. As usual, there is nothing to say when or how he acquired it; his own catalog merely provides the comment "in alter Abschrift." According to the British Library catalog, the Breitkopf and Härtel edition of these cantatas was published in about 1830; therefore the copy was probably made before that date, and it looks as though it dates from the previous century. The twelve cantatas are all for soprano and alto with figured bass.

10. Bach, Cantata 150, "Nach dir, Herr" [incomplete]

Copyist unknown. Discarded by Brahms.
[In the Vienna Stadtbibliothek manuscript collection, catalog number MH 12105/C. Listed in Brahms's earlier catalog, but not the later one.]

This copyist's version of the Bach cantata is part of a mass of autograph material, much of it letters, which was thrown away by Brahms, rescued and kept by his housekeeper, Celestine Truxa, and later given by her son to the Stadtbibliothek. The manuscript has been torn in two and then taped back together; a bifolio containing pages 17, 18, 31, and 32 is missing, as is half of the sheet with pages 29 and 30. Brahms's markings consist of a reference to Spitta's biography of Bach on the title page and a few corrections; there are no annotations in the chaconne.

This must be the copy of the hitherto unpublished cantata which Philipp Spitta had made and sent to Brahms in January 1874.[157] Once it was published in the *Werke* volume 30 in 1884, Brahms had no further use for the copy.

Spitta drew Brahms's attention specifically to the final chorus of the cantata, calling it "a bold transfer of chaconne form into choral music." The story of the further transfer of the chaconne bass into the Fourth Symphony, which was composed in 1884 and 1885, is told by Specht:

Brahms borrowed [the passacaglia theme] from Bach's Cantata no. 150, where it forms the bass of the *ciacona,* which he played to Hans von Bülow at the house of Siegfried Ochs, accusing him of having no notion of these masterpieces. Bülow had no more than cool admiration to spare for this choral movement, the cunning structure of which Brahms demonstrated to him with enthusiastic eloquence, for to his mind the great climax which according to Bach's conception is inherent in the superstructure built up over this bass could not be fully realized by voices. "The same thing has struck me too," said Brahms. "What would you say to a symphonic movement written on this theme one day? But it is too lumpish, too straightforward. It would have to be chromatically altered in some way." This, it may be seen, is what he afterwards did when he erected one of the most towering Brahmsian movements on the foundation of Bach's bass.[158]

Printed Books and Music

Brahms's collection of books on nonmusical topics has been completely catalogued and described by Kurt Hofmann.[159] However, the best catalogs made so far of his printed music and books on music are the two he compiled himself (see pp. 9-10). In them, the music and books on music are not separated from one another in any way; however, they are physically separated in the Archiv and sometimes the reasons why a particular publication was assigned to one category or another is rather difficult to fathom.

The books on music may be easily and rapidly examined, since they are kept together. Their Archiv catalog numbers all show a second figure between 201 and 204, which describes the shelf area in the book room. Although I have looked at most of the books in this shelf area, I have chosen to list only a few, which seem to me to be those on early music that Brahms used the most, or that are in some other way related to the topic of this investigation.

The part of the collection that is classified as music is more completely covered here, because its contents are more difficult to locate in the Archiv. Orel's catalog was used to compile a master list of works related to the topic of early music,[160] and items on the list were located through the card catalog. During 1975-76, the Archiv staff was in the process of recataloguing the music collection: new catalog numbers begin with the letters H or Q (for hoch or quer format), and old numbers begin with Roman numerals which were assigned on the basis of genre. The only categories of "early music" left out of the search were works of purely instrumental music, such as music by Domenico Scarlatti; music by pre-Classic composers such as C. P. E. Bach; and nineteenth-century settings for voice and piano of folk songs from earlier periods.[161]

Some of the items listed in Orel's catalog cannot now be found in the Archiv. The problem has already been discussed in connection with the various editions prepared by Franz Wüllner (see above, p. 00). Other missing works are the following:

1. *Carissimi's Werke*. Erste Abtheilung: Oratorien. Edited by F. Chrysander, no date. [*Denkmäler der Tonkunst* II]

There are two copies of this volume in the Archiv, but neither is the one Brahms owned. His copy of a performance edition of *Jephta* is still there, however (see below).

2. Couperin, *Pièces de Clavecin*. Premier et Second Livres. Edited by Johannes Brahms. Issued in 1871 as volume IV of Chrysander's series *Denkmäler der Tonkunst*

The Archiv owns another copy of this volume; Brahms's copy is missing. Chrysander's letters to Brahms show that because the *Denkmäler* had been sent to Brahms's father in Hamburg instead of to Vienna, Brahms had in 1876 not yet seen the published version of his own edition.[162] He received it later, however, and it appears in both his catalogs.

3. *Denkmäler der Tonkunst in Oesterreich* II, part 1. Fux, Motetten

The Archiv has another copy, but the one listed in Orel's catalog is missing, as is another volume in the series, III, part 1, containing keyboard works by Gottlieb Muffat.

4. "Lotti, Antonio, Terzett Lamento 6 Blatt [handschriftlich]"

This entry appears in Orel's catalog, but not in Brahms's earlier one; the square brackets are Orel's. Another entry under Lotti in Orel's catalog was added to Brahms's revised catalog after his death by Richard Fellinger; it reads "Duett für 2 Soprane: Partimento in amore 1 Blatt." No trace can now be found of either of these works, unless the "Lamento" is related to A130, 27-29 in some unexplained way.

5. "Nicolai, Ein feiner kleiner Almanach, 1777, 78, 2 Th. (Berlin)"

Brahms's own copy of this collection would be valuable to anyone working on his folk song settings, since it was one of the most important of his sources.[163] Along with the work of Kretzschmer and Zuccalmaglio, it is the subject of the attacks of those who objected to the fabrication or romanticization of "folk" material.[164]

6. "Singschule oder Solmisation (Wien bei Hohenleitter). (Durante, Porpora, Hasse etc.) siehe: Paris." "Paris, Gesangschule des Conservatoriums in Paris (Peters) (Cherubini, Méhul etc.)"

The same two entries also appear in Brahms's earlier catalog. They refer to the second volume of a three-volume set published by Breitkopf & Härtel (no date, perhaps a later edition than the Peters edition Brahms refers to) under the double title *Méthode de Chant du Conservatoire de Musique à Paris* and *Singschule des Conservatoriums der Musik in Paris*. The Archiv (catalog number Schulen 7099) has the first volume, on how to sing, and the third, a collection of arias, but not the second, "Solmisationen aus den besten ältern und neuen Werken."

7. "Sweelinck, Joh. P., Psalm 150, Amsterdam 1891"

This is the only listing in Orel's catalog for any vocal work by Sweelinck; a collection of keyboard works by Sweelinck and Scheidt is also listed, but was not examined in this study.

Of the missing works, the most valuable to us would probably have been *Chorübungen* III, edited by Wüllner (Munich: Ackermann, 1880), partly because it is the source of so much of the material in "Octaven und Quinten" and was obviously thoroughly studied by Brahms, and also because it contains a large repertoire (105 pieces) of sacred and secular a cappella works, mostly by Renaissance and Baroque composers. Brahms acquired his copy in 1881, too late for its contents to have had any influence on his choral compositions; but his reactions to the music and to Wüllner's heavy editing for performance would have been extremely interesting.[165] Florence May (2nd ed., pp. 197-98) mentions a few early music works which Brahms had owned and then presumably given away to friends. The only one in this category which has been examined by the present writer is the Bach four-part chorales (see below), which Miss May owned in 1905; she also had a manuscript copy, not by Brahms but with a few marks in his hand, of the *Art of the Fugue*. A volume "containing compositions by Orlando di Lasso" was in the possession of Julius Spengel; Brahms probably gave the collection to Spengel during the period around 1890 when they were in fairly frequent contact and Spengel's choir in Hamburg gave the first performance of the *Fest- und Gedenksprüche*. There is no mention of the gift in the letters Brahms wrote to Spengel, but an entry "Lasso, Orlando, Hauptstücke des 51. Psalms" appears in his earlier catalog only.

Brahms also, of course, knew many editions of works of early music which he did not have in his own library. We have already seen that he copied a good deal of material from Winterfeld's *Der evangelische Kirchengesang*. He mentioned another collection in correspondence: in a May 1863 letter to Gänsbacher, a Viennese friend, about the conducting job at the Singakademie, he asked whether the society had much they had not already used in their library, and in addition to that "perhaps larger collections of early sacred pieces—Proske?"[166] Brahms did not own any volumes of Karl Proske's enormous *Musica Divina*, a Catholic church–sponsored collection of liturgical music mostly by Italian Renaissance composers, nor did he use the collection as a source for Abschriften or performance repertoire as far as is known; but it seems certain that he examined at least some of it with a view toward obtaining performance material. It is a pity that we cannot know whether Brahms read or paid any attention to Proske's long introduction to the first volume, where he discusses the background knowledge needed to conduct this music, including a thorough foundation in counterpoint, a theoretical and practical knowledge of Gregorian chant, and an understanding of the church modes. Proske also provides (pp. xxxviii ff.) a detailed and scholarly account of the practices of musica ficta, and describes his own rather cautious but eminently correct editorial procedures.

In the discussion of Brahms's library of printed material which follows, the early music and books on early music are divided into these categories:[167]

1. works printed before 1800, including pedagogical books
2. folk song material, including chorale tunes and settings
3. journals
4. single pieces or collections of works by a single composer, including *Werke*
5. collections of music by different composers, including *Denkmäler*

Within each category, items are arranged alphabetically by composer, author, or editor, except for the *Denkmäler,* which appear as a group under the various series titles. The Archiv catalog number is given for each item, in square brackets. In most cases, principal emphasis in the description is placed on Brahms's annotations in the work.

1. Works Printed before 1800

Albrechtsberger, Johann Georg. *Anweisung zur Composition, mit ausführlichen Exempeln, zum Selbstunterrichte.* Leipzig: Breitkopf & Härtel [1790]. 404 p.
[1439/203]

This is one of the pedagogical works which Brahms used to teach himself counterpoint during the 1850s. It contains a number of his markings, most of which are corrections or queries in the musical examples, or strokes which call attention to specific rules of counterpoint. The front cover page has the pencil signature "Brahms."

Johann Sebastian Bachs vierstimmige Choralgesänge gesammlet [sic] von Carl Philipp Emanuel Bach. Erster Theil. Berlin und Leipzig: Friedrich Wilhelm Birnstiel, 1765. 50 p., plus 2 p. Druckfehler. [British Library: K10.a.39]

This collection of one hundred chorales is the only volume owned by Brahms which the present writer examined outside of the Archiv. It was in Florence May's possession in 1905, and at the time the second edition of her book was published in 1948 belonged to a Mr. Evlyn Howard-Jones. The British Museum acquired it from a Mrs. Jones in 1950.[168]

Brahms signed the title page "Joh. Brahms 1855," and wrote an alphabetical list of the chorale melodies inside the back cover of the book. He also made a number of the corrections printed in the list of Druckfehler, and wrote question marks at the beginning of three chorales which are written in longer note values and harmonized in a simpler style than the others, perhaps querying whether they were really by Bach.

Keiser, Reinhard. *Divertimenti serenissimi, delle Cantate, Duette & Arie diverse, senza Stromenti. Oder: Durchlauchtige Ergötzung über verschiedene Cantaten, Duetten und Arien, ohne Instrumenten.* Hamburg: Greflinger, 1713. 42 p.
[Q3744]

On 30 November 1855, Brahms wrote to Clara Schumann,

> Think of my joy: Avé has a big attic full of unorganized music, the most wonderful things; I often rummage there, and I can take duplicates with me.[169]

This work by Keiser must have been one of these duplicates; the title page bears Avé Lallemant's stamp and below it the signature "Joh. Brahms. Nov. 1855."

The volume is a collection of vocal solos and duets with figured bass, and contains no markings by Brahms except one X in blue pencil where the relation between the bass and the vocal part is poor. This book, along with much of Brahms's library, was left behind in Hamburg after he moved to Vienna. After his father's death, when his stepmother moved out of

Hamburg in 1883, Friedrich Chrysander packed up the things that Brahms still wanted and sent them to him. Chrysander kept out two volumes, however—one from the Handel *Werke* to correct some mistakes, and this one, because he was working on Keiser at the time and wanted to write an article about it. He eventually returned it to Brahms, and was, as its presence in the Archiv shows, unsuccessful in his later attempt to obtain it as a memento after Brahms's death.[170]

Kellner, David. *Treulicher Unterricht im General-Bass.* 3rd edition. Hamburg: Christian Herold, 1743. 96 p. Bound in at the back:

[Mattheson], *Die Kunst das Clavier zu spielen,* durch den Verfasser des critischen Musicus an der Spree. Berlin: Haude und Spener, 1751. 27 p.
[145/203]

On the title page, in ink, there is the signature "Brahms 1848." This evidence that Brahms was already collecting old books about music at the age of fifteen is cited by both Mandyczewski and Geiringer.[171] The volume contains no signs of use by Brahms; the few markings appear to be in someone else's hand, presumably that of a previous owner. Brahms's own catalogs identify the author of the book bound in at the back as Mattheson.

Kirnberger, Joh. Phil. *Die Kunst des reinen Satzes in der Musik.* Second part, second and third sections. Berlin & Königsberg: G. J. Decker & G. L. Hartung, 1777, 1779. 282, 188 p.
[9856/202]

This pedagogical work, which is entirely concerned with "doppelten Contrapunct," has the notation "Brahms / Nov. 1855" on the title page, and is therefore presumably one of the fruits of his search through the Hamburg second-hand bookshops during that month.[172] Brahms read and worked with the book, since there are occasional marginal pencil strokes in it, but he did not give it the same kind of hard use that some of the other pedagogical works received.

Krieger, Johann. *Sechs Musicalische Partien.* Nürnberg: Endter, 1697. The pages of the six pieces are numbered separately. Also bound in the same volume:
Krieger. *Anmuthige Clavier-Ubung* [sic]. Same publisher, 1699. 69 p.
[Q13178]

Both volumes contain keyboard music only. Brahms wrote his name twice in the front and provided dates (1652-1735) for Krieger. There are only a few marks in the music.

Marpurg, Friedrich Wilhelm. *Handbuch bei dem Generalbasse und der Composition* . . . nebst einem vorläuffigen kurzen Begriff der Lehre vom Generalbasse für Anfänger. Berlin: J. J. Schützens Wittwe, 1755. 70 p.
Zweyter Theil (1757) and Dritter und letzter Theil (1758), pp. 71-341, plus examples. On title page in ink: "1855. Brahms."
[383/202]

Another copy, with no signature on the title page, under the same catalog number, has bound in at the back:
Nichelmann, Christoph. *Die Melodie nach ihrem Wesen*. . . . Dantzig: J. C. Schuster, 1755. 175 p., examples.

The copy with Brahms's signature on the title page is otherwise entirely unmarked. He worked in the copy with Nichelmann's book bound into it, as had a previous owner; sections of it contain copious markings, and many page corners are turned down. Marpurg's book is the one which Brahms and Joachim agreed to study at the beginning of their counterpoint project in 1856.[173]

Much of the section for beginners, the first twelve pages, was heavily underlined in ink by the previous owner, especially in the passages dealing with various kinds of seventh chords, and with the preparation and resolution of dissonances. The later sections on ninth and eleventh chords, on inversions and doubling in triads, on dissonances arising from seventh chords, and on the treatment of syncopation, suspensions, and appoggiaturas, receive special attention. Whether Brahms paid any attention to these annotations is, of course, now unknown. His own pencil markings include "NB NB NB" at the head of the chapter on writing figured basses.

Brahms owned two other works by Marpurg in early editions: *Anleitung zur Singcomposition,* 1758 [384/203], which is about setting German, Latin, and Italian texts; and *Einleitung zum Klavierspielen,* 1755 [389/204]. He acquired both volumes in 1855. Neither has any marks.[174]

Mattheson, Johann. *Kern Melodischer Wissenschaft* bestehend in den auserlesensten Haupt- und Grund-Lehren der musikalischen Satz-Kunst oder Composition, als ein Vorläuffer des Vollkommenen Capellmeisters, ausgearbetet [sic] von Mattheson. Hamburg: Christian Herold, 1737. Vorrede, 182 p., Register. On the title page: "Brahms. 1856"

(inside front cover the name of a previous owner, Hieronymus Ro-
senmüller). [410/203]

Another copy was given to Nottebohm by Brahms in 1868, and then belonged to Mandyczewski. It has the same catalog number, but is not
really part of the Brahms Nachlass.

This treatise was later incorporated by Mattheson into Part II of *Der
vollkommene Capellmeister.*[175] In Brahms's copy, a number of passages
are marked with ink brackets, perhaps by the previous owner. Brahms
marked many of the same sections in pencil, adding new annotations, and
occasionally changing words or slightly rewriting sentences to make them
more independent of their context, as though he were thinking of quoting
them.

   Some of the marked passages are aphorisms about music and musicians, including several slighting references to French style and practice.
Others deal with the importance of writing simple, beautiful melodies,
and hiding all that is forced, contrived, or artful, together with rules for
composing such melodies. In a section on ornamentation, Mattheson compares the new French taste for ornate performance with that of earlier
times, and quotes (p. 140) an anecdote from "a Johannes Manlii, unknown to me" about Josquin's wrath when someone performed a colo-
ratura that he had not written in one of his pieces, and his insistence that
if he had not written an ornament in that place because it pleased him,
he did not want one added by an ass. This passage is marked in pencil,
and the words "es heisst" which introduce the story are crossed out.

   Brahms owned several other works by Mattheson in original editions,
including *Der vollkommene Capellmeister* (described below). The only
one examined by the present author was the *Organisten-Probe* of 1719
[408/203], which, according to a note in Brahms's hand, was given to him
for his birthday in 1856 by "Constanze, Lina u. Elisabeth." Inside the
back cover he wrote the numbers of the seven pages where he had made
annotations. One marked passage is a story Mattheson tells (p. 239) of
one of his own piano sonatas, which was said to be too difficult even for
the composer himself to play; however, in a public concert before a large
audience "this untruth was finally brought to shame."

Mattheson, Johann. *Der Vollkommene Capellmeister,* Das ist Gründliche
   Anzeige aller der derjenigen Sachen, die einer wissen, können, und
   vollkommen inne haben muss, der einer Capelle mit Ehren und Nutzen
   vorstehen will: Zum Versuch entworffen von Mattheson. Hamburg:
   Christian Herold, 1739.[176]
   [1197/69B][177]

This copy had been previously owned by the double bass player and composer Johannes Sperger, who signed and dated it Pressburg 1783. It was somehow acquired by Joachim, who wrote in his name and "Hannover Debr. 55," and gave it to Brahms with the note "This book is to be placed next to the German sayings of Grimm, for it belongs to Johannes. Christmas 1855."[178]

There are only a few other annotations, all marginal pencil strokes which call attention to various passages. In a section discussing the affections ("Gemüths-Neigungen," p. 15), two sentences are marked:

> Where there is no passion, no affect to be found, there is also no virtue. If our passions are sick, then they must be healed, not murdered.[179]

Several paragraphs which describe the qualities necessary for success as a composer—natural ability, desire, and diligence—are also noted, together with a rule: "hear many, but imitate few."[180]

Mattheson's comments on avoidance of consecutive octaves and fifths (p. 257) attracted Brahms's attention, not surprisingly: he chides those who would "make an elephant of such gnats" by censuring otherwise good composers who make an occasional slip in this regard, and says that "a practiced musician does not look around much for such things but aspires toward something greater and more important."[181] The relevance to "Octaven und Quinten" is obvious and striking. Another passage marked by Brahms (p. 481), and amusing to those who have had to contend with his handwriting, is one on the importance of writing carefully, and the falsity of assuming that the handwriting of a learned man must be illegible. Mattheson says that such an assumption "almost reminds me of that castrato who presumed that he would necessarily sing beautifully because he had been emasculated."[182]

Muffat, Georg. *Apparatus Musico-Organisticus*. Vienna: van Ghelen, 1690. 66 p. [VII/8583]

Brahms's markings show that he carefully studied the twelve toccatas in this collection, which was left to him by Nottebohm. Other works by the same composer are found in Brahms's copies of *Denkmäler der Tonkunst in Oesterreich.*

The composer Gottlieb (Theophilo) Muffat is represented by a 1727 edition of *Componimenti Musicali per il Cembalo* [Q11387]. Brahms's copy of the *Denkmäler* volume (1896) which contains the same work is missing.

[Printz, Wolfgang Caspar.] *Musicus Vexatus* oder der wohlgeplagte doch
nicht verzagte, sondern jederzeit lustige Musicus instrumentalis, in
einer anmuthigen Geschicht vor Augen gestellet von Cotala, dem
Kunst-Pfeiffer Gesellen. Freyberg: Johann Christoph Mietheu, 1690.
204 p., of which 190 are original and the last few hand-copied.
[9084/202]

Brahms made no marks anywhere in the body of this work, which he
acquired in 1855, but it is interesting nevertheless. One of the stories
Kalbeck tells about Brahms and C. F. Pohl (III, 180n) is that Pohl borrowed this volume, which was missing the last several pages, and kept it
for a very long time. When he finally returned it, he had beautifully copied
the missing material from another copy in the Archiv, and had had the
volume bound in leather. He also wrote a note in the front, identifying
the author and explaining the pseudonym. Brahms added another note,
suggesting that the author might instead be Kuhnau and citing the source
from which he obtained this opinion; Geiringer says, however, that Pohl
was right.[183]

2. *Folk-Song Material, including Chorale Tunes and Settings*

Becker, C. F. *Lieder und Weisen vergangener Jahrhunderte.* Leipzig:
Kössling, 1849 and 1850. Two volumes, bound together:
viii, 78 p.; viii, 80 p. [2796/203]

Texts and tunes only are given in this collection, which Brahms was using
as early as April 1854 as a source for Abschriften (A 128, 1-2). He wrote
in his usual cross references to other collections, and took the texts given
here for his performance versions of "Innsbruck" and "Mein G'müth ist
mir verwirret" (A 134, 43-44). Becker is also the source of both text and
tune of "Von edler Art," which Brahms set for mixed chorus.[184]

Becker, C. F. and Gustav Billroth. *Sammlung von Chorälen aus dem XVI.
und XVII. Jahrhundert.* Leipzig: Karl Tauchnitz, 1831. vii, 80 p. On
title page, signatures "R. Schumann" and "Joh. Brahms." Bound
into the same volume:
Becker, C. F. *Mehr-stimmige Gesänge berühmter Componisten des sech-
zehnten Jahrhunderts.* Dresden: Wilhelm Paul, no date. On title page,
signature "Brahms." [7318/203]

This double volume is included in the folk song and chorale category
because the first of the two works received a great deal more attention

from Brahms than the second. The only things he wrote in the second were his name and, at the back, a table of contents of the chorales in the *first* collection, arranged alphabetically by title.

The volume of chorales contains mostly settings by Calvisius and Schein. Brahms's many markings include corrections, cross references, parallels, and additional texts. In "O Gottes Lamm unschuldig" (no. 36, p. 63), he changed some note values and the bar lines in order to produce a 3/2 meter pattern.

Böhme, Franz M. *Altdeutsches Liederbuch.* Leipzig: Breitkopf & Härtel, 1877. lxxii, 832 p. [3147/201]

Eduard Hanslick gave this book to Brahms in June 1877, and Brahms clearly used it a great deal even though he objected to many of the conclusions reached by Böhme and the other representatives of the "scientific" school of folk-song study. In 1894, at the height of his anger over the collection by Erk and Böhme (see below), Brahms wrote to Spitta that he had studied Böhme's earlier book carefully, and had even lost confidence in its value as a reference work. Spitta replied that he agreed on the weaknesses of insight and taste, but that as a scholar he had to appreciate the great amount of detail supplied.[185]

Brahms's markings in the long introduction are fairly easy to interpret. A stroke in the margin means that a statement is noteworthy; an exclamation point means that he considered it outrageous. Given his prejudice in favor of early music, it is not surprising that he wrote a large exclamation point against a paragraph which says:

> The medieval musical settings of the 15th and 16th centuries, even those of the so-called classic period of counterpoint in Palestrina's and O. Lasso's time, are basically *foreign* to us modern people of the 19th century, and for the public as well as the modern artist who is not exactly accustomed to historic things, have become *tedious*.[186]

In the section containing texts and tunes (there are no polyphonic settings), Brahms's notes show how much work he did in the area of folk song. It is full of cross references and comparisons with other sources, especially Forster and Nicolai. He marked deviations from the other sources, and took note of the sections of Nicolai's tunes which Böhme said were not genuine folk material. In many places he objected to Böhme's procedures or conclusions; and in a Wächterlied (no. 111), where Böhme left out a verse that he said was "zu lüsterne" (too bawdy), Brahms found it in Nicolai and wrote it in.

Deutsches-Evangelisches Kirchen-Gesangbuch. Stuttgart & Augsburg:
J. G. Cotta, 1855. 150 p. [7258/204; listed under "Kirchen-Gesangbuch" in Brahms's catalogs.]

Brahms signed his name in blue pencil on the title page of this collection of 150 texts and tunes. There are a few pencil marks, and a number
of ink blots scattered through the last part of the book, where he was
underlining names of tunes with a troublesome pen.

Erk, Ludwig, and Franz M. Böhme. *Deutsche Liederhort.* I. Halbband.
Leipzig: Breitkopf & Härtel, 1893. lx, 304 p. [3889/204]

This volume of texts and tunes was edited and issued by Böhme from the
handwritten notes Erk left when he died in 1883. It is the collection which
called down Brahms's wrath against the "Pächter des Volksliedes" (folk-
song farmers) and precipitated his publication of the forty-nine folk-song
settings for voice and piano as a response.[187]
He was already thoroughly prejudiced against the whole group of
investigators which included Erk and Böhme, because they had questioned the authenticity of tunes from the collection of Kretzschmer and
Zuccalmaglio that he had treasured since his youth. If this volume of the
Deutsche Liederhort in the Nachlass is in fact the only one that Brahms
examined, it shows his prejudice even more clearly than one might ex-
pect, since most of the pages are uncut.[188] In the introduction, only
pp. xxxiii-lvi are cut, often carelessly, and a few markings appear in the
list of sources. The pages are also cut for the table of contents, which is
just a list of sections of the volume, and from p. 265 to the end. The only
annotations in this last section appear on pp. 277-78, where Brahms
underlined the text and put an exclamation mark in the margin when
Böhme comments, "What wonderful melodies many of our folk songs
have!" Brahms showed his disagreement with this assessment, at least as
far as this collection was concerned, when he wrote to Spitta, "Do you
find in the whole book one bar of music which interests you in the slight-
est, or even comes close to it?"[189] It seems from the appearance of this
volume, however, that Brahms made his judgment of the collection and
embarked on his "Streitschrift" (polemic) against it on the basis of prejudice, rather than a complete examination of its musical contents.

Kretzschmer, August, and Anton Wilhelm von Zuccalmaglio. *Deutsche
Volkslieder mit ihren Original-Weisen.* 2 vols. Berlin: Vereins-Buch-
handlung, 1838, 1840. 558, 694 p. [1808/202]

This collection was given to Brahms by his Hamburg friend Karl Grädener on 8 August 1856, after he was already acquainted with Schumann's copy (see A128, 4, p. 15 above). It was his prime source of folk-song material throughout his life, and remained his favorite collection in spite of the attacks of more scholarly investigators.[190] Brahms's copy shows that he accepted many of the results of their work, however, since it is filled with pencil notations of sources and variants, with references to where he obtained his information (Böhme appears frequently), and corrections where he felt they should be made.

Kretzschmer and Zuccalmaglio gave only the sketchiest of information on the sources of their tunes, and much of that seems to be spurious, inserted to give the impression that they had collected many tunes themselves rather than obtaining them from published editions.[191] Brahms gave the true sources when he could find them; thus, for example, for I: no. 213, he crossed out "Altdeutsch" (after surrounding it with exclamation points) and wrote that the melody had been composed in 1814 to a text written in 1812.

In the song "Ulrich" (II: no. 15), Brahms noticed that the real rhythm is not 3/4 throughout, as it is printed, but rather is two bars of 3/4 followed by two of 3/2. He wrote in the new time signature after the first two bars, and showed where the beats fall in relation to the text accents.[192]

Liliencron, Rochus von. *Die historischen Volkslieder der Deutschen vom 13. bis 16. Jahrhundert.* Nachtrag: Die Töne. Leipzig: Vogel, 1869. 106 p.; Beilage xliv p. [2952/203]

Eitner, in his *Verzeichniss,* calls this the most reliable collection of secular Lied melodies; and Spitta, when he replied to Brahms's attack on Erk and Böhme,[193] excepted Liliencron when he described the group of folksong workers as "mediocre minds" (he said that Böhme, whom he had the dubious pleasure of knowing, was a second-rate mind and a puffed-up fool, and that Erk had been a childlike soul whom it was impossible to dislike).

Brahms did not own the four volumes of complete texts that make up the larger part of this collection. The supplementary volume, which contains tunes and a large appendix of polyphonic Lieder settings, he used mainly as a cross reference for songs he was already interested in, judging from his infrequent markings. These appear in tunes he had set, like "Es flog ein Täublein weisse," or copied into the Abschriften, like Zirler's "Die Sonn' die ist verblichen" (A130, 7-8). "Ach du armer Judas" is also marked; and it is here that the two sheets from *Psalmodia* that were Brahms's source for "O wy arme Sünders" (A135) were found (see chap. 2, n. 127).

Meister, Karl Severin. *Das katholische deutsche Kirchenlied in seinen Singweisen.* Erster Band [no others appeared]. Freiburg im Breisgau: Herder, 1862. 512 p., appendices, including facsimiles. [10.023/124]

This collection, along with Corner's, was a source of the sacred folk songs Brahms published in his 1864 group of four-part settings, as well as for the tune of "O Heiland, reiss die Himmel auf" (Op. 74/2).[194] It was given to him by his Hamburg friend Theodor Avé Lallemant, probably immediately after publication, since Brahms left for Vienna at about that time, and soon became estranged from Avé Lallemant, who did not support him in his effort to obtain the conducting position in Hamburg he wanted so badly.

Brahms studied the volume carefully; there are many pencil notes and many turned-down page corners. In the introduction, Meister gives the locations of his sources, and Brahms marked them if they were in places accessible to him, like Hannover and Wien.[195] References to songs he was interested in are also marked, including several to various Marienlieder. The main section of texts and tunes is filled with the usual cross references, corrections, and queries.

The second appendix is a collection of polyphonic settings. For each one, the text is underlaid only at the beginning, and is then given complete at the end. Brahms supplied the missing underlay in the first piece ("Dich mutter gottes rüff wir an"—one of the texts he had already set in the *Marienlieder, Op.* 22) and part of the second. He also wrote in German translations of the Latin parts of Walther's setting of "Josef, lieber Josef mein."

Tucher, G. Freiherr von. *Schatz des evangelischen Kirchengesangs im ersten Jahrhundert der Reformation.* Leipzig: Breitkopf & Härtel, 1848. Erster Theil, Liederbuch: Kirchengesänge, Psalmen und geistliche Lieder; xvi, 488 p. Zweiter Theil, Melodienbuch: Melodien des evangelischen Kirchengesangs; xxxiv, 452 p. [10.028/204 and 10.029/204]

Tucher's collection was the source of some of Brahms's early copies.[196] He wrote his name on the flyleaf of each volume, but there is no date to show when he acquired them.

The volume of texts has only a few annotations. Brahms wrote in a missing verse of "Ich hab mein' Sach Gott heimgestellt" between verses 14 and 15. In the volume of four-part settings he made more markings, including his usual sources, dates, and corrections. He crossed out some incorrect editorial B flats in no. 507, and in no. 310 rebarred the ends of the first, second, and last phrases to show the triple-meter accentuation which Tucher had ignored. Brhams's observations are discussed further below, pp. 160-61.

Wackernagel, Philipp. *Das deutsche Kirchenlied*. Stuttgart: Liesching, 1841. xxxix, 894 p. [4128/202]

Brahms acquired his copy of this large collection of texts at Christmas in 1862. It contains only a few marginal pencil strokes and cross references. There are no markings in any of the texts he set for chorus. If he did use no. 373, "Zum Begrebnis," as his source for the text of the *Begräbnisgesang* (Op. 13), which was composed in October 1858 in Detmold, he must have used someone else's copy and modernized the spelling himself.[197]

Wackernagel, Philipp. *Kleines Gesangbuch geistlicher Lieder*. Stuttgart: Liesching, 1860. 224 p. [10.022/205]

This collection of texts and tunes was acquired by Brahms in 1864. He marked it throughout with the usual corrections and underlinings. In no. 135, a rhymed version of the verses of Psalm 51 which he had already set in Op. 29/2, "Schaffe in mir, Gott," he underlined the beginning of the word "erhalte," which is the version he himself had used (see p. 118, n 74.).

Brahms also read Wackernagel's notes carefully, even some years later. In the commentary to no. 190, "Es kommt nun leider her die Zeit," he identified the strong resemblance of the tune to one in Forster III, no. 42,[198] although Wackernagel attributed the melody to F. W. Arnold and was extremely complimentary of Arnold's skill in composing a tune which fits the text so perfectly.[199]

3. Journals

Jahrbücher für Musikalische Wissenschaft. Edited by Friedrich Chrysander. Vols. I (1863) and II (1867). Leipzig: Breitkopf & Härtel. [2753/201]

In a letter to Hermann Levi in September 1872, Brahms praised Chrysander's diligence, and then wrote

> I am ashamed not to have the Jahrbücher—I borrowed two copies from Stockhausen and Joachim, and both were uncut! Then I stopped being ashamed, and now I have them too.[200]

The pages of these two volumes are cut, at least, but the few annotations were mostly made by someone other than Brahms. The only marks that may be his are some pencil strokes in the margin in the article in volume I about the organ accompaniment for Handel's *Saul,* which Brahms conducted for the Musikverein.

He also owned a separately bound copy of an article from volume II:

Arnold, Friedrich Wilhelm. *Das Locheimer Liederbuch . . . als Documente des deutschen Liedes.* Edited by H. Bellermann. 224 p. [2753/201]

A number of pencil marks appear in the section containing the tunes and texts. Several of these call attention to songs that Brahms set, including "Wach auf mein Hort"[201] and "All mein gedencken dy ich hab dy sind pey dir."

Vierteljahrsschrift für Musikwissenschaft. Edited by Friedrich Chrysander, Philipp Spitta, and Guido Adler. Leipzig: Breitkopf & Härtel, 1885 ff.

Brahms's enthusiasm for this journal has been cited as evidence of his musicological bent.[202] However, he once hurt Spitta's feelings by admitting that he did not always take the trouble to read it.[203] He subscribed only irregularly (after the very first issue there are no more until the sixth year, 1890), and read only those parts which appealed to him. In each issue the pages containing the table of contents are cut, and occasional titles are marked; but many pages of many issues remain uncut.

An 1890 article on Demant was the source of Brahms's Abschriften of pieces by Demant and Regnart (A 130, 10). The same interest in parallel fifths which led him to copy the Demant piece also prompted him to mark an article on Zacconi by Chrysander in volume 9 (1893), in which the special case of villanelle, where rules on consecutive fifths are deliberately broken, is discussed.[204] In issues from 1892 and 1893, statements on the practice of diminution and cadential ornamentation are marked; but Brahms did not bother to cut the pages of a review of Dannreuther's *Musical Ornamentation.*

4.   *Single Pieces or Collections or Works by a Single Composer,* *including* Werke

Johann Sebastian Bach's Werke. Leipzig: Bach-Gesellschaft, beginning in 1851. [The Archiv has two complete sets: Brahms's set is bound in *brown,* and the set which the Musikverein obtained through its own subscription is bound in *green.*]

Clara Schumann gave Brahms the first volume of the Bach collected edition for Christmas in 1855; he first appeared in the list of subscribers in 1856 (in Düsseldorf); and from then on the appearance of each new volume was an event of major importance to him.[205] In his own copies of the vocal works, he made all sorts of markings: repeat signs show large-scale structure; brackets show the entrances of important themes and imitating voices (sometimes themes are numbered and then identified by their numbers whenever they recur); parallels are marked; years of composition and other information from Spitta's biography of Bach are written in;[206] chorales which appear as cantus firmi are identified and their texts filled in; appoggiaturas and trills are added in a few places; and corrections are made.

In addition to these kinds of markings, which he made almost routinely, Brahms noted a number of features which attracted his special attention. Only a few will be described here; these have particular relevance to the discussion of Brahms's choral works in chapter 3, below.

In Cantata 53 ("Schlage doch, gewünschte Stunde," vol. 12/2, [1863]), he wrote an NB beside the last bar of the first aria, where the final resolution to the tonic is sounded only by the bell. The alto arioso in Cantata 72, "Alles nur nach Gottes Willen," (Vol. 18 [1870]: p. 69) caused him some difficulty when he tried to work out the true rhythm from the complicated text accentuation; he marked several hemiolas, but did not reach a really satisfactory solution and erased them (see Example 39, below). A hemiola in an oboe part is marked in volume 33 [1887]: p. 107.

A particularly striking example of chromaticism coupled with parallel fifths in the bass recitative of Cantata 91 (Vol. 22 [1875]: p. 25), the Adagio section with the expressive text "durch dieses Jammerthal zu führen," inspired him to write "wie schön!"—one of his very few verbal comments—in the margin; in this passage he also crossed out the editor's printed query about another parallel fifth. When he copied the passage into "Octaven und Quinten" (p. 7), he marked both spots, labeling them "absichtliche Quinten" (intentional fifths). The passage is shown in Example 5, without Brahms's annotations; the parts are first and second violins (on one stave), viola, bass solo, and continuo. The fifths that elicited the "wie schön" comment are between viola and continuo at the beginning of the Adagio.

The only performance markings which Brahms made in his own set of the *Werke* are in Cantata 21, "Ich hatte viel Bekümmerniss" (Vol. 5/1 [no date, but probably 1856]: pp. 1-64), which he performed at Detmold and later with the Singakademie in November 1863; and the *Weihnachts-Oratorium* (Vol. 5/2 [1856]), also performed by the Singakademie, in March 1864. In the latter work, he added particularly detailed markings to the Sinfonia of the second cantata (the Pastoral Symphony, pp. 51-58). It seems likely that these more elaborate instructions were intended for use

Example 5

by the copyist at the Gesellschaft der Musikfreunde, where this movement was performed separately on 19 April 1874 under the title "Pastorale," whereas the other performance markings probably stem from the Singakademie season.

In Cantata 21, most of the performance markings have been erased. However, Brahms's analytical markings, which probably date from the Detmold period, remain. In the first chorus he labeled the first exposition of the fugue "I[te] Durchführung" and also numbered the second, third, and fourth expositions, adding the comment "Engführung" (stretto) on the last. He identified important key areas, showed the entrances of the subject, and noted that in the second exposition the voices enter "verkehrt"—in a different order. Most of the entrances "und bist so unruhig" in the second chorus he marked with square brackets; and in the section "dass er meines Angesichtes Hülfe" he assigned a number to each of the initial melodic patterns that appear in the vocal parts and in the oboe, up as far as 5, and then labeled most of the entrances with the appropriate numbers.[207]

Brahms evidently preferred not to clutter his own copies with performance markings for the Musikverein concerts, and consequently most of them appear in the set which was owned by the Gesellschaft der Musikfreunde and was available to its conductors. Cantatas 4 ("Christ lag in Todesbanden"), 8 ("Liebster Gott, wann werd' ich sterben?"), and 34

("O ewiges Feuer, o Ursprung der Liebe") all have Brahms's performance instructions. Because these copies were also used by other conductors, some works which Brahms performed contain their markings in addition to his own. Cantata 50 ("Nun ist das Heil") is one such case; and another copy of Cantata 4 [catalog number III/25479], a reprint from the collected edition, contains not only Brahms's markings, which he transferred from volume I of the Archiv's complete set in a more detailed form for use by the copyist, but also many annotations from another conductor, who kept some of Brahms's instructions, changed others, and added a great number of his own. The *St. Matthew Passion* volume belonging to the Archiv's set has performance markings from at least four different conductors; a number of them resemble Brahms's but may actually be Franz Schalk's.[208] Brahms's own copy of the *St. Matthew Passion* was clearly used by him as a guide for the organist; it contains his sketchy instructions and the organist's additions. Separate organ parts, partially prepared by Brahms, survive for the Passion [III/1935] and for Cantatas 8 [III/25427], 34 [III/25463], and 50 [III/25454].[209]

Bach. *Sechs Motetten*. Neue Ausgabe. Leipzig: Breitkopf & Härtel, [1853, according to Wüllner in his notes to the *Werke, 39* (1892)]. [III/2749]

The signature "Johs. Brahms" on the title page and the annotations in this volume suggest that Brahms acquired it quite early in his career, studied the music carefully, and returned to it repeatedly. By contrast, his copy of the 1892 edition is not much marked.

He wrote in his usual repeat signs to show large-scale repetitions, and indicated imitative entries with his characteristic square brackets. In "Komm, Jesu, komm," the brackets are inverted when the subject is inverted. Parallels are marked as usual, and Brahms may have felt that the large number in "Lob und Ehre und Weisheit" was accounted for by the note (from Spitta II: 820) "unächt," which he wrote in at the beginning. Other notes from Spitta's *Bach* appear frequently. In "Der Geist hilft," in addition to the usual structural signs, Brahms marked the last first soprano phrase, "Seufzen, mit unaussprechlichen Seufzen," which is particularly angular and chromatic.

"Jesu, meine Freude" contains markings of the usual type, including notes on text alterations and sources taken from Spitta. In the fifth section, "Trotz dem alten Drachen," which uses the third verse of the chorale text, Brahms wrote a note at the beginning, "NB Variation des Chorals!" and then showed the structure of the chorale tune by writing in fermatas at the ends of all phrases in addition to his normal repeat signs. This was certainly an independent observation: in his copy of Spitta's

Bach (II: 431-32), Brahms underlined and questioned the statement that this verse is a free treatment, and that the chorale lines are used only in general as motives, without a strict connection to the original melody.[210]

There are a number of additional markings in "Jesu, meine Freude," including dynamics, rehearsal letters, and tempo indications. These are not in Brahms's hand, and were presumably made by a conductor at the Musikverein who used this copy for a performance at some later time.[211]

Carissimi, Giacomo. *Jephta*. In's Deutsche übertragen von Bernhard
    Gugler und mit ausgesetzter Orgel- oder Pianofortebegleitung bear-
    beitet von Immanuel Faisst. Leipzig and Winterthur: Rieter-Bieder-
    mann, 1878. Score, 40 p. [H22077]

In the introduction Faisst explains that this edition is meant as a practical performing supplement to Chrysander's scholarly *Denkmäler der Ton-kunst* edition (Brahms's copy of that edition is missing). Therefore it is provided with a translation, dynamics, a realization of the continuo with suggested organ registrations, and modern clefs. Brahms made no marks in this score, but he folded two sections of programs from concerts where the work was performed into it, and made pencil alterations in the German translations provided in both of them. He may have earlier considered performing *Jephta* with the Musikverein, since he wrote to Wüllner in 1874 asking if he might borrow a copy of the score.[212]

Clemens non Papa. *Souter Liedekens*. Published as Tom. XI of *Collectio
    Operum Musicorum Batavorum Saeculi XVI*, edited by Franz Com-
    mer. Berlin: Trautwein (M. Bahn), 1857. 120 p. [H27295, cata-
    logued under Commer]

This collection of three-voice psalm settings by Clemens non Papa (there are also ten settings by Susato, who first published the collection in 1556 and 1557[213]), and the introduction by Commer, contain only a few markings by Brahms, all calling attention to parallels. He used this volume as the source for one of the "Ick seg adieu" versions he copied into A130, 13-14.

Eccard, Johannes, and Johannes Stobäus. *Preussische Festlieder auf das
    ganze Jahr für 5. 6. 7. u. 8. Stimmen*. Edited by G. W. Teschner.
    Leipzig: Breitkopf & Härtel, [1858]. Two parts: 67, 95 p. Bound into
    the same volume:
Eccard, Johannes, *Geistliche Lieder auf den Choral* oder die gebräuch-
    liche Kirchenmelodie gerichtet und fünfstimmig gesetzt. Edited by

G. W. Teschner. Leipzig: Breitkopf & Härtel, [1860]. Introduction and two parts: viii, 49, 59 p. [XVII/32132]

On the title page of the first volume, where the *Preussische Festlieder* are identified as coming from editions of 1642 and 1644, Brahms wrote "1598 zuerst erschienen," and then signed his name. He numbered the pages all the way through both volumes, up to a total of 279. In the second volume, the chorale settings, the only annotations he made apart from the page numbers are in no. 6 of the first part, "Resonet in Laudibus," where he noted that there are both German and Latin texts, and wrote in the German one.

There are copious markings in the first volume, the *Preussische Festlieder*. Three pieces have performance markings, most of which have been partially or completely erased. They are all from the second part: no. 1, Eccard's "Der Christen Triumphlied aus Osterfest" (text "Wir singen all mit Freuden Schall"), which Brahms performed with the Singakademie on 6 January 1864; no. 2, Stobäus's "Aufs Osterfest" (text "Sollte denn das schwere Leiden"), which there is no record of his ever having performed;[214] and no. 18, Eccard's "Übers Gebirg Maria geht," which has already been discussed in connection with Clara Schumann's Abschriften in A134, 29-34. This, Brahms's copy of Teschner's edition, with his own dynamics and some changes in the text which he took from Clara's copy, is the source for the parts made by the Musikverein copyist for the performances in November 1872.[215]

Apart from the performance instructions, there are a number of other annotations in the first volume. Repeat signs which help to clarify the structure of a piece occur frequently, as do brackets which point out imitative entries. Two particularly interesting rhythmic markings appear in part 1, nos. 9 and 10, "O Freude über Freud' " and "Die grosse Lieb' dich trieb." In no. 9, which is barred in 3/2, Brahms shows the hemiola structure at the text "Wir hab'n erlebt die Zeit"; and in no. 10 he points out the reverse pattern, where the true meter is briefly triple against the barred 4/4 at both appearances of the text "dies betrübte Leben." These rhythmic features are discussed further below (see p. 161).

Händel, Georg Friedrich. *Werke.* Edited by Friedrich Chrysander. 96 vols. Deutsche Händel-Gesellschaft, 1858-94. [The Archiv has two sets, with no catalog information about which belongs to the Brahms Nachlass. Brahms's set is bound in *black,* and the Archiv set, 39 volumes of which were purchased from a London dealer in 1923, is bound in *green.*]

Brahms was a subscriber to the complete Handel edition, but he did not value this music as highly as that of Bach,[216] and there is very little handwritten material to be found in his own copies.[217] The *Klavierstücke* in volume 2 (1859) did receive some attention: a few fingerings, some notes on the sources of pieces, and occasional question marks and corrections are written in; and Fugues I, III, and IV (pp. 161-70) have subject entrances marked.

Brahms's markings for the performances he conducted are all written into the copies which already belonged to the Gesellschaft (those bound in green). In order of performance, they are the *Dettingen Te Deum*, the organ concerto no. 4 in D minor (8 Dec. 1872), *Saul, Alexander's Feast,* and *Solomon* (see Appendix 1 for dates). In all of these works, the markings were intended for the use of the copyist as well as Brahms himself; they therefore contain more precise instructions in the instrumental than the vocal parts, with particular attention given to string articulation. In *Saul,* which has the most elaborate performance instructions, dramatic texts are predictably emphasized by dramatic dynamics, with crescendos used to bring out expressive dissonances, many of which are suspensions.[218]

Brahms also owned a facsimile edition of the autograph of *Messiah* (published by the Sacred Harmonic Society in June 1868, from an original in Buckingham Palace), which he acquired in 1869. Chrysander was very scornful of it in the foreword to his own facsimile edition, which was published in 1892 with the support of a fund arranged by Brahms and Bülow. The only mark in the 1868 facsimile is a pencil date 1741 written at the end of the Hallelujah chorus.

Lassus, Orlandus de. *Psalmi Poenitentiales*. Berlin: M. Bahn, [no date]. 88 p. [H27155]

This is the same edition of seven penitential psalms (published in 1584) as that listed by Eitner with the information that it was edited by S. W. Dehn and published by Crantz (Trautwein) of Berlin in 1838. No date shows when this reprint was issued, but Brahms identified Dehn as the editor in his own catalogs, even though the information is missing from this volume. He wrote his name on both the outer paper cover and the title page, but no date.

There are only a few pencil marks, including brackets for imitative entries and a correction. Two short sections of music are marked with NB's, one (p. 27) probably because of a number of implied parallel fifths which are avoided by the exchange of voices,[219] and the other (p. 29) perhaps for a tight series of entries in strict imitation followed by the interesting use of a pedal tone in the soprano.[220]

Lotti, Antonio. "Crucifixus a 6." No. 7 (published separately in score)
    from Vol. 1 of *Musica Sacra*. Berlin: Schlesinger, [1852]. 3 p.
    [H27168]

This is the only piece from Schlesinger's *Musica Sacra* collection which
Brahms himself owned (see A130, 27-29 above, for a discussion of the
collection and the Abschriften Brahms made from it). The only markings
in this copy are bass figures which were at one time written in on the first
page only and later erased. A recent edition of this work appears in
Wüllner's *Chorübungen* (1954), no. 38.

Kade, L. Otto. *Mattheus le Maistre*. Mainz: Schott, 1862. 160 p. text; 70
    p. music. [5126/203]

This book about the composer Mattheus le Maistre (d. 1557) is included
in the music list because of the collection of musical examples published
with it. Brahms studied these examples and marked a few parallels.
    There are only two marks in the text. Brahms questioned the opinion
that Winterfeld, in *Der evangelische Kirchengesang,* had given too much
space to his favorites, neglecting other important composers, and that in
particular Hassler rather than Eccard should have received more attention. His other mark calls attention to Kade's complaint that too few
reliable editions of early music are available.

Schütz, Heinrich. *Sämmtliche Werke*. Edited by Philipp Spitta. 16 vols.
    Leipzig: Breitkopf & Härtel, 1885-94. (See p. 136 below for the con-
    tents of Vols. I-XI.)

Brahms's delight when the critical edition of Schütz finally began to appear has already been mentioned, and his Abschriften from volumes I,
II, and IX have been described (A130, 21-24). Although at this stage of
his career he was no longer seeking or preparing works for performance,
his copies of the *Werke* are also evidence of the care with which he studied
this music for its own sake. There are too many of his markings for any
sort of complete list here, and therefore a summary will have to suffice.[221]
    In general, Brahms continued to notice the same sorts of things that
had always, almost routinely, attracted his attention. He corrected errors;
noted parallels (even in a piece with as many as twenty-two voices);
traced chorale tunes and texts; provided references and cross references;
and marked structural repetitions, ground bass patterns, and imitative
entries. In two places he noticed ingenious uses of diminution: one is
melodic, when in *Symphoniae Sacrae* II, no. 21 (VII: 132 [SWV 361]),
the first bass has an ascending figure on "zechen," first in half notes and

then in eighth notes; and the other is harmonic, when in *Symphoniae Sacrae* III, no. 7 (X: 74 [SWV 375]), the harmonic rhythm at the cadence on "geopfert" is twice as fast the second time it occurs.

To a nineteenth-century musician, even one well acquainted with the early music that had so far been published, many of Schütz's harmonic progressions must have been startling. The early Baroque period was largely unexplored, and Brahms's previous experience with this sort of unpredictable chromaticism was probably limited to such works as Lasso's "Aus meiner Sünden Tiefe" (A130, 9), Rovetta's "Salve Regina" (A134, 25-28), and the few works by Marenzio, Monteverdi, Gesualdo, and Schütz himself printed (almost all incomplete) in Winterfeld's *Gabrieli*.[222] The lush, smooth chromatic writing of Corsi, Durante, and Lotti, or the logical, even if striking and original progressions of Bach (many of which Brahms marked in the *Werke*), would not have prepared him for much of Schütz.

Brahms marked conventional dissonance treatment occasionally; for example, in the *Aufferstehung* (SWV 50) in volume I, only three sections are marked, and they are all duet passages constructed as chains of suspensions. For the most part, however, he noted striking examples of unconventional chromaticism or dissonance. A few of these are listed here:

1. IV: 125, in "Domine ne in furore," downward leaps of a diminished octave in S and A at "miserere mei" (SWV 85: *Neue Ausgabe* 9: 94).

2. VI: 197-98, in "Quem admodum desiderat," the entire section "ita desiderat ad te," which is dominated by an ascending chromatic figure in close imitation in all voices (SWV 336: *Neue Ausgabe* 12: 70-71).

3. VIII: 50, in "So fahr ich hin," the phrase "so schlaf' ich ein und ruhe fein" is marked, probably both for its chromatic harmonic progression and its text painting, where long notes and slow motion conventionally depict rest (SWV 379: *Neue Ausgabe* 5: no. 11).

Two cross relations are marked in a way which suggests that Brahms thought they might have been errors. One occurs in VI: 57, in "Siehe, mein Fürsprecher ist im Himmel," where he wrote several X's in the next-to-last bar (SWV 304: *Neue Ausgabe* 11: 109, m. 90); see Example 6.[223] The other (Ex. 7) is in VIII: 44, in the first triple-meter bar of "Die mit Thränen säen" (SWV 378: *Neue Ausgabe* 5: no. 10, m. 12), where he suggested that the third note in Soprano 1 should be lowered a half step to eliminate the cross relation. The countless other cross relations appear not to have disturbed him; and indeed we have already

Example 6

Example 7

speculated that they may have contributed a special interest to some of the passages he chose for his Abschriften.

5. *Collections of Music by Different Composers, including* Denkmäler

Archives curieuses de la Musique. Two parts: Musique Religieuse; Musique de Chambre. [No editor given.] Publications de la Revue et Gazette Musicale, [no date]. 9, 8 p. [V/42591. Catalogued under "Verschiedene."]

This small collection contains pieces ranging from a Hucbald organum to a Josquin motet in the first part, and from a rondeau by Adam de la Hale to a Willaert madrigal in the second. All sources, whether primary or secondary (several pieces come from Burney or Kiesewetter), are cited. There are no marks of any kind from Brahms. The examples of medieval music in this collection are the only ones he owned outside of journal articles or books on music history.

Denkmäler der Tonkunst. General editor, Friedrich Chrysander. Bergedorf bei Hamburg: Expedition der Denkmäler (H. Weissenborn). [Each volume catalogued separately.]

Brahms's own copies of two volumes from this series with works by Carissimi and Couperin are missing (see p. 70 above). All three which may still be found in his Nachlass were apparently published in 1871; the information is not always given in Brahms's copy, however, and has been obtained from other sources.

Volume I [H21568] is Palestrina, *66 Vierstimmige Motetten* (Liber primus, Rome, 1563; Liber secundus, Venice, 1581), edited by Heinrich Bellermann, 334 pages plus a table of contents. Brahms made only a few of his typical marks in this collection. Imitative entries are marked in several places, as are examples of parallel fifths, mostly occurring across a rest in one voice.

Volume III [uncatalogued] is the first part of Arcangelo Corelli's *Werke*, edited by Joseph Joachim, which contains forty-eight trio sonatas. It has no marks from Brahms at all.

Volume V [H21624] is Francesco Antonio Urio's *Te Deum*, edited by Chrysander "als Quelle zu Händel's Saul, Allegro, Dettinger Te Deum, etc." This is the work which Brahms called to Hermann Levi's attention, saying "It will amuse you amazingly! At once on the first two pages, Handel's Saul, and Te Deum, very striking."[224] The only marks Brahms made in this volume are two notes of parallel fifths. Another copy [H21625], not from the Brahms Nachlass (the Archiv owns three copies altogether), contains a note from Mandyczewski: "Von Johannes Brahms erhalten. Wien 12. März 1883. Eusebius."

Denkmäler der Tonkunst in Oesterreich. Vienna: Artaria, 1894 ff. [I/36788]

Brahms is one of the signers of the letter, dated October 1893, which appears at the beginning of the first volume and contains the introductory remarks by the sponsors of the series. According to Orel's catalog, he owned copies of each of the first seven publications; however, volume II/1, motets by Fux, and volume II/3, Gottlieb Muffat's *Componimenti Musicali per il Cembalo,* are missing.

Judging from the small number of marks Brahms made in these volumes, he did not use them very much. Volume I/1, masses by Johann Joseph Fux, has only one query of a possible wrong note and one mark for a repetition. While volume I/2, Georg Muffat's *Florilegium Primum* (1695), a set of suites for string orchestra, has the pages cut but no other signs of use, Muffat's *Florilegium Secundum* (Vol. II/2) has a few marks in the composer's introduction on performance practice. Brahms apparently did not read all the way through the music in volume III/1, Johann Stadlmeyer's *Hymnen* (1628), since one pair of pages is uncut and there are no marks. In the prologue and first act of Cesti's *Il pomo d'oro* (III/2),

Brahms indicated a ground bass pattern, and showed another repetition with a long "vi . . . de" across two pages—a comment which he often made to show correspondences. The last part of this volume, after page 120, and the back cover are missing.

Denkmäler deutscher Tonkunst. Leipzig: Breitkopf & Härtel, 1892 ff.
    [XVII/27866]

In the letter at the beginning of the first volume, Brahms appears as one of the founders of the series, along with Chrysander and Spitta. Orel's catalog lists only volume I (1892), but volume II (1894) is also part of the Brahms Nachlass.

Of all the Denkmäler, this volume I, Samuel Scheidt's *Tabulatura Nova,* shows the most evidence of careful study by Brahms. His annotations, which show canons, imitative entries, and corrections, are found throughout the work. The second volume, which begins the publication of Hans Leo Hassler's *Werke,* has only one mark which looks simply as if Brahms had dropped his pen.

Kästner, H. *Chor-Gesänge ohne Instrumenten Begleitung.* Hannover, 1851.
    28 p. [H27302. Catalogued under "Verschiedene."]

This collection has already been mentioned as the source for Brahms's Abschrift of the "Ave Maria" attributed to Arcadelt (A137). His only marking is the note "NB Kästner in Hannover" on the first page; the title page is missing. The collection contains twelve works by Palestrina, Anerio, "Arcadelt," Eccard, Gabrieli, Hassler, Praetorius, Lotti, Bach, and Michael Haydn. All are printed in open score, with a piano reduction and German singing translation provided below the score.

Rochlitz, Friedrich. *Sammlung vorzüglicher Gesangstücke.* Mainz: Schott,
    1835. Vol. I, divided into two separately-bound parts, each with its own introduction: 19, 37 p.; 25, 74 p.; with 6 p. corrections. [H27303. Catalogued under "Verschiedene."]

Although Robert Schumann owned a copy of this collection, and Clara made her Palestrina Abschriften from it (A134, 29-34), Brahms presumably did not acquire these volumes until sometime after 1868. Each of them has the date August 1868 written on the flyleaf, and each has the names of clefs written in one piece, evidently as an aid in transposition. None of the dates or annotations looks like Brahms's hand, however; they appear to have been written by a previous owner. There is no way of knowing how long after 1868 or in what way Brahms acquired the collection.

Rochlitz, a "Romantic critic" who was active in the first stages of the nineteenth-century early music revival,[225] published the three volumes of his *Sammlung* in the 1830s. The first half-volume contains works said to have been composed between 1380 (Dufay) and 1550 (Lasso); and the second covers the years 1550 to 1630.[226] Two other pieces which appear among the Brahms Abschriften are found here, although the collection was not his source in either case: they are Gabrieli's "Benedictus" (A130, 1-6) and Gallus's "Ecce quomodo" (A130, 18-19, etc.), which is here called "Passionsgesang."

The first volume contains only a few corrections in Brahms's hand. In the second, all of his annotations appear in the Gallus piece, one he knew well. At the beginning, where Rochlitz has a note saying that the piece was disseminated in "more or less changed" forms, Brahms underlined the words "weniger verändert" and wrote in the margin, "hier sichre falsch" (here surely wrong). He wrote a number of NB's in the music where there are differences from the version he already knew, and made several pencil corrections.[227]

Winterfeld, Carl von. *Johannes Gabrieli und sein Zeitalter.* Berlin: Schlesinger, 1834. 3 volumes (1st and 2nd bound together): Erster Theil, xii, 202 p.; Zweiter Theil, iii, 228 p.; Dritter Theil, 157 p. of musical examples. [1624/204]

Although Winterfeld's large and important work is classified as a book in the Archiv, and the first two volumes (bound into one) are text, it will be described here as a music collection, because the third volume was such an important source of music-historical examples to Brahms. We have already seen that this volume (or perhaps one belonging to one of Brahms's friends) may have been the source of the Abschriften in A130, 1-6. Brahms's own set was given to him by Avé Lallemant in 1858, according to a note inside the front cover of volume III.

In this work, Winterfeld was not only the first nineteenth-century scholar to call musicians' attention to the Venetian school,[228] but he also accomplished a virtual rediscovery of Schütz. As Moser says,

> Despite his old-fashioned prolixity, Winterfeld . . . produced a portrait of Schütz to which for half a century German romanticism could look up in reverence, until the brothers Spitta ushered in a new age of Schütz investigation.[229]

Brahms may not, at the age of twenty-five, have been fully aware of the work's historical importance, but he certainly read the text and studied the music carefully, as his markings show.

Winterfeld's introduction and the sections of volume I which deal with the history of Venice and San Marco, with Gabrieli's life, and with Gregorian chant, have very few marks. The chapter on the church modes, however, attracted more of Brahms's attention. A long paragraph on pp. 87-88 dealing with the characters of the various modes is marked with heavy pencil stripes in the margins. In a long, lyrical prose flight, Winterfeld calls the Ionian mode bright and cheerful, complete in itself; the Mixolydian also cheerful, but with a note of striving and longing like the Christian's longing for rebirth and return to an earlier innocence; the Dorian sadder and softer, but comforting and encouraging, with a quiet and holy seriousness that is suitable for the most sacred songs; the Aeolian covered by a shadow of deep sorrow; and the Phrygian enveloped by a still deeper darkness which seems to express only profound need and remorse. Next to the Phrygian mode, however, stands heavenly comfort, since the deeper man's sin, the more fervently he feels the blessedness of his redemption. Therefore since the earliest days of the church, the Phrygian mode has been used not only for penitential psalms, but also for solemn songs of praise. Winterfeld's pseudo-scientific derivation of this system and his other statements are sometimes inaccurate and rather amusing, but his sincerity is undeniable. He reflects not only his own Lutheran enthusiasm but also the historical perpective of the 1830s—and these ideas of early music are, after all, those that Brahms first learned.

The remainder of the first volume, containing chapters on Willaert's students and successors, on rhythm, and on the early part of Gabrieli's career and his relation to Palestrina and Lasso, has no Brahms annotations except a few underlinings of sources of music and a mark against Rovetta's name in the list of the Maestri della Capella at San Marco.

The second volume of text does not contain many markings either. In the first section, on the new direction of music at the beginning of the seventeenth century, Brahms corrected a few notes in an example from a Monteverdi madrigal given to show how rules of counterpoint could be broken to illustrate the text in a highly emotional passage. A section on the chromaticism of Marenzio and Gesualdo contains a cross reference to Marenzio's "Voi che sospirate," which appears as an appendix to volume III; in that volume Brahms wrote another cross reference and the German translation provided in volume II. Winterfeld (II: 89) calls this piece "enharmonic," and discusses the great difficulty of singing it in tune.

Chapters on accompanied song (with sections on playing the organ and other instruments, and on ornamentation) and on oratorio have no Brahms annotations. In the important chapter on Schütz, he corrected a date which is obviously a misprint; his only other mark is in Winterfeld's description of "Saul" (p. 198), which calls attention to the passage where the tenor soloist continues the call "Saul, Saul" on long notes in an ascending scale (marked in the margin), through the *major* tonalities of *F* and *G* (underlined by Brahms).[230] Winterfeld's authority for matters of terminology and performance practice in Schütz's music is Praetorius; he also includes a section on passion and resurrection oratorios, mentioning composers as far back as Obrecht. Brahms made no further annotations in this section, or in the final chapter, a general review and conclusion.

Winterfeld's third volume contains no table of contents. Because his collection of examples made such an important contribution to the development of nineteenth-century awareness of the early Baroque period, and because it was also especially important to Brahms, a complete list of its contents is given in Table 4.[231]

Winterfeld labeled his examples with Roman numerals to show which volume they illustrated, and with letters A or B to denote complete examples and fragments of pieces respectively; but in volume III he provided no cross references back to his discussion of each piece in the text. Brahms wrote in these cross references to the text volumes for fifteen of the examples; and in thirty pieces he wrote in the German translation of the Latin or Italian text which Winterfeld had provided in one of the earlier volumes. Pieces identified with asterisks are those in which Brahms made markings in addition to these or to his other routine kinds of annotations—corrections, queries of possible errors or of the voice leading, and notes on parallels. For each example, Winterfeld's example number, the page number, the composer, and the title or beginning of text (which is sometimes from the middle of a piece in the case of a fragment) is given.[232]

Table 4.   List of Examples from Winterfeld, *Johannes Gabrieli,*
Volume III

Winterfeld's Example No.	Page No.	Composer	Title or Beginning of Text
I.A.1.	3	Gabrieli*	Ego dixi Dominus
I.A.2.	7	Gabrieli	Deus meus
I.A.3.	11	Gabrieli*	O Domine Jesu Christe
I.A.4.	15	Gabrieli	Domine exaudi
I.A.5.	18	Gabrieli	Magnificat (1° toni)
I.A.6.	24	Gabrieli*	Sancta Maria

Winterfeld's Example No.	Page No.	Composer	Title or Beginning of Text
I.A.7.	29	Gabrieli*	Beata es virgo Maria
I.A.8.	32	Gabrieli*	Jubilate Deo
I.A.9.	42	Gabrieli*	Benedictus (a 12, in 3 choirs)
I.A.10.	46	Palestrina*	Surge illuminare Hierusalem
I.A.11.	51	Palestrina	O Domine Jesu Christe
I.A.12.	53	Lasso	Magnificat VIII (6° toni, 1st section)
I.A.13.	54	Lasso	Te prophetarum
II.A.1.	55	Gabrieli	Miserere mei
II.A.2.	58	Gabrieli*	O quam suavis
II.A.3.	62	Merulo	Toccata (7° tono)
II.A.4.	65	Gabrieli	Canzone per l'organo[233]
II.A.5.	66	Gabrieli	Sinfonia & "Et Dominus de caelo intonuit"
II.A.6.	73	Gabrieli*	In ecclesiis
II.A.7.	82	Schütz	Fili mi Absalon [SWV 269]
II.A.8.	87	Schütz	Was betrübst du dich, meine Seele? [SWV 335]
II.A.9.	92	Schütz*	Saul, Saul [SWV 415]
I.B.1.	99	Gabrieli*	Surrexit pastor bonus
I.B.2.	100	Gabrieli	. . . Hodie spiritus sanctus [Hodie completi sunt]
I.B.3.	101	Gabrieli	. . . Ascendit Deus [Omnes gentes]
I.B.4.	104	Gabrieli	Psalm 8, Domine Dominus noster
I.B.5.	105	Gabrieli	Angelus Domini descendit
I.B.6.	107	Gabrieli	. . . Ego dormivi [Angelus ad pastores]
I.B.7.	108	Gabrieli	Kyrie (alto & instruments)[234]
II.B.1.	108	Monteverdi	Dal ballo delle Ingrate
II.B.2.	109	Monteverdi	Combattimento
II.B.3.	112	Monteverdi	Dixit Dominus
II.B.4.	114	Monteverdi	Deposuit
II.B.5.	115	Marenzio	Psalm 78, verse 3
II.B.6.	117	Gesualdo*	Moro lasso
II.B.7.	118	Gesualdo	Moro, moro e mentre sospiro
II.B.8.	118	Gabrieli	Sonata per tre violini
II.B.9.	119	Gabrieli	Canzon noni toni
II.B.10.	120	Gabrieli	. . . Qui crediderit [Hodie completi sunt]
II.B.11.	122	Gabrieli	O Jesu mi dulcissime
II.B.12.	124	Gabrieli	Magnificat sexti toni (first verse)
II.B.13.	126	Gabrieli	Salvator noster
II.B.14.	133	Gabrieli	Timor et tremor
II.B.15.	136	Gabrieli	a) . . . Quando coeli movendi sunt b) . . . Tremens factus sum ego [Exaudi me Domine]

Winterfeld's Example No.	Page No.	Composer	Title or Beginning of Text
II.B.16.	137	Gabrieli	. . . In pace recipe animam meam [Domine Deus meus]
II.B.17.	139	Schütz	Ego sum tui plaga doloris [SW 57]
II.B.18.	141	Schütz	In te Domine speravi (a 4) [SWV 66]
II.B.19.	143	Schütz	. . . Miserere nobis [SWV 65; in new ed. "miserere mei"]
II.B.20.	143	Schütz*	In te Domine speravi (alto & instruments) [SWV 259]
II.B.21.	146	Schütz*	. . . Quia amore langueo [SWV 264]
II.B.22.	147	Schütz*	. . . Surgam et circuibo [SWV 272]
II.B.23.	150	Schütz	. . . Cantate ed exsultate [SWV 276]
II.B.24.	150	Schütz	. . . Christus ist hie, der gestorben ist [SWV 329]
II.B.25.	152	Schütz	Sei gegrüsset, Maria [SWV 333]
II.B.26.	153	Schütz	Mein Sohn, warum hast du uns das gethan? [SWV 406]
II.B.27.	155	Schütz	. . . Steh auf und nimm das Kindlein [SWV 403]
No. 28.	156	Marenzio*	O voi che sospirate (complete)

*Pieces in which Brahms made special markings.

Most of Brahms's markings, apart from the references and the German translations, seem to describe his own observations or ideas, rather than being related to Winterfeld's discussion in the text volumes. Many are analytical: they help to clarify the contrapuntal structure by pointing out entrances, sometimes identifying different head motives with differently shaped brackets or with numbers; they also emphasize chordal passages and major section divisions. The many page references back to the text volumes suggest, however, that Brahms also found Winterfeld's comments useful in his study of these works.

A few correlations with Winterfeld's text are of particular interest. In Gabrieli's "O Domine Jesu Christe," Brahms underlined the word "felle" (gall); Winterfeld comments on the "bitterness" of the Phrygian cadence. Winterfeld also discusses the changing harmonies in a section of this piece where there are several varied repetitions; Brahms delineated the sections with repeat signs. Another Phrygian cadence is identified by Winterfeld in Gabrieli's "Beata es virgo Maria" (the piece is in A130, 1-6) by underlining the words "intercede pro nobis." He points out that this pattern is then present continually in one or another of the voices until just before the end of the piece; Brahms marked all of the appearances of this ostinato. One of the incomplete examples, Gabrieli's setting of Psalm 8, for which Brahms provided a cross reference to the text, is included by Winterfeld specifically to illustrate the fact that the true rhythm which comes from word accents may have no relation to the position of editorial bar lines. In the text (I: 172), he quotes a passage from Sebald Heyden, and mentions that this freedom from implied metric accent can take place when the beat remains constant and "no proportion in the sense of the older music theory occurs."[235]

Brahms marked several striking dissonances; noted a few six-four chords, of which he evidently disapproved in their context;[236] added many accidentals, mostly in places where Winterfeld had obviously left them out;[237] and changed the text underlay occasionally. In one of the pieces which shows Gabrieli writing in the new style, "O quam suavis," are two markings which call attention to the interval of a diminished fourth.[238] The same interval clearly drew Brahms's disapproval in Gesualdo's "Moro lasso," where he marked a melodic diminished fourth with "X NB," and then wrote another X and a bass figure when he noticed one used harmonically.

Brahms performed two works from Winterfeld's volume of examples with the Singakademie in his unsuccessful concert of 6 January 1864 (p. 3 above); they are I.A.9, Gabrieli's twelve-voice Benedictus, and II.A.9, Schütz's "Saul, Saul." His original performance markings, mostly erased but some still legible, are found in this volume in the Archiv.[239] He did not erase several changes he made in the Schütz piece after consulting the original partbooks of *Symphoniae Sacrae* III (1650) in the Hofbibliothek. These changes consist of a few corrections, the tying over editorial bar lines of some notes in the continuo part, and the addition of some original dynamics. Brahms wrote a note, "Original-Ausg./Hofbibl.," at the bottom of page 93 to show where he had found them.

3

The Effects of Brahms's Study of Early Music on His Choral Writing

The Choral Works of Brahms: A Chronological List

Writers of composers' biographies exhibit a tendency to divide their subjects' work into periods, and the present writer is no exception. For our purpose, the most useful division of Brahms's career is into three periods—an early period up to about 1863, a middle period to 1885, and a late period.[1] It is, of course, impossible to be precise about these dividing dates, since many of Brahms's ideas matured in his mind over a period of years; in particular, several of his middle-period works were begun in the first period and not finished until much later, or incorporate musical material from the first period. Further confusion arises because a number of pieces were not published until many years after they were written, and it is not usually known how much revision they underwent at the time of publication.

Tables 5, 6, and 7 list the choral works of Brahms in approximately chronological order. The dates of composition come from Kross, unless other references or explanations are given. Asterisks identify works which Brahms published for women's voices.[2] The only works without opus number listed are the *Missa canonica* and the folk-song settings for mixed voices found in the *Werke* XXI: nos. 1-22, some published by Brahms in 1864, and others which first appeared after his death.[3]

Brahms's Early Choral Works

The early choral works of Brahms include those which were composed roughly through the 1863-64 season he spent as conductor of the Singakademie, when he turned away from his north German background and toward Vienna and a wider area of activity. This first period of choral composition contains the surviving pieces written in connection with his study of counterpoint, all of the works for women's voices (except for a few later canons), and most of the folk-song and chorale settings.

Table 5.   Brahms's Early Choral Works

Work	Opus No.	Date of Composition
Kyrie and "Missa Canonica"[4]	unpubl.	Feb.-June 1856
Geistliches Lied	Op. 30	April 1856
Folk song settings 2. Mit Lust tät ich ausreiten 3. Bei nächtlicher Weil 8. In stiller Nacht 9. Ich fahr dahin 10. Es pochet ein Knabe 11. Die Wollust in den Maien 13. Es ist ein Schnitter	publ. 1864	1857[5]
Folk song settings 15. Ach Gott, wie weh tut Scheiden 16. Wach auf, meins Herzens Schöne 17. Erlaube mir, feins Mädchen 18. Es wohnet ein Fiedler 19. Da unten im Tale 20. Des Abends kann ich nicht schlafen	publ. posth.	1857?[6]
Ave Maria*	Op. 12	Sept. 1858
Begräbnisgesang	Op. 13	Oct. 1858
Canons* 3. Sitzt a schöns Vögerl 4. Schlaf, Kindlein, schlaf! 5. Wille wille will 6. So lange Schönheit 7. Wenn die Klänge nah'n	Op. 113	1858
Drei geistliche Chöre* 1. O bone Jesu 2. Adoramus te, Christe	Op. 37	before summer 1859[7]
XIII. Psalm*	Op. 27	Aug. 1859
Marienlieder 1. Der englische Gruss 2. Marias Kirchgang 3. Marias Wallfahrt 4. Der Jäger 5. Ruf zur Maria 6. Magdalena 7. Marias Lob	Op. 22	summer 1859 (except no. 3) 1860?

Gesänge für Frauenchor* 1. Es tönt ein voller Harfenklang 2. Lied von Shakespeare 3. Der Gärtner 4. Gesang aus Fingal	Op. 17	winter 1859-60
12 Lieder und Romanzen* 1. Minnelied 2. Der Bräutigam 3. Barcarole 4. Fragen 5. Die Müllerin 6. Die Nonne 7. Nun stehen die Rosen in Blüthe 8. Die Berge sind spitz 9. Am Wildbach die Weiden 10. Und gehst du über den Kirchhof 11. Die Braut 12. Märznacht	Op. 44	1859-60
3 Gesänge für 6-stimmigen Chor 1. Abendständchen 2. Vineta 3. Darthulas Grabesgesang	Op. 42	1859-60
Zwei Motetten 1. Es ist das Heil 2. Schaffe in mir, Gott	Op. 29	summer 1860 (begun 1857)
Canons* 1. Göttlicher Morpheus 2. Grausam erweiset sich Amor 8. Ein Gems auf dem Stein 10. Leise Töne der Brust 11. Ich weiss nicht, was im Hain 12. Wenn Kummer hätte zu tödten	Op. 113	1860-63
5 Männerchorlieder 1. Ich schwing mein Horn 2. Freiwillige her! 3. Geleit 4. Marschieren 5. Gebt acht!	Op. 41	1862 (except no. 1) 1860[8]
O Heiland, reiss die Himmel auf	Op. 74/2	1863[9]
Folk song settings 1. Von edler Art 4. Komm Mainz, komm Bayrn 5. Es flog ein Täublein 6. Ach lieber Herre Jesu Christ 7. Tröst die Bedrängten 12. Wach auf, mein Kind 14. Es wollt gut Jäger jagen	publ. 1864	1863
Regina coeli*	Op. 37/3	Dec. 1863

*Works published for women's voices.

Brahms's Middle-Period Choral Works

Works composed during the years from about 1864, when Brahms began to establish himself in Vienna on a fairly permanent basis, to 1885, when he finished the Fourth Symphony, are included in the middle period of his choral writing shown in Table 6. This long period not only combines Kross's next two divisions, the "orchestralen Grossformen" (1863-71) and "die Werke der mittleren Lebensjahre" (1872-82), but extends into the period he defines as late to include Opp. 93a and 93b. Thus all the large works with orchestra are encompassed, from the *Requiem* and *Rinaldo* to the *Gesang der Parzen*,[10] as well as the two groups of a cappella secular works, Op. 62 and Op. 93a, many of which share a generally lighthearted and folk-like character that has little in common with Brahms's later, more serious secular choral works.[11] By the same token, Op. 93b, the "Tafellied," one of Brahms's few occasional pieces, certainly belongs to the middle period.

The works for solo quartet and piano, the *Quartette* Opp. 31, 64, 92, and 112 nos. 1 and 2, the *Liebeslieder* Op. 52 and *Neue Liebeslieder* Op. 65, and the *Zigeunerlieder* Opp. 103 and 112 nos. 3-6, the majority of which fall into this period, are not listed. They can also be very successful small-scale choral works; but considerations of space, together with the fact that they are thoroughly modern works with much more the character of Brahms's chamber music and Lieder than his other choral music, prevent their inclusion.[12]

Table 6.   Brahms's Middle-Period Choral Works

Work	Opus No.	Date of Composition
Ein deutsches Requiem	Op. 45	1854-68
Rinaldo	Op. 50	1863-68
Canon* 9. An's Auge des Liebsten	Op. 113	1868 or 1869[13]
Alt-Rhapsodie	Op. 53	1869
Schicksalslied	Op. 54	1868-71
Triumphlied	Op. 55	1870-71
Folk song settings 21. Wach auf, meins Herzens Schöne 22. Dort in den Weiden	publ. posth.	early 1873?[14]
7 Lieder für gemischten Chor 1. Rosmarin	Op. 62	finished 1874[15] 1873-74

2. Von alten Liebesliedern		1873-74
3. Waldesnacht		1873-74
4. Dein Herzlein mild		1873-74
5. All meine Herzgedanken		1873-74
6. Es geht ein Wehen		early
7. Vergangen ist mir Glück und Heil		1860
Warum ist das Licht gegeben	Op. 74/1	1877-78[16]
Nänie	Op. 82	summer 1881
Gesang der Parzen	Op. 89	summer 1882
Lieder und Romanzen	Op. 93a	1883
1. Der bucklichte Fiedler		
2. Das Mädchen		
3. O süsser Mai		
4. Fahr wohl		
5. Der Falke		
6. Beherzigung		
Tafellied	Op. 93b	Jan. 1885

*Works published for women's voices.

Brahms's Late Choral Works

The group of late choral works listed in Table 7 is small, consisting of only three complete sets of pieces, all a cappella. With a few exceptions, they employ more than four voices; and all but one of the works with sacred texts are for double choir. Although the Op. 109 motets were, like the *Triumphlied,* written at least partly for patriotic reasons and first performed on a ceremonial occasion, their tone is not strident; in them the double choir medium is treated with the same flexibility that characterizes these other late works. The secular songs of Op. 104 and the motets Op. 110 share the mood of autumnal sadness and resignation that stamps so much of the music of Brahms's later years.

Table 7.   Brahms's Late Choral Works

Work	Opus No.	Date of Composition
5 Gesänge für gemischten Chor	Op. 104	summer 1888
1. Nachtwache I		(except no. 5)
2. Nachtwache II		
3. Letztes Glück		
4. Verlorene Jugend		
5. Im Herbst		1886

Canon*	Op. 113	summer 1888?
13. Einförmig ist der Liebe Gram		
Fest- und Gedenksprüche	Op. 109	summer 1888
1. Unsere Väter		
2. Wenn ein starker Gewappneter		
3. Wo ist ein so herrlich Volk		
Drei Motetten	Op. 110	1889
1. Ich aber bin elend		
2. Ach, arme Welt		
3. Wenn wir in höchsten Nöten sein		

*Works published for women's voices.

A Review of Brahms's Choral Compositions in Relation to His Study of Early Music

Before the chronological discussion of Brahms's choral compositions is begun, the limits of his enthusiasm for early music should be considered briefly. Notwithstanding the statements of some of his biographers, his interest was actually something less than universal, especially in the area of vocal music. Although he made periodic attempts to learn foreign languages, especially Italian, he was comfortable and confident only in German. His only published compositions in another language are the Op. 12 and Op. 37 efforts in Latin, clearly written under the influence of E. T. A. Hoffmann's Romantic ideal of sacred music;[17] they are among Brahms's least successful choral works. His experience with these pieces and with the canonic mass, which Joachim criticized for faulty accentuation,[18] did not stimulate him to further study of the language.

This disinclination to learn foreign languages may also have resulted in part from Brahms's strong, positive feelings of patriotism, sentiments shared by nearly all his German contemporaries. Pride in their national heritage played a large part in their enthusiasm for the rediscovery (sometimes the invention) and perpetuation of folk songs, and in the revival of the music of Bach, Schütz, Eccard, and other German Renaissance and Baroque composers. Brahms enjoyed the fruits of these discoveries by the German musicologists who were his friends, but he did not himself pursue knowledge of the past into unknown areas.

His library of early music reflects both his enthusiasms and his limitations, as well as those of the German-speaking musical community of his day. There is no vocal music by French or English composers except for Byrd's "Non nobis Domine" (in A131) and the tune of "Il me suffit" (in A134, 39-40), which appears only as the original version of a German chorale melody.[19] Much music by Italian composers appears, especially in the Abschriften that Brahms made early in his career; but this is mostly sacred music, in Latin, and it may show more clearly the limits of what early music was available at that time than the limits of Brahms's interest. The only vocal works in Italian among the Abschriften are Cesti's *Serenata* (A130, 30-37) and the fragments from Schütz's Italian madrigals (A130, 21). In the area of early instrumental music, which is, of course, independent of language, Brahms made the Frescobaldi Abschriften of A130, 25-26, collected a great number of works by Domenico Scarlatti in early editions,[20] and, with Chrysander, edited the Couperin edition for *Denkmäler der Tonkunst.*

Brahms's tastes in early music developed very early in his career. As he grew older and learned more they became better defined, and he was more selective in his acquisitions, copying or adding to his collection works which appealed to his national pride, his collector's enthusiasm, or his pedagogical instinct. The choral compositions he published during the course of his career show a parallel development and refinement of taste; Brahms became more critical and selective in his evaluation of his own music, just as he did in his study of the music of earlier times.

It is not at all surprising that we should find a correlation between Brahms's acquisition of works of or about early music and his development as a choral composer. It was stated at the outset that students of his choral writing since Philipp Spitta, and including Kalbeck, Hohenemser, Geiringer, Kross, and Beuerle among others, have pointed out the inspiration he derived from Renaissance and Baroque music, and have often cited specific composers and works as the sources of that inspiration in particular cases. However, since Brahms himself said and wrote so little about the sources of his ideas and his methods of composition, the attributions of influence have nearly all had to be based on guesses, some more plausible than others.[21]

The examination of his library for the present study has produced no striking new solutions to these mysteries. It has, however, provided documentary evidence of what works of early music Brahms knew, an approximate chronological record of when he acquired them, and some information on how he studied and performed them. What value he actually placed on individual works remains, of course, largely a matter for conjecture.

The interpretation of his annotations is, in particular, a subject that needs to be approached with great caution, lest the prejudices of the investigator rather than Brahms's own reactions to the music provide the conclusions. It is for this reason that the present writer has tried to describe the contents of the library as fully as possible, so that the reader may reach his own conclusions—although limitations of space and time prohibit the provision of a complete list of the annotations. The reader is therefore still dependent on this writer's judgment for the choices which have been made; but on the whole, an attempt has been made to present information objectively.

In the material which follows, now that the description of Brahms's library is complete, the writer's subjective opinions must play a significant and unavoidable part. One general rule may be stated: whenever an early music connection is cited, the work referred to is part of Brahms's library and has been described in chapter 2 unless a specific statement is made to the contrary.

The Early Period (1856-64)

Brahms's earliest surviving choral compositions are canons. Evidence of his interest in canons by other composers may be seen in the Abschriften A131, the earliest of which were copied in 1854. There are no examples in Brahms's collection of the sorts of complex Renaissance canons that Kross seems to suggest as influences on Brahms when he compares his canonic writing with that of Josquin.[22] It is possible, of course, that Brahms might have read the accounts of Glarean's work that were given in the histories by Forkel and Kiesewetter, as Kross says. He did not own either of these histories himself, though he did have a copy of Forkel's Bach biography; but Schumann had Kiesewetter's *Geschichte der Musik* in his library.[23]

Although the canons of the "Geistliches Lied," the first section of "Schaffe in mir, Gott," and the Benedictus from the canonic mass may have been written originally as exercises, each is as successful musically as it is technically.[24] However, the canons of Op. 37, especially the first two, do not work out so well. The dates of their composition are not established; they could have been composed in this earliest period, around 1856, or as late as when they were first sung in 1859.[25] They were published along with the later-composed no. 3 during Brahms's first years in Vienna, when he badly needed the money.

The first, "O bone Jesu," is stiff and stilted;[26] and the second, "Adoramus te, Christe,"[27] though somewhat less awkward—possibly because the canonic section is not so elaborate—is noticeably lacking in stylistic unity. One is forced to wonder whether Brahms's critical judgment might have been impaired by his sentimental recollections of the happy days with the uncritical ladies of the Hamburg choir, who were all probably a little in love with their young conductor, when he allowed it to be published. Up to the end of the canon there is some melodic and harmonic resemblance to Palestrina;[28] perhaps Brahms first constructed the canon this far as an exercise without providing it with a proper conclusion. The problems arise in the last fourteen measures, which he may have added at some later time. Bars 24 and 25 (see Ex. 8a) sound as though they were written under the immediate influence of several passages in Bach's Cantata 4, "Christ lag in Todesbanden," which Brahms studied with the Detmold choir in the autumn of 1857;[29] but in bar 25, the harmony takes a turn away from a Bach-like cadence on D minor (a possible cadence is suggested in Ex. 8b).[30]

Example 8a

Example 8b

For the remainder, Brahms seems to recall the chordal Palestrina of Clara Schumann's A134 copies, except for the anachronistic dominant seventh in the fourth-to-last bar. Beuerle defends Brahms against the charge of eclecticism in this piece as in others. I feel, however, that in this case eclecticism is precisely what causes the work to fail; with a different ending the canon might have been salvaged. On the other hand, Op. 37/3, "Regina coeli," which is mirror-canonic in the two solo voices, sounds rather contrived, but is on the whole more successful than the others because of its freely written choral parts and the more unified style.[31]

The other earliest canons which Brahms decided were worth keeping do not have the problems of the Op. 37 group; certainly by the time of their 1891 publication in Op. 113 he would not have released any work that he felt would not do him credit. Even so, he wrote to Joachim after their publication: "Of course the canons are to sing and not to hear! I make an exception for the Leiermann if it is sung really enthusiastically [fanatisch]."[32]

During Brahms's study of canon and counterpoint, when the early choral works were composed, he acquired a number of eighteenth-century pedagogical books; but his own collection of actual works of polyphonic early music was limited until about 1857 to a few Abschriften from Schlesinger's *Musica Sacra* and from Winterfeld's *Der evangelische Kirchengesang,* the "Palestrina" Responsorien, the *Missa Papae Marcelli,* and perhaps the copies that Clara Schumann made for him. The only printed books containing this sort of music which he himself owned were Becker and Billroth's collection of chorales and the first volume of the Bach *Werke.* Also he had, of course, studied the works of early music in Schumann's library.

Once Brahms was given the conducting job at Detmold, he had a practical reason both to add to his library of choral literature and to contribute his own efforts to the genre. He realized in short order that he had very little knowledge of how to write for chorus, and said in a letter to Joachim in December 1857, "How little practical knowledge I have! . . . My things are really extremely unpractically written!"[33]

Some of the first choral composing he did during the Detmold period is an early manifestation of his lifelong interest in German folk music. Kretzschmer and Zuccalmaglio's collection was his main source of texts and tunes for these first choral folk-song settings. He acquired his own copy in 1856 (see p. 81 above), and it remained his favorite source of folk-song material for the rest of his life, in spite of the attacks on the authenticity of its contents. All of his earliest settings are from this collection except no. 8, "In stiller Nacht," and no. 17, "Erlaube mir";[34] they are straightforward chordal presentations of the melody, which is invariably in the top voice. Brahms chose seven of these early settings for publication in 1864 along with some of the settings he had just composed for the Singakademie. He may have revised the Detmold settings at that time, or may have chosen them for inclusion in the set in the first place because their arrangements were originally somewhat more sophisticated than those which were not chosen and therefore remained unpublished until after his death.[35]

Most of the early folk-song settings are distinguished from similar work by other composers only by the somewhat greater attention Brahms gave to writing interesting inner parts. For example, in no. 15, "Ach Gott, wie weh tut Scheiden," the alto is spared a dull part in bars 10-12 by the otherwise unnecessary crossing with the tenor. None of these settings shows any consistent use of contrapuntal choral writing. At this stage of his life, when Brahms wanted to write vocal counterpoint, he wrote canons and put them in works with sacred texts.

Through the years in Detmold and Hamburg and his first year or two in Vienna, Brahms studied early music more diligently and added a wider range of it to his library than he did at any other time in his life. In the Abschriften we see that he pursued the study of folk music into its appearance in sophisticated polyphonic Renaissance Lieder, investigated a number of German chorales, copied more examples of canons, and explored post-Renaissance Italian church music. His most important acquisitions of printed early music at this time were Winterfeld's *Gabrieli,* Meister's collection, and the successive volumes of the Bach *Werke;* the Handel *Werke* also began to appear during this period.

Brahms wrote a good deal of choral music in the years immediately after the early folk-song settings, much of it clearly designed to be "practical"—that is, not too difficult, and with an immediately pleasing external effect.[36] Much of the music for the Frauenchor falls into this category, including the 13th Psalm (Op. 27), which in its most appealing moments strongly resembles Mendelssohn, but also suffers from the same eclecticism as Op. 37/2; the four songs with horns and harp (Op. 17), which have also often been compared to Mendelssohn; and the *Lieder und Romanzen, Op.* 44. The latter set, in addition to its surface appeal, shows a much more fluent use of contrapuntal techniques to enrich the part writing and the overall vocal interest than we have seen so far in Brahms's secular choral writing; yet the details are added in a way that does not interfere with the overall impression of charm and simplicity conveyed by this group of songs.[37] For example, in no. 4, "Fragen," the character of the simple, repetitive Slavic folk text is in no way distorted by the use of short bits of Vorimitation in each of the first two verses, or by the canonic writing in the two middle voices with a series of suspensions in the third and fourth bars before the end.[38] In no. 5, "Die Müllerin," the melody has a strong flavor of the Phrygian mode, snatches of Vorimitation are used, and in a striking example of text painting, Brahms uses an ostinato of unison octave leaps in the second soprano and second alto to describe the mill wheel turning in the wind.[39]

Many of the works of this period exist in forms both for women's and for mixed voices, although usually Brahms published only the latter versions.[40] However, two of the pieces published for women's voices in Op. 44 also survive in mixed chorus arrangements in Brahms's hand in the Vienna Stadtbibliothek;[41] unfortunately no information is available to tell when they were made. No. 5, "Die Müllerin," appears in A minor with the bass doubling the alto an octave below in the mill-wheel bars; and no. 6, "Die Nonne," is in F minor with a number of changes in details of distribution of the voices. In general, this discussion will deal only with the version for mixed voices of any work which exists in both forms.

An early work of this period which was certainly written for mixed voices in the first place is the *Begräbnisgesang,* Op. 13. The commentators have nearly all called it a forerunner of the *Requiem*; and indeed its initial melodic idea resembles not only no. 2 ("Denn alles Fleisch") of that work[42] but also the similar line found in other works associated with death, such as "Magdalena" in the *Marienlieder* (Op. 22/6) and the beginning of the first of the *Vier ernste Gesänge* (Op. 121). A number of the Brahms biographers have called Op. 13 a setting of an old German chorale tune,[43] but in reality only the text is old.[44] Brahms himself wrote to Julius Otto Grimm, when he sent him the work in the autumn of 1858, "I hardly need to tell you that I haven't used any chorale or folk melody."[45] Grimm was very favorably impressed with the work, and noticed the resemblance of the middle section, "Die Seel'," to "Den Tod" from Bach's Cantata 4;[46] this section also shows a discreet and effective use of canon in the vocal parts. Grimm rehearsed the piece with his choir in Göttingen for a performance in early 1860, and Florence May (2nd ed., p. 264) reports that Philipp Spitta took part in the performance. She also repeats a story told her by Carl von Meysenbug, a friend of Brahms from Detmold who was a student at Göttingen:

> As Grimm was distributing the parts of the "Ave Maria" and the "Begräbnissgesang" at one of the practices, . . . my neighbour, a glib University student with the experience of several terms behind him, said to me in a surprised tone: "Brahms! who is that?" "Oh, some old ecclesiastic of Palestrina's time," I replied—a piece of information which he accepted and passed on.

It would take a very credulous student to accept the "Ave Maria" as a work of early music.[47] Perhaps the idea is not quite so ludicrous in the case of the *Begräbnisgesang,* nor is the supposition that the tune belongs to an old chorale; but nevertheless the work, in innumerable details of harmony, rhythm, part writing, and instrumentation, especially in the C major middle section, demonstrates that it is the product of Brahms as a composer of his own time. Even though parts seem to be deliberately cast in an archaic mold,[48] the *Begräbnisgesang* does not leave the listener with the same impression of patched-up historical imitation as do those works in which Brahms displays an uncritical eclecticism.

Brahms himself described the *Marienlieder,* Op. 22, to Simrock: "The poems are beautiful old folk songs and the music somewhat in the style of old German church and folk songs."[49] Kalbeck feels that they may have been inspired by Eccard's "Übers Gebirg Maria geht";[50] and certainly they belong to the long German tradition of Marian legend songs of which the Eccard work and the folk texts chosen by Brahms are examples. Brahms was attracted by such texts, as the markings in his folksong collections show, and he liked the Eccard piece enough to perform it more than once (see A134, 29-34, above). However, the seven settings he made of similar texts in Op. 22 have little in common with "Übers Gebirg";[51] they are, on the whole, *less* richly romantic than Eccard's remarkably sweet five-part setting, except for "Ruf zur Maria" (no. 5), which is a wonderful example of nineteenth-century chromatic harmony.

The other six *Marienlieder* have a drier quality which, if it can be compared to anything in Brahms's library at all, is perhaps closer to Praetorius's simple "Maria zart" (A130, 15), probably copied during this period, or to some of the earlier chorale settings published in the first volume of Winterfeld's *Der evangelische Kirchengesang*. Most of the early sixteenth-century settings have their tunes in the tenor; we cannot know whether Brahms was consciously imitating the style when he set "Marias Kirchgang" with its Dorian melody in the alto, the next lowest of four voices in every verse but the sixth. In the sixth verse a new melody in E flat major moves from soprano to tenor, and the ringing of bells is imitated in an exuberant display of text painting. That Brahms was not attempting to write a mere imitation of sixteenth-century style is shown clearly by his setting of no. 4, "Der Jäger," an attractive and purely Romantic hunting song full of horn calls and secondary dominants.[52]

The Marienlieder occupy a middle ground between sacred and secular works. The two remaining groups of entirely secular pieces written before Brahms left Hamburg for Vienna include Op. 41, his one set of songs for a cappella men's chorus. Four of the five are military songs—that staple of the men's chorus repertoire—with texts taken from a book of Carl Lemcke's poetry published in 1861 and acquired by Brahms the next year.[53] As in the Op. 44 set for women's voices, the pieces of Op. 41 sound like what is expected in their medium, and yet are filled with contrapuntal details that make them interesting to sing. The rhythmic patterns of no. 2, for example, with triplets and duplets alternating and overlapping, along with the imitative complexity of the part writing, redeem a rather mindlessly patriotic text.[54] The songs contain many instances of both obvious and subtle text illustration; and one wonders whether knowledge of the historical "diabolus in musica" may have prompted Brahms to write the unison melodic tritone on the word "Teufel" in no. 4.

The first song in the Op. 41 set, "Ich schwing mein Horn ins Jammerthal," was first written for the Frauenchor in 1860; Brahms also published a version for solo voice and piano (Op. 43/3) with the text "Ich schell mein Horn." This song, along with another composed at about the same time, "Vergangen ist mir Glück und Heil" (Op. 48/6 for voice and piano, and Op. 62/7 for mixed chorus), are the only examples in Brahms's published choral output where he appears to have deliberately attempted imitations of sixteenth-century polyphonic Lieder. Even in the 1863 folksong settings, where a more active contrapuntal style is used in conjunction with genuinely old melodies, he does not write the open fifths found here, use triads exclusively in root position,[55] or write the long notes of Renaissance notation.[56] The melodies which he invented for the two ancient texts and placed in the top voice in each case are both good imitations of old tunes;[57] and "Vergangen ist mir Glück und Heil" is even in the Dorian mode. Kalbeck detects a resemblance to "Innsbruck" in the melodic outline of the cadence of "Ich schwing mein Horn."[58] A number of commentators point out the long notes at the beginning of each phrase as a feature which these melodies have in common with many sixteenth-century Lieder; examples may be found in Brahms's Abschriften not only in "Innsbruck," but also in three out of the four Tenorlieder of A130, 7-9, copied later. In the early works, however, the long notes occur only at the beginning of each piece, not at the beginning of every phrase as they do with Brahms.

A wholly different secular style is found in the three songs for six-part mixed chorus, Op. 42—indeed, three quite different styles appear. Kross (p. 175) says that in these three pieces, with their varying influences, we see most clearly Brahms's "central artistic problem," the reconciliation of the divergent principles of historicism and of nineteenth-century Romanticism. The three works do have some common features. For example, all are in six parts, with two alto and two bass parts, although the way in which the six parts are used varies widely among them. The ease with which Brahms wrote for six-part choir is universally attributed to his acquaintance with early music. We have seen that he copied a number of works from Winterfeld's *Gabrieli* (A130, 1-6); part of his object in doing so may have been to study the distribution of the parts in the many-voice texture. Examples of text painting are plentiful throughout Winterfeld's collection; and all three pieces in Op. 42 employ madrigalisms in illustration of their texts, which are different in character but among them contain many of the ideas of "classic" Romanticism.

The commentators agree that "Vineta" is a work of purest Romanticism;[59] they also agree in general on the effect of "Darthulas Grabesgesang," which in Hans Gál's words,

> . . . begins and ends like an antiphonal chorus of the sixteenth century but has a
> middle section in the romantic lieder style. And yet, because the musical construction

flows so naturally from the words and their expression, one never has any sensation of discrepancy.[60]

"Abendständchen," however, elicits a variety of opinions, ranging from those who say that both it and "Vineta" are in the style of the Romantic part songs of Schumann,[61] to Kross, who bases his discussion of the piece on the influence of pre-Baroque choral music, though at the same time he uses the highly romantic image of a sleepwalker's security to describe Brahms's success in his first venture into the realm of the Chorlyrik.[62] A more reasonable assessment is perhaps that of Beuerle, who feels that all three of these songs, but "Abendständchen" in particular, demonstrate the incorporation of techniques derived from sacred music into the service of lyric expression, and thus point the way to Brahms's last Chorlieder, Op. 104.[63]

The two motets Op. 29 clearly illustrate Brahms's use of techniques from early sacred music in the medium which might be considered their natural place. Apart from his general studies in counterpoint, and specifically in canon, if we are to speak of a principal early music "influence" on these motets it must be Bach's Cantatas 4 and 21, which Brahms had performed with the Detmold choir in 1858 and 1859. He may also have acquired his copy of the Bach motets by this time.

In "Es ist das Heil" (Op. 29/1), Brahms follows a fairly straightforward chorale setting in the style of Bach[64] by a chorale motet with cantus firmus in which nearly every available contrapuntal device is used.[65] This sequence of movements is never used by Bach,[66] but examples of both types of movement are found in Cantata 4, "Christ lag in Todesbanden." In particular, Brahms's chorale motet resembles Bach's verse 4, "Es war ein wunderlicher Krieg," in an astonishing number of details.

"Schaffe in mir, Gott" (Op. 29/2) began, at least, as a contrapuntal exercise. The first section must have been composed in the summer of 1857, because Grimm asked Brahms for a copy of it in September of that year.[67] At the end of the 1858 season at Detmold, Brahms wrote to Joachim that he proposed to work on Bach's Cantata 21;[68] he also studied and marked his copy of the cantata carefully (see pp. 86 above). Beuerle makes a case for the direct influence of Bach's cantata on Brahms's motet (pp. 134-35); I agree with him in general but feel that a more useful comparison with Brahms's second section, "Verwirf mich nicht von deinem Angesicht," might be not Bach's initial chorus, but the section of the cantata where the chorus sings "dass er meines Angesichtes Hilfe und mein Gott ist." These two fugues have not only the word "Angesicht" in common, but a similar exposition structure (Bach's is much shorter, but the initial presentation of the voices is similar).[69] The final fugues in both works have a similar fanfare character. Overall the contrapuntal design in both the cantata and the motet is more rigid and operates on a smaller scale than is usual in choral works for either of these composers. Bach's cantata is one of his early works, and the choral movements are divided into short sections, each with its own contrapuntal layout. Brahms's motet is divided into a canon, a fugue (with much canonic material, especially at the end), another canon, and a closing fugue.

In spite of all the similarities between these works of Bach and Brahms, there is another piece of early music that Brahms probably knew, although he did not own a copy of it, and may also have had at the back of his mind when "Schaffe in mir, Gott" was composed. It is a setting for SSATTB and continuo of the same text by Andreas Hammerschmidt (1611-75), which was published in Bote and Bock's *Musica Sacra* series in both volumes 3 (1843) and 5 (no date), and also in the second volume (1856) of Schlesinger's *Musica Sacra*.[70] Since the text, three verses from Psalm 51, is very well known among German Lutherans,[71] Brahms probably learned it as a child rather than from Hammerschmidt's setting; but especially if the Biblical verses already appealed to him, he could hardly have avoided noticing this setting in one or another of the publications where it appeared. The fact that the three verses are usually thought of as a unit suggests that he may have had the idea for the entire motet at the time the first canon was composed, and may even have worked on the remaining sections at this early date.[72]

There are a number of resemblances between Hammerschmidt's and Brahms's settings. In both, the first two verses are in duple meter and the third is in triple meter. Most of the Hammerschmidt piece is chordal, but the "Verwirf mich nicht von deinem Angesicht" section, which is much longer than either of the others, is set in short points of imitation interspersed with chordal passages. The six voices of the Baroque version are used in a number of quasi-double-choir combinations, and at "Tröste mich wieder mit deiner Hilfe" tend to divide into high versus low groups similar to the opposing groups of men's and women's voices which Brahms uses at this point.[73] In the latter part of this section, where the men repeat the text "der freudige Geist erhalte mich,"[74] the listener hears Brahms's use of parallel thirds and sixths in the two upper voices more noticeably than he does the continuing canon at the seventh below between tenor and second bass. Then in the final fugue on the same text, the strings of parallel thirds which develop from the second measure of the subject are a prominent feature. Hammerschmidt writes no final fugue and has no fanfare theme, but his entire "freudige Geist" section is constructed from pairs of voices moving in parallel thirds in a generally chordal structure built up by the pairs' entrances in close imitation. These resemblances could all have been accidental, and do not prove that Hammerschmidt's work had a direct (whether conscious or unconscious) effect on Brahms's own setting of the same text. They do, however, show that Brahms's approach to that text was similar to the seventeenth-century composer's way of thinking; and it is hard to imagine where he could have learned this approach except from his study of early vocal music.

The remaining motet from the period before Brahms turned his attention to the large oratorio works is "O Heiland, reiss die Himmel auf" (Op. 74/2), composed in about 1863, soon after he arrived in Vienna, but not published until 1879.[75] The structure, a set of five variations on selected verses of the chorale, resembles Bach's Cantata 4, the only one of his chorale cantatas where the melody appears in every verse. Brahms did not forget about this cantata after he performed it at Detmold in 1858; in March 1873 he gave the first Viennese performance with the Gesellschaft der Musikfreunde.[76] Another Bach work that Brahms probably knew before 1863, the motet "Jesu, meine Freude," contains five different settings of the chorale melody (the sixth verse uses the same music as the first), just as this Brahms motet does. However, in its musical style "O Heiland, reiss" is not nearly so dependent on Bach as the other chorale motet, "Es ist das Heil." In fact, its five verses are not only a compendium of almost all the early music techniques Brahms had used in his choral writing up to this time, but they exhibit the use of additional resources that he had not yet drawn upon in choral music. Since this work has been largely neglected by other writers on Brahms, it will be examined in some detail here.

The first verse is a straightforward imitative setting of the chorale melody, which is in the soprano. This is the first consistent use of Vorimitation in Renaissance style that we have seen in Brahms's music; it also appears in most of the folk-song settings for mixed chorus that were written for the Singakademie at about the same time. Models for this style may be found in Zirler's "Die Sonn' die ist verblichen" (A130, 7-8) and other works in the collection of Tenorlieder from which Brahms copied it, probably at close to the time he was working on the motet (see above, pp. 62-63.). The first verse and Brahms's 1863 folk-song settings are different in that the modality of the F Dorian melody is not disguised by the setting of the chorale. A few D flats are added; and in some cases D naturals prove to be part of melodic F minor scales. Several D naturals do occur with a modal connotation, however; and verses 2 and 3 also have a number of them. The 3/2 meter of all three of these verses may also have a consciously archaic implication.

In the second verse the same smoothly flowing harmonies are maintained along with the points of imitation structure and the Vorimitation supporting the unadorned melody in the soprano. The speed of the lower voices is doubled, however, from the basic half-note units of the tune to quarter notes, in a procedure reminiscent of Sweelinck and those who followed him in the German organ school.[77] The process of intensification and thickening of the contrapuntal structure which culminates in the canons of the last verse and the Amen begins here.[78] The verse ends, as does the first, on an open fifth.

The first two verses are both rather neutral in their presentation of the text, though perhaps a case can be made for discreet text painting in the smooth flow of the parts coupled with the text image of dew pouring from heaven. In the third and fourth verses, however, text representation becomes the dominant feature, and even affects the chorale melody itself. The tenor has the melody in the third verse, and begins without ornament against staccato chords in the other three voices. As the text speaks of the earth flowering, the tenor also flowers into ornamental triplets, imitated by the other voices. Mountains, valleys, and the image of the Savior springing from the earth are met with predictable leaps and arpeggios in the three accompanying voices and more flourishes in the tenor melody. This exuberance, coupled with the Dorian D naturals, which here have a Lydian flavor because of the predominance of A flat major in the verse, makes an overall impression of enthusiastic innocence which exactly matches the character of the text.

At the same time, the seeming naïveté of this third verse disguises Brahms's careful craftsmanship and also obscures details of changes in the chorale melody itself which reflect early music practices. It is probably going too far to compare flourishes at the end of each of the phrases with Renaissance cadential ornaments, since all the evidence available in Brahms's library points only to an acquaintance with aspects of Baroque keyboard ornamentation practice at this stage of his career. These same flourishes, however, occur in the course of cadential hemiola structures which Brahms must have planned deliberately, because this verse, alone of the five, is lengthened by precisely the number of measures necessary to accommodate them; in the first two phrases he even repeats words in order to make the patterns work.

In the fourth verse the meter changes to 4/2 (Adagio) and the cantus firmus moves to the bass, in C minor. The key change is accomplished for all four voices in a smooth transition in the first three bars of the new verse, and the key signature remains three flats, so any modal quality disappears. It is replaced by a chromaticism which is expressive of the text as a whole as well as in specific madrigalisms. The contrapuntal interplay of the accompanying voices begins with a canon by inversion between tenor and soprano, but this strict beginning soon loosens into a free but strongly interconnected structure. In the first line, "Hie leiden wir die grösste Not," the bass moves slowly through the chorale melody, with one added passing tone and a low G interpolated between the last two notes to provide a standard V-I cadence. The upper voices move in a quarter-note pattern dominated by the sighing figure (*Seufzermelodik*) so well known as a Baroque symbol of sorrow;[79] chromatic tones which intensify the expression are gradually introduced into the Seufzermelodik. In the second phrase, "vor Augen steht der bittre Tod," the bass picks up these chromatic tones and introduces them into the chorale melody in a manner which foreshadows Brahms's addition of a chromatic passing note into the chaconne bass of the Fourth Symphony, composed many years later in 1884 and 1885.[80] A specific instance of word-painting is the sharp dissonance of the word "bittre" in the eighth bar. This is immediately followed by another madrigalism as the alto, soprano, and tenor enter on "ach, komm, führ uns" on an ascending series of notes—E flat, F, and G—in a manner reminiscent of the descriptive passage "Leite mich in deiner Wahrheit" in Bach's Cantata 150;[81] the bass melody is also changed to provide A flat, the next note in the series. In this phrase, the use of chromaticism is correlated very closely with the text: it dissolves with "mit starker Hand," reappears for "von Elend," and then is resolved to a final C major chord (the first major chord for the end of a verse) at the consoling conclusion, "zu dem Vaterland."

That chord serves as dominant for the return to F minor in the last verse. Although the key signature remains the same, there is now no trace of the Dorian mode. The canonic structure of this verse is not obvious to the ear, but it is nevertheless strict: soprano (with the chorale melody in a version ornamented with passing and neighbor tones) and bass have a canon by inversion throughout the verse; and in the final Amen the alto and tenor join them in a mirror canon of their own, imitating the melodic material of the continuing soprano-bass canon.[82] The meter of this verse is a tramping 4/4, the text a straightforward expression of praise, and the effect one of startling contrast to the previous verse. The quickening of motion to eighth notes and the buildup of contrapuntal intensity through the Amen help to relieve the sensation of anticlimax which is almost inevitable after the emotional high point of suffering and release is reached in the fourth verse. However, the maintenance of intensity through the transition to the last verse and on to the end of the piece is certainly the most problematical aspect of its performance. It is clearly necessary to consider the canonic structure of the final verse as an expression of the eternal stability and firmness of the "starker Hand" which leads "zu dem Vaterland" and the certainty of the final Amen.[83] With this idea in mind, one can see that in spite of the strophic structure, where only the chorale tune apparently serves to bind disparate sections together, and with a variety of techniques derived partly from early music and partly from his own creative intelligence, Brahms here constructed one of his most imaginative choral works, the first of the motets in which this fusion of old and new ideas is truly successfully accomplished.[84]

The collection of fourteen folk-song settings for mixed voices which Brahms published in 1864 with a dedication to the Singakademie includes seven which he had only recently composed from material found largely in Corner's 1631 *Gesangbuch* (A128, 14-21). Three of these settings appear as complete or partial sketches among the Abschriften. In contrast with those composed during the Detmold years, the new ones show a much greater familiarity with the techniques of the sixteenth-century German polyphonic Lied. This style is exemplified by the Tenorlieder by Zirler, Stoltzer, Greitter, and Senfl in A130, 7-9, together with the collection from which they were copied, and by Isaac's "Innsbruck" (A134, 43-44, and elsewhere), Scandellus's "Schein uns, du liebe Sonne" (A130, 9), Praetorius's "Maria zart," (A130, 15), and Eccard's "Übers Gebirg Maria geht" (A134, 29-34). Meister's *Das katholische deutsche Kirchenlied* (see p. 82 above), which was probably given to Brahms in 1862 and is the source of some of the folk-song material, contains a large appendix of polyphonic settings; it is the only printed collection of this sort of music that Brahms owned. It seems certain that exposure to the Corner and Meister collections and to Nottebohm's transcriptions of Tenorlieder, linked with his renewed association with a choir of mixed voices, spurred Brahms to the composition of this group of settings. The one song from a source other than Corner and Meister is also a genuinely old melody; it is "Von edler Art," the only secular song, which Brahms took from Becker's *Lieder und Weisen vergangener Jahrhunderte* (in the Nachlass), and which is found in polyphonic settings by Senfl and Schönefelder in several sixteenth-century collections.[85]

Morik has classified and analyzed all Brahms's folk-song settings, including the a cappella choral settings (pp. 126-64), and it is unnecessary to repeat the process here. However, a few additional remarks based on more recent chronological information and on the sketches in the Corner sheets are in order.

Of this group of seven settings, "Tröst die Bedrängten," "Komm Mainz, komm Bayrn," and "Ach lieber Herre Jesu Christ" fall into the first two categories of Morik's classification: the first is listed with those settings which have the simplest possible relation to the melody (these are mostly very early compositions); and the latter two appear in the middle category, where harmonic color and counterpoint assume greater importance.

"Tröst die Bedrängten" is found in the Corner sketches in ink in precisely its published form, complete with dynamic markings. It is unique among this group in that Brahms apparently never even considered a more elaborate setting for it; and indeed, it is hard to imagine any elaboration in the accompaniment of such a straightforward tune and text. The original tune has no sixth degree to tell us whether it is Dorian, and Brahms moves away from G minor only to turn at bar 12 to the relative major instead of the expected dominant of G minor (which had appeared in the corresponding place at the end of the first phrase). This change leads him to write parallel fifths between alto and tenor[86]—an unexpected liberty from the Brahms who so carefully marked all the instances of forbidden parallels he noticed in his copies of early music. The autograph also contains the Dorian E natural in bar 14 of the alto which is missing from the Peters edition, as noted above (Chap. 2, n. 37).

The long note values of "Ach lieber Herre Jesu Christ" have already been mentioned in connection with Brahms's "reconstructions" of Renaissance style (see Chap. 3, n. 56). This setting differs from the two pieces examined there in that the modal implications of the tune, which is Phrygian in this case, are completely ignored; and the part writing, though homophonic, is very smooth, with generally conjunct motion and many first inversion chords. Morik (pp. 138-42) decides to place the setting in his second category in spite of its homophonic style because of what he sees as a sophisticated "Harmonik der Gegenbewegung" (harmony of contrary motion) in which the harmonic structure, full of "Nebendreiklänge" (triads other than I, IV, or V) and unusual progressions involving IV and V chords, is derived from overriding contrapuntal considerations, rather than being related to the more usual functional harmony of the nineteenth century;[87] he relates this technique to the practices of sixteenth-century polyphony.

The third of the simpler settings, "Komm Mainz, komm Bayrn," is a particularly interesting case. Morik placed it in his middle category, but had no way of knowing that if Brahms had followed an earlier plan, it would have been a more elaborate setting. The sketch in the Corner sheets (pp. 16-17 above) shows clearly that Brahms at one point thought of introducing the refrain with a fairly long stretch of Vorimitation. Before he had fixed all the details of this version, however, he discarded it in favor of a single bar of Vorimitation, with the contrapuntal activity carried on until the soprano had reached the second bar of the refrain. Finally he settled on the simple chordal harmonization which appears in the published version but not in this sketch.

Brahms's very first idea, a brief Vorimitation by tenor and bass in unison, has been identified by Bozarth.[88] The next two stages are im-

mediately apparent when one looks at the sketch: the second version
(Ex. 9), in two staves below the original two, is the longest, and was
crossed out by Brahms in pencil. He tried out the tenor and bass parts
of the shorter third version (Ex. 10) in the empty first measure of the
upper stave of Example 9, drawing a curving bar line down to show how
it fits together with the upper voices in his original copy; this version is
not crossed out, and is the one he intended for a time to send to his
publishers.[89] The version he finally settled on and published is shown in
Example 11.

Example 9

Example 10

Example 11

The sketches show that at this time Brahms's first inclination was to try
to set old tunes in a manner clearly affected by his experience of the old
style—indeed, that in a case such as this he heard the melody in a po-

lyphonic context almost at once, and only later decided that here, at least, a simpler setting would be more satisfactory.[90]

The remaining four of the seven settings belong to Morik's last category, works that have in common a striking use of more artful, elaborate techniques.[91] Morik says that they share the "spätmadrigalisch" characteristic of staggered vocal entries, applied in a variety of ways; and he describes the pieces one at a time, largely from this point of view. When he writes of the influences of early music on these settings, however (pp. 159-60), he cannot account for the resemblances he finds to German Renaissance polyphony, because his information on Brahms's knowledge of early music comes from the correspondence, from Kalbeck, and from lists of music—nearly all of it sacred Italian Baroque—studied or performed by Schumann. Morik feels that the principal influence derived from this music must have been the way in which the façade of polyphony is maintained as a gesture of respect to the past, while in fact the real content of the music is mainly homophonic; its most important attribute is the effective use of the body of sound as a whole rather than the maintenance of independent voices.

This description of the folk-song settings is a good one, even though Morik's account of influences on them is incomplete because he had no information on the remainder of the contents of Brahms's library. In the light of the knowledge of Brahms's acquaintance with German Renaissance music, Morik's comparison of Brahms to the Italian Baroque composers may be adapted and a new analogy suggested: Brahms took sixteenth-century polyphonic Lieder for his models as the Baroque Italians took the music of Palestrina; he then applied the aims and techniques of his own time to produce a generally successful hybrid that bridges the gap between historical styles.

One of these four settings, "Wach auf, mein Kind," appears as a sketch in the Corner sheets of A128. In the sketch, in ink, Brahms first hunted for a solution to the problem of placing the bar lines; he had also attempted to determine the natural rhythm of the tune in his first copy from Corner's *Gesangbuch,* but was evidently dissatisfied with the result. Once he had made a decision about the the rhythm, he began to put in a few ideas for counterpoint in pencil. He did not complete the setting in this sketch; but there is enough to show that Morik (pp. 154-55) is right in saying that it is largely derived from the canonic techniques of imitation, augmentation, and inversion applied to phrases from the melody. All of Brahms's pencil additions are precisely these sorts of canonic experiments. The imitation of the soprano by alto and tenor of the middle bars 11-15 is fully laid out; and the bass augmentation of bars 4-6 appears in strict form, with a half note in bar 4 rather than the quarter note of the final version. On a staff below the sketch, Brahms wrote a bass clef and then an inversion beginning on E flat of the soprano melody of bars 11-13. He must never have found a place where he could fit it in, though, because it does not appear in the final version. The inversion in bars 2-4 at the beginning of the tenor part does appear; but there is no trace of the two bars of Vorimitation in the bass and alto which disguise the tonality of the piece for several measures.[92]

The motet Op. 74/2, the seven new folk-song settings, and the canonic "Regina coeli" (Op. 37/3), written for a group of women singers in Vienna, are the last choral works Brahms composed before he turned his attention to the large-scale works of the middle period. Once the success of the *Requiem* had assured his financial security, he never again had to publish music with which he was not completely satisfied simply because he needed the money. We are therefore denied information about any works he may have written primarily for study or experiment. Another probable reason the number of smaller works dropped after the early years is that Brahms no longer produced many short pieces for the use of choirs he himself was directing. He still felt impelled to write for chorus, though, as is clearly shown by the amount of choral music he composed when there was no longer an external compulsion to do so.

The Middle Period (1865-85)

There is less evidence of a connection between Brahms's choral compositions and the additions he made to his library of early music during this period than either of the others. It has been assumed that the additions he made to the Abschriften from works he found in Vienna were copied fairly soon after his arrival there, so that they really belong with the early group of choral compositions. They include the folk songs from Corner's *Gross' Catholisch Gesangbuch* and the Tenorlieder (A130, 7-9), whose effects we have already seen; the various exercises in transcription of early notation, which include the Calvisius and Schütz transcriptions of A130, 11-12; the partial copy of Cesti's *Serenata fatta in Firenze* (A130, 30-37); and Bach's "Es ist genug" (A130, 17). The Bach preludes and fugues copied from autographs (A130, 41-42) may also belong to the 1860s. There are no surviving early music Abschriften at all from the 1870s, unless some of the copies without dates might have been made during that decade.

Brahms's main acquisitions of printed early music during this twenty-year period were the accumulating volumes of the Bach and Handel *Werke,* and he made heavy use of both series in his three seasons of performances as conductor of the Musikverein. He continued to study German folk

song with the collections of Liliencron and Böhme, subscribed to Chrysander's *Jahrbücher* and *Denkmäler der Tonkunst,* and acquired Carissimi's *Jephta* in a performing edition. In 1881 he was given Wüllner's
large collection *Chorübungen,* volume III.[93]

The bulk of this early vocal music is large-scale Baroque cantata and
oratorio compositions, just as the bulk of Brahms's choral output from
the middle period is large-scale works with orchestra. Because he first
won widespread fame in this genre, the large choral works have until
recently received a much larger amount of critical attention than the a
cappella works.[94] They will therefore be given correspondingly little attention compared to the a cappella pieces, in which, after all, choral
writing, the main concern of this study, is the sole means of expression.

Of the seven large works, only the *Requiem* and *Triumphlied* have
sacred texts. *Rinaldo,* with a text written by Goethe specifically for use
as a cantata, and the *Triumphlied* are optimistic, but "everywhere else we
are confronted with the ideas of Fate and Death."[95] From our point of
view, the *Requiem* is the most interesting work, because its somber religious texts inspired Brahms to create settings in which he expanded his
accumulated knowledge of early music into the largest possible framework. This is quite the opposite of the way in which "O Heiland, reiss
die Himmel auf" exemplifies its distillation into concentrated form.

The Biblical texts which Brahms chose for the *Requiem* present an
interesting problem in relation to his study of early music. Kalbeck (II:
247) points out the existence of Schütz's "Selig sind die Toten" without
suggesting that Brahms knew the work; and Kross feels that it is "at least
worthy of mention" that several of the texts had already been set by
Schütz.[96] As a matter of fact, three of the *Requiem* texts appear in the
works of Schütz, and there is evidence which suggests that Brahms knew
of at least two of them.

In *Symphoniae Sacrae* III, no. 4 (SWV 401), Schütz begins with a
text from Luke, "Mein Sohn, warum hast du uns das gethan?" and then
continues with the "Wie lieblich sind deine Wohnungen" text from
Psalm 84, using precisely the verses which Brahms chose for the fourth
movement of the *Requiem.* The first part of the Schütz work appears as
example II.B.26 in the third volume of Winterfeld's *Gabrieli* to illustrate
tone painting of the word "Schmerzen" by chromaticism and suspensions. In his detailed discussion of the piece (II: 199-200), Winterfeld gives
the remainder of the text and praises Schütz lavishly for his knowledge
of the Bible and the skill with which he combined texts from different
sources—remarks which are strongly reminiscent of many that have been
made about Brahms.[97] Judging from the thoroughness with which Brahms

studied Winterfeld, it seems certain that he was aware of Schütz's setting of this text, and of his choice of the particular verses.[98]

In the case of "Selig sind die Toten" (*Requiem,* no. 7), there is no direct evidence that Brahms knew of Schütz's six-voice setting from *Geistliche Chormusik* (SWV 391). However, it was published at least twice before 1865—in the second volume of Rochlitz's collection (where it lacks Tenor 2), and in Bote and Bock's *Musica Sacra* XIV. Brahms did not own either of these volumes, but he might very easily have studied either, since both were widely available.

The section of Psalm 126 beginning "Die mit Tränen säen" (*Requiem,* no. 1, second section) was set twice by Schütz, in the *Psalmen Davids* (SWV 42) and again in the *Geistliche Chormusik* (SWV 378). There is no evidence that Brahms was aware of either setting; indeed, his reaction to a cross relation in the *Geistliche Chormusik* version published in the *Werke* in 1889 suggests that he had not seen it before (see p. 92 above). A fragment of Schein's setting of this same text, "und bringen ihre Garben," is given by Winterfeld (I: 170) as an example of a series of implied parallel fifths which fall on strong beats; but the remainder of the text is not quoted, nor is Schein's work identified beyond the statement that it is from *Israelsbrünnlein,* 1623.

Regardless of whether the existence of these early Baroque settings had any influence on Brahms's choice of texts for the *Requiem,* the long history of its composition covers the period of his most intense study of early music.[99] By the time the work was complete, he had so thoroughly incorporated techniques learned from this study into his own style that countless examples of their use may be found throughout it, and indeed in all of his compositions.

Even *Rinaldo* (Op. 50), the most nearly operatic of Brahms's choral works and thus the farthest from sacred style, contains examples of Baroque cliches: cadential hemiolas (mm. 95-100) and Neapolitan sixths (m. 1128) are used quite automatically, and there are numerous examples of text illustration. Brahms began the work in 1863 for a men's choir competition, but did not finish it until after the *Requiem* was completed. The other work which uses male-voice choir with a soloist is the *Alto Rhapsody* (Op. 53), also on a Goethe text, a piece written for no external purpose, but because it had great emotional significance for Brahms. In it recitative, text painting, rhythmic ambiguities, and canonic techniques are all employed in ways which are clearly related to Baroque practice but have none of the superficial or automatic quality of their use in *Rinaldo.*

The *Triumphlied* (Op. 55) is a grandiose occasional piece, a patriotic extravaganza written to celebrate the German victory in the Franco-Prussian war of 1870-71. In it, as Wagner wrote, Brahms donned the "Halleluja-Perücke Händels.''[100] Wagner meant to be scornful, but all subsequent comments on the piece, no matter how laudatory, have agreed at least with the Handel comparison. Frequently the *Dettingen Te Deum,* which Brahms performed in his first concert with the Gesellschaft der Musikfreunde in 1873, is cited specifically,[101] perhaps because when Brahms was planning the *Triumphlied* in late 1870, he wrote to Reinthaler that he wanted to write "ein gutes Te Deum.''[102] The work has been evaluated in widely differing ways through the years: in 1912 Evans could write (p. 249), ''No dissentient voice has ever, or is likely ever to be raised as to the immense grandeur of this work; even the critics for once agreeing among themselves and uniting in its praise.'' Since World War I it has been more coolly evaluated, and Kross describes it as bombastic, saying that it is too much a product of its own time and circumstances to be thought of so highly today.[103] The most successful parts are those where Brahms uses procedures from early music in conjunction with his characteristic voice: the long dominant pedal at the end of the first movement, the canon by inversion at ''und die ihn fürchten'' in the second, and the rhythmic complexities throughout (see p. 163). Least successful are those where the imitation of Baroque behavior seems to overcome his judgment, such as the rapid, almost ludicrous pattern of ''ein König aller Könige'' in the last movement. Brahms himself described the *Triumphlied* as ''not difficult, only forte.''[104]

The *Schicksalslied, Nänie,* and *Gesang der Parzen,* though they were composed over a span of about fifteen years, may be thought of as a group because their texts, from Hölderlin, Schiller, and Goethe respectively, are all based on the legends of classical antiquity. In its tone of comfort to the living, *Nänie* (Op. 82), written as a memorial to the painter Anselm Feuerbach,[105] is very similar to the first and last movements of the *Requiem,* and the chorus and orchestra are treated in essentially the same way. Except for the introduction, the orchestra serves mainly in an accompanying role; and once the choir has made its first fugal entrance, the rich, smooth vocal counterpoint carries the message of the text. Brahms was concerned about the difficulty of setting the hexameters of the poem;[106] but the flowing 6/4 of most of the piece, with the frequent use of both cadential and internal hemiolas, provides a flexible and successful solution.

The two songs of fate, in different ways but with some obvious similarities, depict the blessed state of the gods and their indifference to the unfortunate human race. In contrast to the *Requiem* and *Nänie,* the orchestra is dominant, going far beyond reflecting the mood or echoing the thematic material of the chorus. The problematical postlude of the *Schicksalslied* (Op. 54), which actually contradicts the meaning of the poem, has elicited reams of commentary, and sometimes even the conclusion that Brahms intended it to carry a Christian message. More interesting from our point of view, however, is the violently agitated middle section, which depicts the plight of man. Though the piece as a whole is less obviously influenced by early music than any of the large works except *Rinaldo,* this middle section contains a number of Baroque practices which serve the function of text painting. Often one word at a time is illustrated in the manner of some madrigals, but on the whole the old techniques are used in a thoroughly modern way. For example, the one section of choral imitation in an otherwise homophonic setting serves to give the impression of restlessness, of no place to settle ("doch uns ist gegeben, auf keiner Stätte zu ruhn")—and at "ruhn" there is brief repose, contrary though it may be to the general sense of the text. The famous hemiola rhythm at "wie Wasser von Klippe zu Klippe geworfen" illustrates the words clearly; less obvious, perhaps, are the pounding hemiolas in the woodwinds against the rhythm of the chorus in bars 126-27 and 288-89, which increase the confusion of "leidenden Menschen." There are no cadential hemiolas here to create a false sense of stability. Security and peace are reserved for the gods, to whom Brahms even gives a Baroque bass pattern; several writers[107] have pointed out how closely the pizzicato cello and bass line accompanying the first entrance of the full choir resembles the bass of the renowned "Air on the G string," taken from Bach's third orchestral suite.

In the years between the composition of the *Schicksalslied* and the *Gesang der Parzen* (Op. 89), Brahms studied and performed a great deal of the music of Bach, and the latter work seems to me to be heavily indebted to that study, for all its large forces and pagan theme. From the very beginning the orchestration gives the impression of a massive organ work permeated with Baroque-style counterpoint, and melodic lines are often reminiscent of Bach. For example, the chorus in bars 49-51 speaks of dissension and has a jagged line full of diminished intervals; and in bar 84, where the breath of Titans rises from the abyss, the bass voices and instruments move upward in a syncopated chromatic line that not only depicts the words, but also sounds remarkably like the bass line in the final chorus of the first part of the *St. Matthew Passion.*

Aside from these and other resemblances to Bach, the *Gesang der Parzen* has links to earlier music. Although the choral writing is mainly homophonic, the six voices are often divided into various kinds of opposing groups, most often women's voices against men's voices in the arrangement used in "Darthulas Grabesgesang" (Op. 42/3) and "Schaffe in mir, Gott" (Op. 29/2). Text painting occurs frequently, sometimes rather illogically; Kross (p. 402) points out the incongruity of the treatment of "ein leichtes Gewölke" (mm. 93 ff.). Semitone relations are used almost obsessively in a manner which is unusual in Brahms's choral music, and much of the harmonic structure of the piece as a whole is based on them. The remarkable last section (mm. 162 ff.) consists entirely of a circle of major thirds (D—F sharp—B flat) connected by augmented sixth chords, and finally ends on an open fifth. The effective avoidance of functional harmonic relationships in this conclusion has more in common with a much earlier—or later—period of music than with Brahms's usual choral style.

The small choral works written in Brahms's middle period comprise much less music than the large oratorio-style pieces. Apart from the vocal quartets with piano, there is only one accompanied work, the "Tafellied" (Op. 93b), which Kross (p. 419) calls a "liebenswürdige kleine Werkchen." It is a charming occasional piece, much like some of the lighter quartets, one of Brahms's few concessions to the purely social function of most nineteenth-century German singing societies.

The two choral folk-song settings which Brahms wrote during this period are probably occasional pieces also, produced (or perhaps revised from earlier versions) for the Singverein when he was its conductor in the 1870s. Each of the these songs, "Wach auf, meins Herzens Schöne" and "Dort in den Weiden," was set five different times by Brahms, more than any other folk songs; and each first appeared among the early settings.[108] These versions for mixed voices were published after Brahms's death from the only surviving source, the individual parts in the Archiv;[109] thus we can only guess that they were newly composed in the middle period. The tunes come from Kretzschmer and Zuccalmaglio, and that of "Wach auf, meins Herzens Schöne" is actually by Reichardt, although the text is old.[110] Both settings bear a strong resemblance to the group composed around 1863 for the Singakademie, and are assigned by Morik to his third category, the most elaborate settings. In his discussion, he describes the "rhythmic canon" in "Dort in den Weiden" as an example of Brahms's extension of imitative practices.[111]

The earlier setting of "Wach auf, meins Herzens Schöne," one of the group probably composed at Detmold, is simpler than this later one. In the later version we find a different arrangement for the third verse, as before, and the same fragments of Vorimitation used to bridge the gaps between lines; but the parts are more independent of one another, and the two Stollen of the third verse are set with the tune in the tenor rather than the soprano. Morik (p. 159) says that Brahms probably realized that this Tenorlied form was an anachronism when he used it with an eighteenth-century tune, but felt it was worthwhile as an enrichment of his medium. Whatever his intent, or his later opinion of these two settings, they remain attractive and enjoyable to sing.[112]

The two groups of secular choral songs from this period, Opp. 62 and 93a,[113] contain a number of pieces that also have a folk-like character, all of them settings of traditional texts. In them, according to Beuerle (pp. 268, 279, 294), Brahms continued to transform "Lieder im Volkston" (i.e., songs in the manner of folk song) into true choral art songs by tightening the rhythmic and motivic organization of the pieces and connecting the settings more closely with the texts. Thus "Rosmarin" and "Von alten Liebesliedern" from Op. 62 and "Der bucklichte Fiedler," "Das Mädchen," and "Der Falke" from Op. 93a share a formal concentration and complexity which are entirely new in nineteenth-century choral music of this type and are probably by-products of Brahms's work on the instrumental music of this period, which is characterized by a much greater economy of style than his earlier works.[114] The effect is that these relatively objective, story-telling poems are given an equally objective but highly intellectual musical treatment.

In setting the more subjective texts among these two sets—that is, those with no connection to folk tradition—Brahms tends more often to use practices derived from early music. As we have already noticed, he wrote interesting vocal parts almost from the beginning of his career, and even in completely homophonic works the lines often have real melodic character. But why, for example, he should have chosen to write strict canonic passages in expressive works like "Waldesnacht" and "All meine Herzgedanken," unobtrusive though they are, remains a puzzle. He had amply proved he could do so in the sacred works; perhaps he remained intrigued by the challenge of seeing how many ways he could write effective music in the form of canons. Similarly, he no longer needed any specific reason for choosing to use other techniques of early music; they had become completely integrated into his personal style and were no longer introduced as foreign elements.

In only one of these pieces does the technique seem to take control of the musical expression. This is "Beherzigung" (Op. 93a/6), Brahms's title for a text by Goethe which says that timidity and vacillation are of no use in trouble, but defiance and refusal to give in will receive the help of the gods. It seems likely that Brahms constructed the setting with its several canons in order to convey the sense of certainty of the text; perhaps the same reason accounts for the resounding hymn-like conclusion. Unfortunately the ultimate effect is that of a pompous sentiment pompously expressed.[115]

"Fahr wohl" (Op. 93a/4), which was sung by the Singverein as Brahms's funeral procession went by the Gesellschaft der Musikfreunde, is a simple strophic setting of a gentle, bittersweet text by Rückert. Although there are touches of sentimentality reminiscent of Mendelssohn,[116] the unobtrusive but cleverly constructed canonic section in the middle is wholly Brahmsian. "Dein Herzlein mild" (Op. 62/4), a model of concise motivic organization with passages of canonic imitation, is also strophic, but it has a variation at the end of the last verse, a three-measure expansion of the final cadence. These three bars, which illustrate the image of the heart as an opening flower bud, are built from overlapping hemiolas and a momentary Neapolitan which is unexpected because the harmonic orientation of the piece throughout has been strongly—and unusually for Brahms—toward the dominant side.

The remaining three songs, "Waldesnacht" (Op. 62/3), "All meine Herzgedanken" (Op. 62/5), and "O süsser Mai" (Op. 93a/3), are part of the stream of development that leads from Op. 42/1 to Op. 104. The first and last, each in four parts,[117] have in common the poetic view of nature's power to lighten one's troubles, as well as an appearance of simplicity disguising remarkable motivic unity and a wealth of contrapuntal activity. The canon in "Waldesnacht" results in expressive dissonance; and in "O süsser Mai" the Vorimitation and hemiola cross rhythms which appear as the poet turns away from the beauties of nature seem to exemplify the confusion and contrariness of his mind. The old techniques are here used with thoroughly modern connotations.

"All meine Herzgedanken" is the only one of these middle-period songs in six parts (Brahms's customary SAATBB). It has a straightforward quality that seems to link it more with the earlier than the later Chorlieder, though there is no evidence that it was written before 1873. The division into groups of men's and women's voices,[118] the long, arched phrases, and the rich diatonic harmony are all immediately apparent. Small-scale motivic development plays no significant role here. Examples of early music practices are abundant; but the details of the double chorus treatment, some Vorimitation, the canonic imitation of the middle section, the many suspensions, and the highly independent part writing all disappear into the texture, leaving the listener with a beautiful and romantic impression, but no particular awareness of the skill required to produce it. Brahms came close to this effect earlier, in "Abendständchen," and reached it again in the two "Nachtwache" poems of Op. 104; thus "All meine Herzgedanken" forms a link between his early and late Chorlieder in more ways that just the use of the six voices.

The motet Op. 74/1, "Warum ist das Licht gegeben den Mühseligen?" has attracted as much critical attention and admiration relative to Brahms's other small-scale choral works as the *Requiem* has relative to all his other choral music.[119] Whether the work was meant as homage to Bach, as Spitta concluded from the inclusion of the final chorale,[120] we cannot know. Brahms himself wrote only, when he sent a copy of the motet to Otto Dessoff, that it showed off his knowledge of the Bible and perhaps preached better than his words could—and that he had "gone walking with it a lot," which meant that he had worked very hard on the piece.[121] The comment about preaching does suggest that he intended to convey a definite message, and the texts themselves and the way he treats them give the same impression. The message is not, however, the Christian idea of redemption, any more than is that of the *Requiem;*[122] no answer is offered to the question "Warum?"—but God is said to be mericful, and death is seen as a release.

The sectional construction of the work, and its closing chorale, certainly resemble the motets of Bach.[123] The first movement, with its recurring "Warum," has been compared by Leichtentritt to a motet by Schein, "Siehe nach Trost war mir sehr bange," which he correctly says Brahms could scarcely have known.[124] The strictly organized chromatic fugue at the start, the free counterpoint of the middle part, with its change from chromatic to diatonic expression as the text lightens temporarily, and the return at the end to the thematic material of the fugue, without its contrapuntal structure and in a different meter, form the outline of a movement which in many details utilizes practices of an earlier era, but which in its entirety belongs to the late nineteenth century.

The second and third movements form a unit: they are both in six parts (SSATBB), and the texts describe the mercy of God on those who have suffered with patience. The music which makes up the second movement and ends the third is an expansion of the four-part Benedictus canon which Brahms had composed in February 1856 in Düsseldorf and had written about to Clara Schumann, saying that it sounded "recht hübsch" to him.[125] He had intended it originally for women's voices, but Grimm, who often complained about the low range of Brahms's second alto parts, suggested in 1860 that it would sound better for SSAT; it appears here in that form.[126] The canon is sung through once completely; on the second time around it is joined by the two bass parts and transformed into free imitative counterpoint which lasts until the end of the movement. We do not know whether Brahms decided to use the canon after he had chosen the texts for this motet and realized how admirably it would fit the idea of hands reaching up toward God, or whether he may have been looking for an appropriate use for the "recht hübsch" sound of the canon which he had composed so long before. Regardless of the order of events, its diatonic certainty, after the chromatic questioning of the first movement, sounds like an act of simple faith.

Beuerle suggests that the canonic movement gives the same impression of ceaseless praise of God as the Sanctus movements of Palestrina masses;[127] and we have seen that shortly after Brahms's Benedictus canon was written, he copied the *Missa Papae Marcelli* (A134, 1-16), which he may already have studied. The Sanctus of this mass is set for all six voices and employs the rising scale of a fifth as an important element; the Benedictus is for four voices (SATT) and contains much quasi-canonic writing. There is, of course, no evidence of any direct connection in Brahms's mind between the two works, but we do know that he was occupied with the study of Palestrina, along with many other activities, at this time.[128]

The beginning of the third movement sounds like an elaborate chorale harmonization. Brahms here provided his own "chorale" melody, much as he did in the earlier *Begräbnisgesang* (Op. 13) and "Vergangen ist mir Glück and Heil" (Op. 62/7), or the later "Wenn wir in höchsten Nöten sein" (Op. 110/3). The five lower voices surround the G Dorian tune with free imitative counterpoint. This accompaniment is not only thematically unrelated to the melody, but also avoids any suggestion of modal harmony; rather it is solidly in C major as the dominant of F major. The triple meter and F major tonality of the canon return, and after a short double choir passage (divided S_2TB_1/S_1AB_2) the canon itself reappears unobtrusively. The movement ends in the same way the second movement did, though with a different text.

The final harmonization of the chorale "Mit Fried und Freud ich fahr dahin" has somewhat less rapid harmonic motion than Bach's two harmonizations.[129] Brahms's version seems to have a more settled tonal feeling, especially in the long C major middle section, whereas Bach's setting is more restless and unpredictable. The reasons for Brahms's decision to include the chorale at all have been explained by the commentators in a number of highly ingenious ways;[130] my own feeling is that if there must be an explanation at all, the most likely one is Spitta's comment with reference to the whole body of Brahms's sacred choral music:

> Its basis is the religious feelings of the people, such as have been expressed in Luther's Bible and sacred poetry for centuries. . . . The question is not whether the tidings of the Bible and the prayers of church songs form the foundation of his personal beliefs. As the forms of expression of the outlook and perception of the people, they are decisive factors for him.[131]

On the basis of the general expectation—and Brahms's—of what a motet should be, it was simply a reasonable step to conclude with a chorale which would summarize the message of the entire work.

The Late Period (1886-89)

The most notable addition to Brahms's library of early music during the later years of his life was the complete Schütz edition, which began to

appear in 1885 (see pp. 91-93 above). By 1888, when most of the secular
songs Op. 104 and the *Fest- und Gedenksprüche* (Op. 109) were composed, seven volumes had been published; they were the following:

I	(1885)	Passions, Aufferstehung, Die sieben Worte
II	(1886)	Psalmen Davids (1619), part 1
III	(1887)	Psalmen Davids (1619), part 2
IV	(1887)	Cantiones Sacrae (1625)
V	(1887)	Symphoniae Sacrae I (1629)
VI	(1887)	Kleine geistliche Concerte, I and II (1636, 1639)
VII	(1888)	Symphoniae Sacrae II (1647)

In 1889, the year of Brahms's Op. 110 motets, the *Geistliche Chormusik*
(1648) appeared as volume VIII.[132]

In addition to the Schütz volumes, Brahms continued to accumulate
the Bach and Handel collected editions; and he acquired some issues of
the *Vierteljahrsschrift für Musik,* mostly after 1890. The only surviving
Abschriften from this period are those from the Schütz volumes I, II, and
IX (1890) in A130, 21-24; the Hassler, Regnart, and Demant pieces in
A130, 10; and any material added to "Oktaven und Quinten" (A132) during
these years.

It may indeed be the case that Brahms's sudden activity in writing
works for a cappella mixed chorus with large numbers of voices was
stimulated by the Schütz edition, especially by the polychoral *Psalmen
Davids.* We must remember, however, that Brahms had written for six
voices frequently, usually in the combination SAATBB, and we have already seen how freely and flexibly he could use this number of voices.

The Chorlieder Op. 104 are the culmination of Brahms's development
of the secular choral song for mixed voices which had begun with the
Op. 42 songs composed nearly thirty years earlier. The only one in four
parts, no. 5, "Im Herbst," was written two years before the rest of the
set, and belongs to the series of settings of nature poems which includes
"Waldesnacht" and "O süsser Mai." It has less motivic concentration
than the other works in Op. 104, but is harmonically much more adven-
turous. Even the "enharmonischen Schwierigkeiten" which Spitta noted
in "Darthulas Grabesgesang" (Op. 42/3)[133] pale before the difficulties
found here, particularly at the unexpected turn to the relative major at
the beginning of the third verse, and the series of augmented sixth chords
which follows. Considerable unobtrusive text painting occurs also, but it
does not illustrate individual words so much as the content of whole
phrases; it fits the text remarkably well, even with the exact musical
repetition of the first two strophes.

The other strophic musical structure in Op. 104 occurs in no. 4,
"Verlorene Jugend," a five-part setting (SATBB) of a folk text. The only

variation between the strophes is that the two-part canon forming the first section of each takes place between alto and soprano in the first verse, and between soprano and first bass in the second; the other parts are changed around accordingly. Rhythmic motives are prominent, and several are two beats long in the triple meter and thus form a pattern of overlapping hemiolas which sometimes runs counter to the text accents.

In "Letztes Glück" (no. 3), the six voices are often divided into groups of men's and women's voices without, as Beuerle says,[134] at all creating any sense of archaic double choir writing; instead, the distribution seems to occur as a natural consequence of expression of the mood of the poem. No attempt is made to illustrate specific words—indeed, the tightly organized repetitive structure of the setting precludes detailed text painting. Beuerle's analysis centers on the concentration of melodic motivic material, and on the way in which Brahms transforms a rather undistinguished poem into a remarkable piece of music. The limitations of the text are overcome, and it takes on new meaning in conjunction with its effective setting.

The pair of Rückert settings, each entitled "Nachtwache," have over the years attracted most of the attention and enthusiasm directed towards the Op. 104 songs. In particular, the second, built on calling and answering horn signals, has always been recognized as "a pearl among the part songs," as Elisabeth von Herzogenberg wrote in a letter to Brahms.[135] She wrote about the other, "The first *Nachtwache* would have more chance if she had not so dangerous a rival in the second, which promptly spoils one for anything less perfect," and went on to ask whether in the first setting "the delicate but rather pianistic than chorally inspired entries will ever sound perfectly in tune and natural." In both songs, old techniques of opposition of groups of high and low voices, imitative entries, and explicit text illustration are used in combination with all the resources of Romantic harmony and intense motivic concentration to produce a thoroughly satisfying result.

In the two late sets of motets, one work appears to stand closer to some of the earlier Chorlieder, and especially to the *Marienlieder*,[136] than to Brahms's other motets. It is "Ach, arme Welt" (Op. 110/2), which is a four-part, mostly homophonic, strophic setting of an old chorale text. The only variations in the strophic structure come in the third verse: one more line is added early in the verse, and the final chord has a major instead of a minor third. Behind its outward simplicity, however, the piece contains a remarkable concentration of emotional expression attained by the use of a variety of techniques, some with a long history from early music, and some from nineteenth-century practice.[137]

Beuerle (p. 201) feels that all style elements of the composition could come from seventeenth-century works, and that only their combination is new. A phrase like that in bar 5, however, where an augmented fifth is used in a purely Romantic context, immediately tells the listener which century he is in. Another of Beuerle's observations seems to err in the opposite direction: he says (p. 202) that the chord change from C major to A flat major between bars 4 and 5 (between the end of the second phrase and the beginning of the third) loses its archaic coloration through the functional harmony of the preceding two phrases and therefore conveys a sense of the mediant relationship. However, here the brief tonicization of C major functions as the dominant of F minor; thus the A flat major which follows instead of F minor is, for the ear accustomed to early music, a normal progression. (Brahms uses it elsewhere; see, for example, Op. 110/1, mm. 16-17.)

A good example of the fusion of old and new styles may be seen in bar 7, where the same soprano text and melody that appeared in bar 5 are accompanied by a different harmony, whose Neapolitan chords unmistakably intensify the emotional effect of the repetition.

The first phrase of Brahms's melody makes use of what is certainly the best-known whole-tone scale in music history, the first four notes of the chorale melody "Es ist genug."[138] As we have seen, Brahms copied and performed this chorale in settings by both Bach and Ahle (see A130, 16 and 17, above). An interesting issue is raised here by Kross's statement that the chord Brahms uses on the word "Welt" is unexpected and at first sounds wrong, since what he expects is a G major triad as dominant of C minor, and the logic of what actually happens is not apparent until the next chords are heard. The surprise is accentuated by a sforzando on "Welt" and the register change in the tenor and bass (Ex. 12).

Example 12

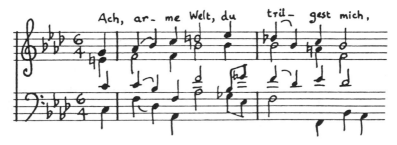

If Brahms's beginning is transformed into Kross's expected progression (leaving aside the question of what would happen afterwards), the phrase shown in Example 13 is obtained; here a seventh is added to Kross's suggested triad.

Example 13

However, the shock of Brahms's progression is not nearly so severe as that produced by Bach's in "Es ist genug" (Ex. 14) which, starting from the relative major (here transposed down a half step for easier comparison), moves abruptly to the same chord Kross suggests as the logical conclusion of Brahms's first phrase, and does apply it as dominant of C minor.

Example 14

A much less startling result is obtained by moving to Brahms's chord after Bach's beginning (Ex. 15).

Example 15

The only predictable harmonization, given the peculiar nature of the melody, is Ahle's, transposed down a whole tone in Example 16.

Example 16

It is possible to set Brahms's melody to Ahle's harmonization, graft an E flat minor chord onto it in place of the E flat major at the beginning of the second phrase, and move smoothly on to Brahms's B flat minor, as shown in Example 17.

Example 17

At the beginning of the third verse, where he turns briefly to the relative major, Brahms seems to be planning to use a version of the hypothetical progression of Example 17. However, he then changes the sense of all previous uses of the D natural by using it as part of a melodic F minor scale, which continues upward (Ex. 18). The whole-tone melody is repeated in the next measure by the bass[139] as the text echoes "du arme Welt," before the B flat minor of the first two verses is finally reached.

Example 18

While it cannot be known, of course, whether Brahms had any of these possible historical models in mind when he was composing "Ach, arme Welt," especially since the "Es ist genug" performances had taken place fifteen years earlier, the different ways in which the three composers handle the same basic problem are thoroughly interconnected.

In the remaining five motets of Opp. 109 and 110, the effects of Brahms's study of the music of Schütz may be more readily discerned than in the smaller-scale Op. 110 no. 2. Their full double choir settings are an obvious point of resemblance, although Brahms's treatment of the medium is like Schütz's in the *Psalmen Davids* only when he divides the group for long periods into two equal SATB choirs or into choirs of high and low voices, and then alternates one of these combinations with true eight-voice texture. Brahms's way of using a number of different, overlapping combinations does not appear in the Schütz *Werke* until the six-voice pieces in *Geistliche Chormusik* (Vol. VIII, published in 1889). The flexibility of Brahms's writing for many voices is something he learned not from Schütz but probably from the many available models he studied much earlier, particularly the pieces by Gabrieli and Palestrina he copied from Winterfeld's *Gabrieli* (A130, 1-6), Palestrina's six-voice "Haec dies," which he prepared for performance (A136); and Eccard's "Der Christen Triumphlied aufs Osterfest," which he performed with the Singakademie (p. 89 above).

Another characteristic of Brahms's late motets for double choir, and especially of Op. 110 nos. 1 and 3, is a freer use of dissonance and unconventional voice leading than appears in his earlier choral works. Chromaticism in the manner of Bach is found frequently in the earlier motets, but now combined with it is a kind of unpredictability, coupled with moments of extreme simplicity, which seems illogical by comparison with Bach or the younger Brahms but does resemble early Baroque practice.

Even the *Fest- und Gedenksprüche* partake to some extent of this Schütz-like quality. On first hearing, these three pieces have an elemental grandeur which seems far removed from Brahms's usual complex habits of thought. However, closer examination reveals details which show that they are among his most carefully and ingeniously constructed choral works. He himself rated them low compared with the Op. 110 motets;[140] perhaps this preference for the later set may be accounted for partly by the fact that their texts express his frame of mind at this time of his life better than the rather sententious certainties of the *Fest- und Gedenksprüche*. While it may be true that nationalistic enthusiasm inspired him to write the Op. 109 pieces in the first place, they convey a much less self-satisfied impression than the *Triumphlied,* composed for similar reasons.

By this time in his life, Brahms viewed even his own patriotic feelings with irony and detachment, and this objectivity protected him from any excess of sentiment.

To a large extent the texts Brahms chose for the *Fest- und Gedenksprüche*[141] preclude any illustration more specific than a depiction of the general mood, expressed by the diatonic ceremonial sound of the full body of eight voices, the antiphonal exchange of two mixed choirs, or occasionally by the solemn martial quality of the men's voices alone. The subdominant tendency of the harmony reinforces the hymn-like character, as does the Handelian, conventional use of cadential hemiolas. The closed three-part form of each movement is determined musically rather than by the structure of the text. When an opportunity for detailed text painting does occur, though, in the middle of the second motet, Brahms seizes it for a spectacular display of expressive skill, culminating in the cascade of notes (and tonalities) at the passage "und ein Haus fället über das andere." Here the logical process of text illustration, coupled with a perfectly regular series of entrances on descending fifths, conveys a convincing picture of chaos in spite of the strictness of the method with which it has been produced. The recovery from this confusion is not finally accomplished until the return of the material from the beginning of the piece along with its triple meter, because although the harmony of the section "Wenn ein starker Gewappneter" which precedes this return is clear and very slow-moving, its rhythm is ambiguous and disorienting (bars 51-55; also see p. 164 below).

In the first and third of the Op. 110 motets, the complexities which are hidden in Op. 109 rise to the surface. These are difficult works, lacking the immediate appeal of the *Fest- und Gedenksprüche,* with their full-bodied diatonic confidence.[142] Although neither is at all fugal, they may perhaps best be compared in their effect on the listener with the chromatic contrapuntal movements in Op. 29/2 ("Verwirf mich nicht von deinem Angesicht") and Op. 74/1 ("Warum ist das Licht gegeben"), rather than with any examples of Brahms's earlier writing for a large number of voices, because of their subjective, questioning content and chromatic harmonies. Each piece has a structure determined to some extent by the choice of text rather than by external considerations: "Ich aber bin elend" (no. 1) is through-composed, and "Wenn wir in höchsten Nöten sein" (no. 3) is strophic, with some variation.

The strophic structure of this third motet is unusual in that each of the first two verses is set quite differently;[143] the third verse repeats the musical material of the first exactly;[144] and the fourth is a variation and expansion of the second. Beuerle (p. 194) speaks of the strong "Affektenkontrast" between lament and praise in the texts of the pairs of strophes, which leads to the arrangement of the setting. He is right in that Brahms's decision to diverge from a simple strophic structure was probably determined by the varying moods of the verses; however, the texts of the second and fourth verses in particular have little in common to suggest that they should be set in the same way. An instance of specific word painting occurs in the second verse, where the text says that our only hope in time of trouble is to call on God "zusammen ingemein"; at this point block chords employing all eight voices appear for the first time. There is no similar text motivation for the appearance of these chords in the fourth verse, but they are heard anyway; the variation of this verse does not begin until just afterwards.

This variation consists of a long expansion of the third text phrase, the admonition "gehorsam sein nach deinem Wort" (be obedient to Thy word), which sounds the only note of caution in the general praise of the last verse. The many slightly varied repetitions of this phrase hammer home the note of warning,[145] but even with this reason for the long insertion, it tends to throw the piece out of balance. The musical structure of the expansion is reminiscent of Schütz in that two distinctly different musical ideas associated with two text phrases are combined in a number of ways.[146] One of many examples from the works of Schütz occurs in "Wann unsre Augen schlafen ein" (SWV 316), from part 2 of the *Kleine geistliche Konzerte*. Brahms called attention to this piece in his copy of the *Werke* VI by marking its beginning, perhaps because the stepwise chromatic motion at the start appealed to him. Toward the end of the piece, where the text is "halt über uns dein rechte Hand, dass wir nicht falln in Sünd und Schand," the first phrase appears in long notes on a descending scale, while the words "dass wir nicht falln," in shorter notes, are set against it[147] in a way quite similar to Brahms's setting of the line "nach deinem Wort" in a single voice against the chords of "gehorsam sein nach deinem Wort."

In part, "Ich aber bin elend" resembles some of the works of Schütz even more closely.[148] At first glance its three connected sections appear to have as little in common as the separate movements of the "Warum" motet. The first and last parts, whose texts come from a single verse of the 69th Psalm, are mostly true eight-voice writing—the first minor, chromatic, and complaining ("Ich aber bin elend"), and the last major, diatonic, and affirmative ("Herr Gott, deine Hilfe schütze mich"). On the other hand, the middle section, a setting of a much longer passage from Exodus, is strictly divided into two SATB choirs and clearly intended to give the impression of responsive psalmody, with one choir chanting the text, and the other continually replying "Herr, Herr Gott."

The contrast between styles is intensified in this middle section because the reciting choir sings only simple triads in root position (except for the brief dissonant syncopations where the basses anticipate the words "Missetat" and "Übertretung" in illustration of the text), while the responding choir has increasingly elaborate flourishes in a much more modern harmonic idiom to accompany its basic motive of a rising fourth. This motive arises initially from the first simple call of the reciting choir, but in the elaboration it moves from voice to voice of the responding choir and eventually provides the transition to the last section.

The psalmody of the reciting choir (Choir 1) resembles a number of sections in Schütz's *Psalmen Davids;*[149] a good example is the first fragment which Brahms copied from volume II of the *Werke* into A 130, 23-24.[150] In this passage from Psalm 110 (see Ex. 19, reduced from Brahms's four staves), Schütz characteristically uses an irregular rhythm which adheres closely to the text accentuation of the homophonic phrase.

Example 19

Brahms sometimes forces the text into a rhythmic pattern that is against the word accents, especially in bars 19-21 (Ex. 20).

Example 20

In the following phrase, however (see Ex. 21), if one assumes that the word accent on "*Gna*-de" and not the bar line determines the rhythm, there is a temporary turn to triple meter which is entirely in the tradition of Schütz—and also, of course, of Brahms.[151]

Example 21

The passage shown in Example 19 immediately precedes a section of falso-bordone, unmeasured homophonic psalmody sung by all thirteen voices. This kind of writing, a part of church tradition, may also have been in Brahms's mind when he composed these homophonic passages in the motet.

In addition to the resemblance to Schütz at his simplest that occurs in the middle section of "Ich aber bin elend," there are clear if less obvious connections between the remainder of the motet and some of Schütz's other works which Brahms was studying at around the time it was composed. The first section, with its angular melodic lines, prominent diminished fourths, and cross relations, has many similarities to the expressive writing of Schütz. A good example from the passages which Brahms copied into A130, 23-24 (see Table 1) is the first phrase of Psalm 130, "Aus der Tiefe" (Ex. 22), which contains upward octave leaps in the soprano and bass lines similar to Brahms's, a harmonic diminished fourth where Brahms has both melodic and harmonic ones, and a conspicuous cross relation.[152]

Example 22

The last section of Brahms's motet conveys the same full-voiced major-mode assurance that God will hear and respond with his protection found in Schütz's setting of "mein Gebet nimmt der Herr an" in Psalm 6, "Ach Herr, straf mich nicht mit deinem Zorn" (SWV 24), a work which Brahms marked for special attention in his copy of the second volume of the *Werke*.

In comparing this Brahms motet to works by Schütz, we can see that Brahms here followed the sense of the text as he composed his setting in the same kind of detail that Schütz did in many of the works Brahms studied. Like Schütz, Brahms was able to combine the heterogeneous elements in the motet into a coherent whole because of the naturalness with which he was able to express himself in the style suitable to each section of the text.[153]

Techniques of Early Music in Brahms's Library and in His Choral Music

A number of practices which Brahms may have derived from early music have already been mentioned in the previous section of this chapter in connection with particular pieces where they appear. In the following final section, his use of a few specific techniques which can be directly related to his study of early music will be discussed briefly. The main source of information on his knowledge of early music is, as usual, his own library—and in particular his Abschriften and the annotations in his volumes of printed music.[154]

In connection with the use of his library as evidence, one issue with no satisfactory resolution must be mentioned. One tends to assume, or perhaps to want to assume, that Brahms received ideas which were new to him from his examination of the early music in his library, and that he then chose to incorporate some of these ideas into his own compositions. However, an additional possibility should be considered—that much of what he marked was in no sense new to him, but may instead have been clever uses of old methods, or simply examples of practices which already interested him. He may already have used some of these ideas in his own compositions, and been struck by the coincidental examples in the music of earlier composers. It cannot be stated positively that Brahms was "influenced" by any given work of early music, but it can certainly be said that his Abschriften and his annotations are conclusive evidence of his interest in the music of Renaissance and Baroque composers and some of the specific techniques they used to attain their results.

As we have already observed, Brahms's knowledge of early music was necessarily limited to what he could obtain in nineteenth-century published editions or manuscript copies. In only a few cases did he learn works of Renaissance or Baroque music from the original editions. His view of this music must therefore have been conditioned by the editorial practices of those who transcribed and published it. In some cases the editors explained their procedures;[155] but often they added bar lines and accidentals, altered note values and text underlay, and provided performance dynamics without any indication of what the original form of the piece had been.

Brahms's earliest Abschriften contain all editorial additions along with the music, with no suggestion that he realized that some of what he was copying was not genuine. As scholarly standards improved with the appearance of the Bach *Werke,* the sophistication of all students of early music grew rapidly. We see this in Brahms in some of his Abschriften of folk songs (A128, 5-12) and chorale melodies (A134, 39-40), where he questions the rhythms implied by editorial bar lines, compares versions, and suggests solutions to editorial problems. His copy of Tucher's *Schatz des evangelischen Kirchengesangs* not only contains some alterations in rhythms, but also shows that he was aware of the possible incorrect use of editorial accidentals. He added some accidentals of his own to his volumes of Forster's *Liedlein,* but he was not consistent in doing so; for example, he did not raise the leading tones in his transcription of "O wy arme Sünders" (A135). In Kade's book on Mattheus le Maistre, he marked a passage where the author complains that few reliable editions of early music are available.

In just one piece of early music, Gallus's "Ecce quomodo moritur justus," Brahms's own editorial decisions throughout the process of transcription and preparation for performance may be seen.[156] Because he never published the final performance version, we do not know how punctilious he might have been in a printed edition in the matter of distinguishing his own contributions from the original material. We also have no information on what he might have told the members of the Singverein in their rehearsals—for example, whether he suggested that they disregard his regular editorial barring in 4/2 in favor of natural accentuation of the text. His performance dynamics have nothing to do with the word accents, but serve to emphasize the musical structure of phrases and to bind the piece together as a whole. Whether he would have paid closer attention to the demands of individual words in a piece with a German text is a matter for conjecture.

In his own compositions, the mere fact that Brahms wrote such a large amount of choral music, particularly a cappella works, is in itself remarkable. No other composer of the nineteenth century wrote so much of such high quality and of such different kinds. In this respect he is like the early composers for whom writing for groups of singers was simply routine, and who treated voices on an equal and often interchangeable basis with instruments. Brahms did not, like Bach, write for voices as though they *were* instruments; but he did treat them instrumentally in that he learned to write especially for their strengths, using their capabilities to the full without exceeding their limitations. He also wrote for choral singers as though they were as intelligent and competent within their medium as instrumentalists—an unusual assumption for a nine-teenth-century composer and an important reason why Brahms's music has remained so popular with choirs.

In a similar way, he seems to have expected instrumental parts to make as much sense as vocal lines. Mattheson advised such an approach to instrumental writing in *Kern Melodischer Wissenschaft* in a passage which is marked in Brahms's copy:

> All playing is an imitation and associate of singing; yes, a player, or one who com-poses for instruments, must observe everything which is required for good melody and harmony even more diligently than a singer or one who composes for voices; for in singing one has the articulate assistance of words, whereas they are, of course, lacking in the case of instruments.[157]

Brahms heeded this counsel; his instrumental lines exhibit the same kind of melodic and contrapuntal logic that characterizes his vocal writing.[158]

Mattheson's insistence on the importance of writing good melodic lines, and his rules for doing it, are among the other parts of *Kern Mel-odischer Wissenschaft* that are marked (see above, pp. 75-76.). In his pref-ace, paragraph 5, Mattheson wrote, "I always insist above all on a single, pure melody, like the most beautiful and natural thing in the world. . . ." He also warned against displays of contrapuntal virtuosity for their own sake, saying (p. 15) that fugues are acceptable, but that pieces made up entirely of fugues, like many early motets, lack vigor and should there-fore be avoided. This passage is also marked, and, indeed, although Brahms wrote many independent canons, he never published a completely inde-pendent choral fugue, but rather incorporated fugal sections into longer movements, or fugal movements into larger works.[159]

For singers, one of the most pleasing aspects of Brahms's choral music is that all his vocal parts, even the inner ones, are interesting. Much has been said about the great importance he placed on writing a strong bass line.[160] Spitta wrote, with reference to the songs, "With Brahms one can speak again of a general bass";[161] and some of the song sketches, which have only a melody and a figured bass, demonstrate this Baroque, polar orientation.[162] However, even when Brahms was realizing a Baroque figured bass, as he did for his editions of the Handel Italian duets and trios for the *Werke* (Vol. 32 [1870]), he was careful to make the inner voices both interesting and logical. In fact, his care in this direction led him to write realizations that were rather too elaborate and full for the musical content of the pieces. This same tendency, however, makes all of his choral parts rewarding to sing.[163] Even the basses and altos, relegated through the Classic period and the early nineteenth century (except in church-style fugues) to almost nothing but harmonic foundation and filler respectively, again had parts that were more interesting than anything composed since Bach.

To a large extent, this feature of Brahms's choral music arises from his pervasive use of imitation, since in imitative writing everyone has his own melodic line. Evidence of his long study of imitation in early music is everywhere in his library, from the square brackets which point out the various entrances in the Abschriften from Winterfeld's *Gabrieli* (A130, 1-6) and in the printed volume, through the analysis of the fugue in Bach's Cantata 21 in the *Werke,* to the many annotations in the Schütz collected edition.

Imitation in Brahms's own compositions also occurs everywhere, but perhaps its use is most remarkable in the secular works for chorus, where it is least expected. For example, a series of imitative entrances is used in "All meine Herzgedanken" (Op. 62/5) to build the texture up to the full six voices for the first time; the result is a completely natural intensification and blossoming of the choral sound, without any impression that a learned, "historic" technique has been used to obtain it. Even in such a romantic, atmospheric piece as "Waldesnacht" (Op. 62/3), much of what is interesting and effective comes from the ways in which imitation is used.

"Waldesnacht" is also remarkable in that this use of melodic imitation between groups of voices results inevitably in some striking dissonances. In this respect too Brahms works in the same way as the old composers for whom the motion of individual voices can sometimes produce dissonant accented passing tones or appoggiaturas instead of the more usual suspensions, and even lead to unexpected harmonic progressions. Examples of this kind of linear logic occur, of course, throughout early music. Two good examples which appear among the Abschriften come from early and late in Brahms's career: one is in Zirler's "Die Sonn' die ist verblichen" (A130, 7-9), where the conjunct motion of soprano and alto leads to dissonance between the two voices and also with the tenor melody (Ex. 23). The other (Ex. 24) is the first Schütz fragment in A130, 23-24 (see Table 1), where the second tenor, in remaining true to a reasonable line in the last four notes of its own melody, throws the smooth harmonic progress of the final cadence off course.

Brahms would never have let the meaning of a final cadence be called into question in his own music, but many other examples of dissonance resulting from the demands of individual vocal lines may be found. Two,

Example 23

Example 24

again from early and late in his career, come from Op. 30 and Op. 109/3. In the Amen of Op. 30 the voices are no longer in strict canon, but Brahms composed a tenor part which is, as Joachim said, "beautiful in itself,"[164] but which has sharp clashes with the soprano and alto in the seventh bar (bar 59). Joachim continued, in the same letter,

> Your ear is so used to rough harmony and such polyphonic texture that you rarely consider the voices simply as they conflict with one another—because you immediately supply the entire context which surrounds such a clash.[165]

In another Amen, at the end of the *Fest- und Gedenksprüche*, Brahms wrote a series of canonic entrances (although the earlier part of the movement is not canonic) which, as the voices pile up against the bass pedal, results in a number of strong dissonances, all perfectly diatonic and perfectly logically obtained. The effect is not at all one of an intellectual exercise, but of a glorious accumulation of sound, gradually increasing, and then decreasing in tension until the final plagal cadence is reached.

Brahms once said to Henschel, "I love dissonances very much, but on heavy beats, and then lightly and gently resolved!"[166] Judging from his own compositions, he loved them not only in the conventional treatment, complete with preparation and resolution, as they were explained in Marpurg's *Handbuch* (p. 75 above). He also enjoyed those that arise from the motion of individual voices in their owm melodies, on either strong or weak beats, and that, without apparent calculation in the sense of the conventional treatment, produce a remarkably beautiful result. Many of Brahms's most poignant moments come from just this sort of diatonic dissonance, sometimes conventionally prepared but often unexpected, often against a bass pedal, and often at cadences. A good example of a similar phenomenon in his library of early music occurs in the final cadence of Eccard's "Übers Gebirg Maria geht" (A134, 29-34), shown in Example 25. Dissonant notes are circled or marked with X's.

Example 25

Often in Brahms's music, if a singer or listener feels the emotional effect of one of these moments and looks for a possible reason, he will find these unexpected diatonic dissonances; sometimes just a single chord can produce the characteristic warmth. A few of the large number of examples which come from the present writer's own experience. in addition to "Waldensnacht" and the Amens from Op. 30 and Op. 109/3 already cited, are given in Examples 26-29 from the following works (again the dissonances are marked):

Ex. 26.   *Requiem* (Op. 45), no. 6 fugue, mm. 290-94, tenors and orchestra (reduced)
Ex. 27.   "Warum" motet, op. 74/1, mm. 115-17
Ex. 28.   "Der Falke," Op. 93a/5, end of each stanza except the last (the last stanza also provides an illustration)
Ex. 29.   Op. 109/3, the cadence at mm. 79-81

In addition to these uses of often unprepared dissonance, there are countless examples of the more usual treatment of suspensions in Brahms's music, and a good deal of evidence of a special fondness for them in his

Example 26

denn du hast al - le Din- ge er - schaf- fen

Example 27

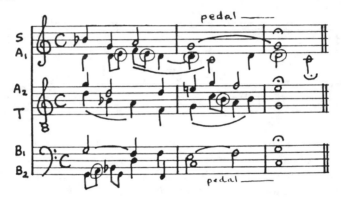

Example 28

library. For example, in the first volume of the Schütz *Werke,* the only passages he marked in the *Aufferstehung* are duet sections, all constructed in standard suspension chains. The performance dynamics he added to the scores of Bach's "Christ lag in Todesbanden" and Handel's *Saul* are clearly designed to emphasize the dissonance in suspensions.[167] Florence

Example 29

May, in her reminiscences of Brahms as a piano teacher and performer, discusses the matter also:

> He loved Bach's suspensions. "It is here that it must sound," he would say, pointing to the tied note, and insisting, whilst not allowing me to force the preparation, that the latter should be so struck as to give the fullest possible effect to the dissonance.[168]

In much of Brahms's choral music, as in that of early composers, dissonance is used along with a number of other melodic and harmonic devices in the service of text expression, either in madrigalisms—illustrations of single words—or in the depiction of the mood or meaning of a phrase or section of the text. Many instances of this kind of descriptive writing in Brahms's music have been cited in the previous section of this chapter,[169] and he was certainly aware of the practice as it was used in early music. For example, in Schütz's "Tröstet, tröstet mein Volk" (SWV 382) in his copy of the *Werke,* volume 8, Brahms wrote "NB unison" and underlined all the parts where the text "ebene Bahn" is illustrated by the voices singing in unison on an unchanging note. He also marked the passage "leite mich" in Bach's Cantata 150 (see p. 121 above).

The use of chromaticism for expressive purposes in early music attracted Brahms's attention particularly. We have already observed a number of instances where he marked striking examples in works in his library, especially in the music of Bach and Schütz. Although a number of highly chromatic works by Italian Baroque composers—Rovetta, Durante, and Lotti[170]—appear among his earlier Abschriften, Brahms's own uses of chromaticism are perhaps more like those of the German composers.[171] The similarity to Bach's melodies is most noticeable in the angular lines of fugal sections in Op. 29/2 and Op. 74/1, as well as in the fugue over the long pedal in the *Requiem,* no. 3. The works of both Bach and Schütz provide many examples, some marked by Brahms, of the kind of stepwise chromatic motion that he used as countersubjects in the fugal motet movements. He also frequently employed chromatic conjunct motion as melodic or counter-melodic material in the Chorlieder; the songs of Op. 62 (nos. 2, 3, 4, and 6) and Op. 104 (nos. 1 and 5) are especially rich in this respect.[172]

Cross relations are another manifestation of chromaticism in early music that Brahms tended to notice and mark, particularly in the Schütz *Werke* and the Abschriften taken from them (A130, 21-24). The kind of relation routinely found between phrases in early music, where the dominant (with raised leading tone) of a minor chord leads not to that expected minor chord, but to its relative major, or where a triad with a raised third is immediately followed by one with the third lowered to the minor, also occurs in Brahms's music, from very early works to late ones.[173] Wüllner at first objected to the cross relation in Op. 109/2, bar 77 (Ex. 30), but Brahms said he could not relinquish it, and Wüllner later became "fully reconciled" to it.[174] This is almost the same relation that occurs in Hassler's "Mein G'müth ist mir verwirret" (Ex. 31). An earlier Brahms work, "O süsser Mai" (Op. 93a/3), contains so many major/minor changes that they must be considered one of the structural bases of the piece.

Cross relations within phrases also appear in Brahms's music, though infrequently. They are not jarring, however, like those he objected to in Schütz's "Die mit Thränen säen" and "Siehe, mein Fürsprecher" in his

Example 30

Example 31

copies of the Werke (see Examples 6 and 7, above). The cross relations in the first section of Brahms's Op. 110/1 have already been mentioned (p. 145 above); but before he had studied most of the works of Schütz he wrote those in "All meine Herzgedanken" (Op. 62/5), which arise from the independent nature of the vocal lines and their imitation structure (Ex. 32). Although these cross relations are apparent on paper, the fact that they occur in the same register and thus result in a smooth chromatic progression softens their effect.

Example 32

In the first "Nachtwache" (Op. 104/1) an accented passing tone (B natural) in the second alto is needed for the melodic line but conflicts sharply with the equally necessary B sharp in the soprano (Ex. 33). In this instance the passing tone has a subordinate function, but the dissonance occurs, like the simultaneous cross relations in early English music, because the melodic integrity of each part is maintained.[175]

Another early music phenomenon which is both melodic and harmonic in nature and which has interesting effects in Brahms's music is the use of the church modes. He marked a passage in Winterfeld's *Gabrieli* on the characters of the various modes (see above, p. 97); and

Example 33

he may have chosen to copy a particular setting of Senfl's "Ich stund an einem Morgen" because it was labeled "Phrygisch"—the only one of the five settings of that tune so labeled in Brahms's source collection.[176] In this case, although the tune is Phrygian, the setting ends not on a Phrygian cadence, but rather with the final tenor note as the fifth of the last chord. True Phrygian cadences are found in the Praetorius "Maria zart" setting (A130, 15); and Brahms also marked several in Winterfeld's *Gabrieli.* Although he was obviously aware of their use, he seems to have decided not to employ them himself, even in some situations where they are expected.

Perhaps Brahms enjoyed writing music with a Phrygian flavor,[177] but for some reason found final Phrygian cadences unsatisfactory. Such an explanation might account for the endings of the duet "Klosterfräulein" (Op. 61/2)[178] and the most startling example, his second organ chorale prelude on "Herzlich tut mich verlangen" (Op. 122/10), which cries out for a Phrygian cadence but instead has the final note of the melody as the fifth of an A minor chord, like Senfl's "Ich stund an einem Morgen." Senfl's ending is satisfactory, however, whereas Brahms's is not.[179] The only example in the choral music where Brahms avoids specific Phrygian implications in a tune is his setting of the folk song "Ach lieber Herre Jesu Christ." There the potentially modal tune disappears into the major scale; the same failure to give a modal setting to a possibly modal melody also characterizes Hassler's "Mein G'müth ist mir verwirret," the original version of "Herzlich thut mich verlangen." Bach's later settings of this melody have led us to think of the tune as Phrygian and to consider a Phrygian cadence as a satisfactory ending—indeed, probably the most satisfactory ending.

It is possible that Brahms's interest in the Phrygian mode may be extended to account for his frequent use of Neapolitan relations, as Spitta suggests when he discusses the derivation of harmonic practices from modal scales.[180] In Brahms's library the examples he marked illustrate the use of Neapolitan chords for expressive purposes in the conventional Baroque sense. One particularly striking example is the section quoted above (see Ex. 5) in the discussion of the Bach *Werke,* "durch dieses Jammerthal zu führen" from Cantata 91. The Neapolitan in that passage is reached by the parallel fifth motion which Brahms marked and labeled "wie schön!" In the chorus of mourning from Handel's *Saul,* he used performance dynamics to set off the two appearances of Neapolitans, both times reducing the volume to pianissimo.

The Dorian mode appears in Brahms's choral writing both in preexistent melodies and in some he composed himself. Sometimes the tunes are harmonized at least partly in accordance with the modal structure, as in "Vergangen ist mir Glück und Heil" (Op. 62/7), the first verses of "O Heiland, reiss die Himmel auf" (Op. 74/2), and the setting of the folk song "Komm Mainz, komm Bayrn." In other works, however, Brahms transforms a Dorian melody to the minor mode or otherwise disguises its modal character in his harmonization, as in the last verse of Op. 74/2, the setting of "Mit Fried und Freud ich fahr dahin" in Op. 74/1, "Marias Kirchgang" (Op. 22/2), and the folk song "Scheiden" from the early group of settings (no. 15).[181]

A few examples in Brahms's library show that he was not exempt from the common tendency to change Dorian patterns to minor scales by adding editorial accidentals. In Heydhammer's quodlibet "Der winter kalt ist vor dem Haus" from Forster's *Liedlein,* volume II (see pp. 61-62 above), he added several E flats in the staff. Example 34 shows one of them, as well as one of the many raised cadential leading tones, placed by Brahms above the staff.

Example 34

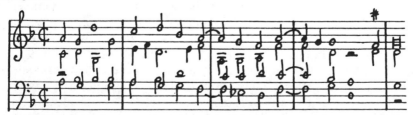

A similar added flat removes the Dorian sixth from the end of the first phrase of Gabrieli's "Benedictus" in Brahms's copy of Winterfeld (p. 101

above); this version was the source of the parts used for performance by the Singakademie (Ex. 35, where the four staves of choir 3 are reduced to two). In this example Winterfeld's editorial accidentals are shown, and Brahms's pencil E flat is circled. The bar lines running through notes are a peculiarity of Winterfeld's edition.

Example 35

The other church modes do not play an important part in either Brahms's library or in his choral music. "O wy arme Sünders" (A135) is Mixolydian; but unless Brahms's tendency to flat the seventh degree of the major scale as he moves toward subdominant areas is a result of modal thinking, as Spitta seems to suggest,[182] this mode is not significant in his own compositions. The Lydian mode is not even mentioned by Winterfeld in his description of the characters of the modes, and Brahms used it in a choral piece only in the witches' dance section of "Der bucklichte Fiedler" (Op. 93a/1).[183]

This witches' dance, in fast triple meter in contrast to the common time of the rest of the piece, may be based on the old model of the Tripla, as Beuerle suggests (p. 292). It was composed in 1883, and Brahms acquired Nottebohm's large collection of early instrumental music, including much dance material, in 1882. Whether there is any direct connection, this insertion of a section in a different meter is a good example of one of the simpler ways in which Brahms treated rhythm freely. Many of his other vocal pieces also have notated changes in the meter, sometimes to suit the requirements of the text for a descriptive purpose, as is the case in "Der bucklichte Fiedler" and also in "Beherzigung" (Op. 93a/6), or to fit the text rhythm more closely, as in "Das Mädchen" (Op. 93a/2), which is based on Serbian patterns. A number of these changes conform to the old dance pattern, duple/slow changing to triple/fast; examples include the last of the *Marienlieder,* the motets "Schaffe in mir, Gott" (and the Hammerschmidt setting cited above, pp. 118-19, as a comparison) and "Warum," and the sixth chorus of the *Requiem.*

An especially interesting meter change is the one from 3/4 to 4/4 in

"Rosmarin" (Op. 62/1) which, as Evans points out (p. 295), could be accomplished with greater fidelity to the text and musical structure if 3/2 were used instead of 4/4. Why Brahms chose the combination of meters he did is not apparent. In a similar situation he did choose the 3/4 to 3/2 arrangement, when he wrote a meter change and new beat patterns into the folk song "Ulrich" in his copy of Kretzschmer and Zuccalmaglio's collection (II, 15; see Ex. 36).

Example 36

In both his vocal and instrumental music, Brahms frequently disregarded the rhythmic patterns implied by his own bar lines and instead wrote rhythms with a freedom and flexibility that has often been compared with the practices of early music.[184] His library shows that he was well aware of these practices.

In several works of early music, Brahms marked conventional hemiola figures. He used brackets (Ex. 37) to point out one of the cadential hemiolas in a triple-meter section of Heydhammer's quodlibet (also cited above, Ex. 35), and also marked them in the Bach *Werke* and in the volume of works by Eccard and Stobäus. Hemiolas are used to broaden cadences throughout Brahms's music—among the choral works, most conspicuously in the *Triumphlied* and the *Fest- und Gedenksprüche,* as befits their ceremonial nature. A more subtle instance of cadential hemiola appears in the third verse tenor of "O Heiland, reiss die Himmel auf" (see p. 120 above).

Example 37

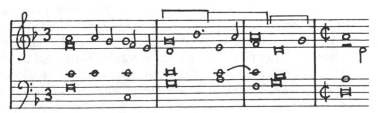

Brahms marked another rhythmic feature in Heydhammer's quodlibet, a triplet pattern of three beats against two (Ex. 38). In this passage, the NBs, slurs, numbers, and the bracket which marks the beginning of a new section in the tenor were all added by Brahms in blue pencil (the Abschrift is in SATB clefs; the alto is tacet in this passage). Examples of this kind of pattern occur frequently in Brahms's choral music, in works as different as the *Requiem*, no. 3 ("Ich hoffe auf dich") and the men's chorus "Freiwillige her!" (Op. 41/2).[185]

Example 38

Internal hemiolas in triple meter, and other types of cross rhythms independent of bar lines, mostly arising in early vocal music from the placement of text accents, attracted Brahms's attention from very early in his career. He realized that editors' or even composers' bar lines did not necessarily determine the real rhythm of a phrase, and experimented with various possible solutions. One such experiment appears in "Ulrich" (Ex. 36 above), and Brahms also recognized and marked a hemiola structure obscured by bar lines in the alto arioso from Bach's Cantata 72. The first half is shown in Example 39; all markings above the staff were added by Brahms in pencil. He exploited a similar fluctuation between triple and duple divisions of six-beat units in the section "Ach, wer heilet die Schmerzen" in the *Alto Rhapsody* (Op. 53).

In the two versions of "Herzlich thut mich verlangen" (the sacred version of "Mein G'müth ist mir verwirret") that Brahms copied in A134, 39-40, he showed Tucher's unvarying 4/2 barring second (ex. 40b). Presumably he realized that it did not conform to the real rhythm of the beginning and end of the piece, which has a regular pattern of hemiolas, because he first copied a version of the tune that he may have obtained from Winterfeld's *Der evangelische Kirchengesang*, which has a more rational barring (Ex. 40a).

Example 39

Example 40a

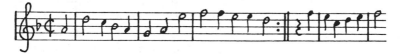

Example 40b

Several other instances where he recognized that the true meter is triple in spite of editorial bar lines in duple meter are found in the collections of Tucher and of Becker and Billroth.

Brahms also was aware that often in early music in duple meter, brief triple-meter patterns may exist and override bar lines. A good example appears in the volume of settings by Eccard and Stobäus (p. 89 above), in Eccard's "Die grosse Lieb dich trieb" (part 1, no. 10), where four of the voices twice have the rhythmic pattern which is shown in Example 41 with Brahms's pencil brackets added above the soprano part.

Example 41

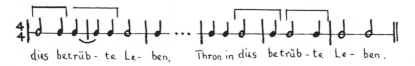

His copy of "Innsbruck" in A134, 43-44 also shows that he was thinking about the true meter determined by the text. The beginning of the soprano line is shown in Example 42 (Brahms used soprano clef); the marks which outline 3/1 measures are in red pencil in the Abschrift.[186] This experiment did not cause Brahms to have the barring altered in the parts used for performance, however.

Example 42

When this kind of independence of the bar line is extended to Brahms's homophonic vocal writing, the result is examples like the previously cited passage in Op. 110/1 (Ex. 21 above). Another good example may be seen in the *Schicksalslied* (Op. 54), where the second appearance of the first main vocal theme, in bars 69-72, seems at first glance to be a case of Brahms's "typical" text misaccentuation (see Ex. 43). However, comparison with the first, somewhat longer appearance of this passage in bars 34-39, where the C of the soprano is clearly a stressed note, and with the phrasing in the violins, which are doubling the soprano and alto lines in bars 69-72, shows clearly that the bar lines should be temporarily ignored in favor of following the true accentuation of the text into triple meter.[187]

Example 43

A natural result of the combination of this kind of rhythmic freedom with Brahms's habit of writing independent, interesting vocal lines is the frequent appearance of cross rhythms between the different parts. Examples may be found everywhere in his choral music; only a few will be mentioned here.

In the second movement of the *Triumphlied* (Op. 55) is a passage where the sopranos of chorus 2 (later joined by the tenors) sing a broad 3/2 which has nothing to do with the bar lines, here nominally marking out 4/4. One can hear the accent structure of the other voices as coin-

ciding with the meter of the second sopranos, with syncopated *Ha*
in the remaining voices of chorus 2 and homophonic *Hall*eluja outbursts
from chorus 1. It is equally possible, however, to consider that the other
voices of chorus 2 have a conflicting 3/2 which is one quarter note behind
the sopranos (thus corresponding with the bar lines), and which is supported by chorus 1 singing Halle*lu*ja. Rhythmic patterns only are shown
in Example 44.

Example 44

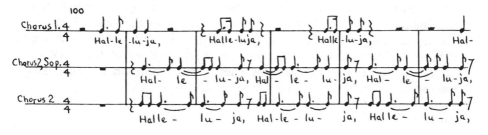

A better-known example comes from the *Requiem*, no. 4, at the phrase
"die loben dich immerdar," which in addition to the implied hemiola
structure underlying the entire section (and underscored decisively by the
orchestra in bars 137- 40), contains a series of overlapping hemiolas in the
vocal parts (bars 143- 48) over the triple meter which prevails in the cellos
and basses. The resulting impression of ceaseless praise is surely exactly
what Brahms intended.

Surprisingly, since German polyphonic Lieder are full of cross
rhythms, there are few examples in Brahms's elaborate folk-song settings
of 1863. Morik (p. 156) points out a situation in "Von edler Art" (mm.
9-10), where the three lower voices are briefly in triple meter against the
soprano's common time; and "Wach auf, mein Kind," in which Brahms
had difficulty deciding on a barring for the tune (p. 125 above), also has
complex independent rhythms in the lower voices.

The other a cappella works contain many interesting cross rhythms.
Early examples occur in the motet "Schaffe in mir, Gott" (Op. 29/2). In
several places in the fugue "Verwirf mich nicht" the imitation is so close
that the bar lines are displaced in single parts for several consecutive
measures;[188] and in the final section, bars 123-25, there are overlapping
hemiola flourishes in parallel thirds in the upper pairs of voices over the
second basses' steady triple-meter dominant pedal.

Examples can also be found in the later motets. The middle section
of the first movement of "Warum" (Op. 74/1) begins with a series of

imitative entrances on "Die des Todes warten." There is no real meter here, though the word "Todes" in most cases has a brief implied triple meter that quickly disappears as other voices make their overlapping entrances; the voices eventually join and re-establish the basic common time of the movement. This passage bears an interesting resemblance to an early work in Brahms's library which also employs the words "des Todes," though death in this instance is a fearful enemy rather than a welcome friend. The earlier example occurs in Johann Stobäus's "Aufs Osterfest," which Brahms marked carefully with dynamics in his copy of the *Preussische Festlieder* (see above, p. 89), but never actually performed. Note the ambiguity of the meter in the section shown in Example 45 (the beginning of the piece), the constant fluctuation in all the voices between triple and duple accentuation, and the cross rhythms of the "und des Todes" entrances (which outline ascending thirds rather than the descending thirds of Op. 74/1[189]). The dynamics are Brahms's.

Example 45

Another example of complex cross rhythms occurs in one of Brahms's late motets, the second of the *Fest- und Gedenksprüche* (see above, p. 142). The confusion of "und ein Haus fället über das andere" (nominally in duple meter, but with many displaced accents which result from the close imitation) is only ended after a prolonged period of rhythmic ambiguity, where each part has its own rhythm and there is no sense of metric organization until the "starker Gewappneter" recovers his triple meter along with the musical material from the beginning of the movement.

Brahms's propensity for writing complex and interesting cross rhythms is illustrated just as frequently in his Chorlieder, where he may have used ideas derived from the independent voices of Renaissance polyphonic Lieder without in any way attempting to imitate other aspects of their style. We have already seen a possible model in "Innsbruck"; other examples occur elsewhere in the Abschriften, though without annotations to show that Brahms realized the rhythmic implications of their melodies or their polyphonic construction. Two good examples are found in A130, 7-9; in both, the bar lines distort the real rhythm of the melody as well as the cross rhythms in the other voices. One is Stoltzer's "Entlaubet ist uns der Walde," where the tenor melody has a changing meter throughout, and the other parts are also extremely irregular. The beginning is shown in Example 46, with the editorial bar lines from Brahms's source. The text appears only in the tenor, both in the source and the Abschrift; so Brahms may not have recognized the rhythmic difficulties in the other voices.[190]

Example 46

The other is Scandello's 1578 setting of "Schein uns, du liebe Sonne," which is, if possible, even more difficult to classify rhythmically, partly because the soprano melody is clearly an ornamented verson of the tune appearing in a simpler form in the tenor. The beginning is shown in Example 47 as Brahms copied it (except for the reduction to two staves from four staves in SATB clefs). The slurs in the lower voices show that he knew where the words were placed. Note the many suspensions, and the

diatonic dissonances in the third bar which give a warm, full sound to the
extended word "Sonne."

Example 47

Brahms does not exhibit such independence from regular meter as
this in any of his Chorlieder. Although he departs from predictable patterns frequently and indulges in complicated cross rhythms, he always
returns to a pattern which is compatible with nineteenth-century expec-
tations before the end of a piece. Thus, for example, we have already
observed (p. 133) that in "Dein Herzlein mild" (Op. 62/4) the expansion
at the end of the last verse is constructed from overlapping hemiolas;
however, an important rhythmic motive from earlier in the piece returns
before the end and clarifies the meter. In "Verlorene Jugend" (Op. 104/4)
the canonic writing of the first half of each verse also leads to overlapping
hemiolas. In this case, the hemiolas of the alto in the first verse are
supported by the lower three voices, but in the second verse the voices
which are not participating in the canon maintain triple meter. The canonic voices continue their ambiguous meter until the end of the section,
which is followed by the homophonic second part of the piece.

"O süsser Mai" (Op. 93a/3), one of Brahms's most romantic Chorlieder, is another work which makes important use of cross rhythms,
again in a central section, so that there is no continuing uncertainty about
the meter at the end of the piece. In this final example (Ex. 48) as in
others that have been mentioned, the hemiola patterns are made clear by
both the text and melodic constructions, and the overlapping results from
close imitation.

For Brahms as for the Renaissance and Baroque composers whose
works he studied and performed, the ideas and sounds of the text to a
large extent determined the construction of a piece of vocal music. Even
when there was no text, however, for him as for them the same kinds of
constructive principles applied, especially the importance and independence of individual lines. The same kinds of results that we have seen in

Example 48

his choral music may be observed throughout his instrumental music as well. To cite only two examples, the first movements of both the Second (Op. 73) and the Third Symphony (Op. 90) contain rhythmic complexities on a scale which far surpasses anything in the vocal music, and yet they are derived from nothing more than hemiola and the freedom from bar line restrictions that we have observed in works of early music in his library.

Studies of Brahms's instrumental music and Lieder from this special point of view will have to await other students of his music and of early music, because the present investigation has demonstrated the magnitude of his debt to the past only for the choral music. Brahms himself realized the importance of its contribution to musicians of his own time, as the examination of his library has shown. He studied early music, assimilated what he found valuable in it, united it with his Romantic imagination and command of nineteenth-century techniques, and composed choral music which is among the most rewarding to sing and to hear of any in musical history.

Notes

Chapter 1

1. Geiringer, *Brahms*, p. 21. See bibliography for complete references.

2. May, 2nd ed., p. 80.

3. A number of writers on Brahms have given Schumann the credit for awakening this interest. See, for example, Kross, *Chorwerke*, p. 562, and Beuerle, p. 65. However, the existence of the Abschriften A130, 27-28 (the copies of Palestrina and others mentioned above) disproves such a statement.

4. Boetticher, pp. 229, 296.

5. Dietrich, *Erinnerungen*, p. 18.

6. *Briefe* I: 73.

7. *Briefwechsel* (BW) V: 123-27, and then occasionally through p. 305 (September 1861).

8. Examples include the first part of Op. 29/2, Op. 30, sections of Op. 74/1, and some of the canons Op. 113. All these works were published considerably later. His determination to destroy unpublished material may have resulted from the fact that one of his closest friends in Vienna was Gustav Nottebohm, the Beethoven scholar. Possibly Brahms observed the studies carried out on Beethoven's sketchbooks and decided that he wanted no such posthumous examination of his own work. See McCorkle, "Obstacles," p. 257.

9. One of these men, Theodor Avé-Lallemant, had earlier, in November 1855, offered to give Brahms any music of which he had duplicate copies. See the Brahms-Clara Schumann *Briefe* I: 156.

10. *Briefe* I: 437; my translation. The entire Singakademie season is described by Kalbeck (II: 93-104).

11. Beuerle, in his discussion of Brahms's choral conducting career (pp. 61-76), says that Brahms's desire to raise himself above his lower-class origin was at the root of his preoccupation with choral music, since choirs were essentially middle-class institutions.

12. Brahms felt strongly about this issue all his life. For example, his only serious falling-out with his friend Franz Wüllner occurred when he refused Wüllner the first performance of the Fourth Symphony in 1885 and unfairly accused him of wanting it because it was a "novelty" (BW XV: 121).

13. Kalbeck III: 268-69. Brahms's first editorial collaboration with Chrysander was the first and second books of Couperin's *Pièces de Clavecin,* which appeared as volume IV of *Denkmäler der Tonkunst* in 1869. In 1870 Brahms provided realizations of six duets and two trios for a Peters edition of Handel. Chrysander later found nine more duets, and asked Brahms to arrange them and to revise the others for the complete edition. One of Chrysander's letters to Brahms makes it clear that he had heard Brahms accompany some of these pieces, realizing the figured bass at sight; see *Monthly Musical Record* 67 (1937): 99.

14. See BW XVI: 88. The correspondence between Brahms and Spitta had lapsed since 1879, until Spitta wrote again in 1888. In his response Brahms expressed his enthusiasm for the Schütz edition and asked when the "grossen Kirchenconzerte" would appear.

15. Kross, *Chorwerke,* p. 457.

16. Hohenemser, writing in 1900 and therefore summarizing the nineteenth-century viewpoint, defined early music for the purposes of his study as that written between the beginning of the sixteenth century and the middle of the eighteenth, except for opera, which has a separate and continuous history. See pp. 9-10.

17. Eduard Hanslick, the Viennese critic who was a close friend of Brahms, ". . . once confessed that he would rather see the complete works of Schütz destroyed than Brahms' *Ein deutsches Requiem,* the complete works of Palestrina than Mendelssohn's, all the concertos and sonatas of Bach than the quartets of Schumann and Brahms, and all of Gluck than *Don Giovanni, Fidelio,* or *Der Freischütz.* 'A shocking confession,' he added, 'but at least an honest one!' " Quoted from the introduction to *Vienna's Golden Years of Music,* p. 2. See also Hanslick's review of a performance of the *St. Matthew Passion,* pp. 97ff.

18. Brahms's unusual freedom from "Historismus" (this German word, meaning historicism, or the too-heavy reliance on historical models, is frequently used as a synonym for "imitation of an earlier style of composition") in spite of his preoccupation with earlier styles of choral composition and his frequent use of older forms, is agreed on by most writers about his choral music. The first to discuss the matter in detail was Philipp Spitta, in his article on Brahms in *Zur Musik,* 1892.

19. See the accounts of the revival of interest in early music in Hohenemser, Besseler (for Renaissance music), Blume (for Bach), Dadelsen, and Kross.

20. See Besseler, p. 8, and Beuerle, p. 57.

21. Hohenemser discusses Mendelssohn's music at length; see pp. 59ff. and 102ff. Also see Beuerle, p. 59.

22. Here the present writer disagrees with Dadelsen, p. 19, who says that because of the virtuoso ideal of the nineteenth century, newly composed music was often too difficult for amateur choirs, and they were forced to fall back on the simpler early music. Brahms himself made a pertinent comment in a letter he wrote to Clara Schumann soon after he took up the job at Detmold (*Briefe* I: 206). Referring to Schumann's "Zigeunerleben," he wrote, "How childishly simple such things are compared to old church music."

23. Dadelsen's dissertation deals with instrumental music. He concludes that much of Brahms's success in this area as well is due to the use of techniques derived from early music, especially those acquired during his counterpoint study in the 1850s.

24. Fellinger, "Grundzüge Brahmsscher Musikauffassung."

Chapter 2

1. Kalbeck IV: 229.

2. Mandyczewski; Kalbeck I: 185-86 and frequent references thereafter; Geiringer, all three articles.

3. Hofmann, *Die Bibliothek von Johannes Brahms*.

4. Now in the Wiener Stadtbibliothek manuscript collection: Signatur 85172 Ja.

5. Robert Pascall dates the earliest entries in late 1854 or early 1855 on the evidence of the placement of a number of Joachim's works, and Brahms's failure to include Schubert in the first series of entries (personal comm., April 1980).

6. Wiener Stadtbibliothek manuscript collection: Signatur 67338 Jc.

7. "Johannes Brahms' Musikbibliothek." Reprinted by Hofmann.

8. Two pocket notebooks dating from the Düsseldorf years are also preserved in Vienna (Stadtbibliothek MS collection: 79560 Ja and 79565 Ja). They contain, in addition to many blank pages, loan lists and a few notes of acquisitions. One of the books shows a loan in March 1856 of works by Keiser and Fried. Bach to "Prof. Jahn in Bonn," and the other contains a short list of works by Schumann in his own hand with a note by Brahms that it had been written during his second visit to Schumann at the Endenich asylum in February 1855.

9. It seems unlikely, however, that items he gave away should appear in Orel's catalog, which runs to the end of Brahms's life. For example, it does not contain an entry for the four-part chorales of Bach, published in 1765 by C. P. E. Bach, although this collection is listed in his earlier catalog. Presumably he had given the volume to Florence May, since it was in her possession in 1905, and thus did not enter it in his revised catalog. The chorales are now in the British Library; see p. 73 below.

10. Kalbeck IV: 229.

11. Volumes II, III, and the "Neue Folge" of *Chorübungen* along with an edition of three of the Schütz *Psalmen Davids* are mentioned in the correspondence in 1877, 1881, 1895, and 1878 respectively (BW XV: 73, 95, 183, 91), although *Chorübungen* II, which contains exercises and works for two and three voices, does not appear in the Orel catalog.

12. Hofmann, p. xxvii.

13. This is the chief reason given by Kalbeck (I: 186), though his list of examples does not contain any for which the statement is true.

14. *Briefe* I: 221, 224. Brahms requested especially German folk songs and vocal works by Eccard and Schütz, whom the editor identifies as "wohl Johann Jakob Schütz . . . (1640-1690)" rather than the far more probable Heinrich Schütz.

15. Orel, *Brahms und Allgeyer,* pp. 13, 15-16.

16. I am grateful to Karl Geiringer for a helpful letter which enabled the Archiv staff to find the volumes, which had been missing. Geiringer mentions the gift in *Brahms,* p. 101.

17. The catalog is published in Mandyczewski's Zusatzband, "Sammlungen und Statuten," to Perger & Hirschfeld's *Geschichte,* but items from the Brahms collection are not separated from the general list. Brahms's own Abschriften do appear on p. 92 at the end of the list of his autographs, but A136 and A137 are not included.

18. Geiringer, "Brahms Library," p. 8, note.

19. See Hancock, "Sources," for a description and classification.

20. The special category of manuscript scores or parts prepared by copyists under Brahms's direction for performances by the Singakademie and the Musikverein, and owned by those organizations rather than by Brahms himself, is mentioned here only in relation to the other Abschriften or printed music. They are described more fully in Hancock, "Performances."

21. See the facsimile of a letter written to his teacher Cossel when Brahms was eight years old (Kalbeck I: following p. 24).

22. Both Robert Pascall and George Bozarth have organized such information in their research and writing about Brahms.

23. Kalbeck (I: 185) uses this reference to Hassler's *Lustgarten* to infer incorrectly that Brahms was using original sixteenth and seventeenth century sources to build up his music collection ". . . before he found Becker's 'Lieder und Weisen vergangener Jahrhunderte' in Schumann's library." The confusion manifest here does not add to our confidence in Kalbeck's judgment when he goes on in the same paragraph to conclude that Brahms observed this music ". . . not through the keenly critical spectacles of the learned historian, but with the unaided eyes of the naive artist . . ." because he had not made a note that this piece is the original version of the Passion chorale. It is much more probable that Brahms copied the tune in the first place because he realized what it was, and felt no need to write down the obvious connection. (Kalbeck also provides a facsimile of a still earlier Abschrift of folk songs, which he dates 1848-50, in I: facing p. 184.)

24. Köster's Papierhandlung was in the Valentinskamp from 1844 to 1866, according to city directories in the Staats- und Universitätsbibliothek Hamburg. Therefore Kalbeck is wrong (II:252) when he says, in connection with the manuscript of the *Requiem,* that Köster's business was at that address from 1860 to 1868.

25. Morik, p. 104.

26. Kalbeck mentions it along with the C. F. Becker collection; see note 23 above.

27. Kalbeck (I: 67) says that two of the Hungarian dances appear here. The incipits of the two tunes in A130, 27-28 are also found in this group.

28. "Liedersammlungen." I am grateful to Prof. Bozarth for the opportunity to read a prepublication typescript of the English version of his article.

29. Arnold lived and worked in Elberfeld, near Düsseldorf; Brahms corresponded with him perhaps as early as 1854 (BW V:33) and certainly in 1855 (Brahms-Schumann

Briefe I: 81), and could easily have visited him at any time before Schumann's death in 1856. There is no reference in the biographies or the correspondence to such a visit, but in a letter to Franz Wüllner written in 1888 (BW XV: 156), Brahms said that he wished he had paid better attention to what Karl Simrock (who worked in Bonn and died in 1876) and Dr. Arnold had had to tell him about the work of Kretzschmer and Zuccalmaglio, who had also been associated with the Elberfeld group (described by Morik, pp. 4ff.).

30. The controversy, with all pertinent references, is summarized by Bozarth in "Liedersammlungen." Morik, who came closest to the right answer, cites an A. Henseler, who worked with Arnold's papers and said he had seen "In stiller Nacht" among them (p. 17, n. 3).

31. Arnold did work in the area of the sixteenth-century polyphonic Lied; see Morik, pp. 8, 17, 36-37. However, Brahms wrote no reference to him on these two pages.

32. Brahms presumably did not yet know all these versions of "Ich stund an einem Morgen" when he set the "romanticized" tune written by Nicolai and adapted by Zuccalmaglio (in A 128, 4) for voice and piano in 1857 or 1858; but see Wiora (p. 20) for a discussion of the possibility that he might have preferred such a version in any case. However, there is no evidence that Brahms was aware at this stage that the version he chose really stemmed from the eighteenth century rather than the sixteenth, as Kretzschmer and Zuccalmaglio claimed. In the 1890s he did deliberately choose to set "Wach auf, mein Hort" in the version of the tune given by Kretzschmer and Zuccalmaglio, even though he knew the tune from the *Lochaimer Liederbuch* and realized that his tune, which was actually composed by Reichardt (Friedländer, p. 220), was not contemporary with the text. See his remarks on the subject to Spitta in BW XVI: 102; and the discussion below of Brahms's copy of the *Lochaimer Liederbuch* (ed. Arnold) in his collection of printed music.

33. Kalbeck III: 164. These sheets have been catalogued by Bozarth, and are described and discussed in "Liedersammlungen" (his sources B1 and B2).

34. BW III: 126-27.

35. This is a different text from the one Brahms used in Op. 22/5.

36. Bozarth, "Liedersammlungen." The appearance of this text in the Corner sheets, with the verses which Brahms set marked, and a reference to Meister for the melody and the first verse of text, disproves Kross's contention (p. 362) that the motet must have been composed in 1860, earlier than the 1863-64 period to which Kalbeck (III: 164) assigns it. Kalbeck used the Corner sheets also, but mistakenly said that both text and tune appear there.

37. There is one discrepancy between the *Werke* and Peters editions of this piece; this autograph agrees with the *Werke* in having an E natural in the alto line at the word "Schaden." See also Mandyczewski's "Revisionsbericht," *Werke* 21: v.

38. Bozarth, "Liedersammlungen." This collection is his source H. Kalbeck (I: 185) says only that it came to Brahms through "ein glücklicher Zufall."

39. Kross, "Volksliedbearbeitungen," esp. p. 20 and note 13. According to Bozarth (ibid.), "Erlaube mir, fein's Mädchen" is in Brahms's hand; he also points out that A 129 was copied too late to have been Brahms's source for the songs he chose to set.

40. *Briefe* I: 52.

41. For a description of this collection, see pp. 62-63.

42. The 1549 edition of Forster III in the British Library corresponds to Nottebohm's "corrected" version. Brahms used an X to point out the correction, written on another stave. Nottebohm employed a form of NB which looks very much like Brahms's but is, in fact, his own; a similar form is sometimes used by other writers also.

43. Brahms's gift volume of Forster I from Karlsruhe was made from the 1560 edition.

44. The secular version of "Es wollt ein Jäger jagen" here is not the same as the early seventeenth century sacred tune included in the Corner sheets of A 128, although they are clearly related.

45. Robert Eitner, "Verzeichniss neuer Ausgaben alter Musikwerke aus der frühesten Zeit bis zum Jahre 1800" (1871). This catalog, one of the first of the reference works produced by the indefatigable Eitner, was an invaluable tool in the effort to track down Brahms's sources for his Abschriften. I am grateful to Rudolf and Uta Henning for drawing my attention to it. All information about holdings of particular libraries comes from Eitner's *Quellenlexikon*.

46. Identified by Bozarth, who subsequently included this sketch in his article "Duets."

47. Mandyczewski (p. 10) exaggerates the amount of music which Brahms transcribed from partbooks.

48. BW VI: 7. Kalbeck (II: 46) mentions the Calvisius setting, in connection with the letter to Joachim, as though Calvisius had composed the tune and this were Brahms's first contact with it. Bozarth, in "Liedersammlungen," points out that it is also in Corner and Meister, and discusses the possible date of composition of Op. 91/2.

49. Brahms used at least the bass book of the set in the Hofbibliothek to check details of Schütz's "Saul, Saul" when he was preparing for the Singakademie performance of 7 January 1864, and wrote a note to this effect in his own copy of Winterfeld's *Gabrieli*, which contains the piece with his performance markings. If he had already used the Archiv books for his transcription, it seems likely that he would also have used them to prepare his performance copy; therefore perhaps these transcriptions were made after early 1864.

50. Information about *Souterliedekens,* with special reference to this piece (printed as an example) and its tenor, is given by Reese, pp. 355-58.

51. The piece does not appear in the index of the Praetorius complete works. A recent edition, with no more information than is given by Winterfeld, is available in the collection *Ave Maria, dich lobt Musica.*

52. No mention is made of any of Winterfeld's books, however, in the partial list from Schumann's own catalog given by Boetticher, p. 296.

53. This could be the unidentified work by Praetorius that Brahms told Joachim he had worked on in the autumn of 1857 in Detmold (BW V: 191); another possibility would certainly be "Es ist ein' Ros' entsprungen," which had been published by Winterfeld and in numerous other collections—then, as now, Praetorius's best-known piece.

54. *Brahms an Spengel,* p. 27, where Brahms referred to it as "ein lieblicher Gegensatz zu dem Bach'schen Choral." Spengel performed "Choräle in Tonsätzen von J. S.

Bach, J. R. Ahle, H. Isaac und M. Praetorius" in the 1887 concert by his Hamburg choir which also included the first version of Brahms's "Im Herbst" (Op. 104/5). Presumably the "Choräle" were the two "Es ist genug" settings and "Innsbruck"; the Praetorius was certainly "Es ist ein' Ros' entsprungen." (Hofmann, Detroit exhibition catalog, no. 154; private comm.)

55. Geiringer (*ZfM*, 1933) has transcribed and published this version.

56. Geiringer's published transcription of this piece and Ahle's setting (ibid.) gives only the final version found in A 130; no mention is made of the stages that Brahms went through to reach it, nor of the subsequent changes made before the performance. See Hancock, "Performances."

57. *The Festschrift der Wiener Singakademie . . . 1858-1908* has lists of all the programs Brahms conducted, pp. 43-44. In the program for 6 January 1864, the last two items are " 'Motette' von J. S. Bach (Liebster Gott, wann muss [sic] ich sterben etc.)" and " 'Choral' von J. S. Bach (Herrsche [sic] über Tod und Leben)." It seems likely that the "Motette" was the first chorus of Cantata 8, and that it and the final chorale were performed without the remainder of the cantata.

58. Hübbe, p. 66; Drinker, pp. 103-4.

59. See A 136 and the later performance versions. These copies and their history are discussed in Hancock, "Performances."

60. The only set in Vienna is in the Archiv, but the Discantus I book is missing. The 1603 edition, from which the Calvisius transcription in A 130, 11-12 was made, contains the Gallus motet also, but the bass figures found here do not appear in that edition.

61. The sketch is only three measures long, and has been thoroughly scratched out in red and blue pencil. The text appears to be "Aus meinem Vaterland verbannt," and the rhythm is the dotted quarter—eighth pattern of several of the Zigeunerlieder and Hungarian dances.

62. These two sheets of Eberle no. 17 paper (Vienna) were originally a bifolio, but they have come apart. Sheet 22 is blank.

63. SWV 3; text "al nostro lamentar vi lamentaste." *Neue Schütz-Gesamtausgabe* 22: 19, mm. 14-16.

64. SWV 11; text "crudelissimo Silvio." *Neue Ausgabe* 22: 78, mm. 9-12.

65. SWV 15; *Neue Ausgabe* 22: 103-9, mm. 1-8, 32-41.

66. Brahms was unhappy with Spitta's decision to use the original clefs in his edition, though he was in general an advocate of the use of SATB clefs in choral music. See a letter to Heinrich von Herzogenberg, in *Correspondence*, p. 400, in which Brahms also mentions the transcription-by-transposition method suggested by Spitta in his introduction to volume IV (1887): xxii.

67. Not by Schütz. See Moser, pp. 660-61; *Schütz Werke Verzeichnis*, p. xi.

68. In the tutti sections of this psalm, the two choruses are reduced onto four staves in the Abschrift.

69. In Psalms 8 and 84, Brahms changed the clefs from Spitta's originals to his preferred SATB clefs, but without any transposition.

70. Brahms copied this text "Wohnungen," the way it appears in his own *Requiem*.

71. Kalbeck I: 286.

72. Giuseppe Corsi, who was active in Rome from 1659 to 1678 (Eitner, *Quellenlexikon*), not Jacopo Corsi of the Florentine Camerata; these two are confused in some editions of the piece.

73. It is in connection with these copies that Kalbeck's error about the possible dates for Köster paper is significant (see above, n. 24). Kalbeck himself noted the date of copying of the Hungarian tunes, however (I: 174).

74. See, for example, Kross, *Chorwerke*, p. 562; Morik, p. 160; and Beuerle, p. 65.

75. I am grateful to the firm Robert Lienau of Berlin for the loan from their archives of a number of the separately published pieces in order that I might determine unequivocally that the collection, now extremely rare, was Brahms's source. Dr. Frese of Robert Lienau informed me that the pieces comprising volume I were published separately beginning in July 1852, and that there is no longer any record of when the collected volume was printed (Eitner's *Verzeichniss* gives a date of 1853). See A130, 1-6 for more information about volume II, published in 1856.

76. Eitner explains this complicated publishing history in his *Verzeichniss*, but gives no reason for it.

77. Three of the four pieces in A130, 27-29 also appeared in the Bote & Bock series: the Lotti is found both in II (1841): no. 19 and V (n.d.): no. 14; and the Durante and Corsi appeared in V: nos. 9 and 10 respectively. A "Misericordias Domini" à 8 by Durante in Bote & Bock's VII: no. 3 is a different piece.

78. If that were the case, he must not yet have developed his decided preference for SATB clefs.

79. "Vere languores nostros" is found in the Stimmenhefte made by the members of the Hamburg Frauenchor (Hübbe, p. 66; Drinker, pp. 103-4).

80. Kalbeck (I: 386) says that Brahms found this piece in the library in Hamburg, and that it provided the inspiration for his own "Adoramus te" for women's voices, Op. 37/2; however, see below, chap. 3, n. 27.

81. Nottebohm also copied some sections of the same work into his large instrumental collection (in the Brahms Nachlass; see p. 66). He may have called Brahms's attention to it in the first place.

82. Hoboken XXIIIc: C19, Pastorella de Nocte, 3rd movement.

83. Both sheets are discussed by Helms in "Brahms und Bach," pp. 60-61.

84. *Clara Schumann-Brahms Briefe* I: 464.

85. Alfred Dürr in *MGG* 5 (1956): col. 1839.

86. Hermann Levi, the conductor in Karlsruhe and a close friend of Brahms until the mid-1870s, wrote to him in February 1869 both to ask him to conduct the *Requiem* and to send him a copy of the *Lukaspassion*, which he had obtained from Hauser. Levi asked Brahms whether he thought the Passion was really by Bach, and if so, whether he would undertake the preparation of an edition for publication. Brahms replied, in letters to both Allgeyer and Levi, that he would not lift a finger to publish

such a work under the name of Bach; that if the handwriting looked like Bach's perhaps there was an ass with the same handwriting; and that the music could only have been written by "our Bach" if he were still so young that he was wetting his bed. The entire exchange appears in BW VII: 33-39, and is quoted by Kalbeck (II: 313ff.). The Passion manuscript is now thought to be a copy made by Bach of some other composer's work.

87. McCorkle, ed., *Haydn Variations*, p. 28. This edition contains a reproduction of the Abschrift. The piece has also been attributed to Ignaz Pleyel.

88. Probably Johann Anton André's *Lehrbuch der Tonsatzkunst*, parts 1 & 2 (1832-40), which contains a section on canons, according to Riemann, *Musiklexikon* (12th ed., 1972) 1: 23.

89. Drinker, pp. 103-4.

90. These appear to be instructions to the printer for the publication of the canons in Op. 113. The canons are no. 5, "Wille wille will" (the end of no. 4, "Schlaf, Kindlein, schlaf" is also found here); no. 10, "Leise Töne der Brust"; and no. 11, "Ich weiss nicht, was im Hain die Taube girret."

91. The many fragments from the works of Bach are discussed but not listed by Helms in "Brahms und Bach," p. 48; Mast gives all sources and exact citations.

92. Mast (pp. 93-101, 191) assumes that Brahms made the transcriptions from partbooks himself. However, the citation of the Musikverein (the Gesellschaft der Musikfreunde) and the tidy appearance of the copies suggest that Brahms was probably copying someone else's transcription, one he had found in the Archiv. (Eitner lists a set of partbooks in the Hofbibliothek.)

93. Wüllner's *Chorübungen* III, which Brahms acquired in 1881, should be in the Nachlass. See p. 10 above.

94. May, 2nd ed., p. 339; *Briefe* I: 426, 428.

95. In the Brahms-Joachim correspondence (BW V), all of Brahms's letters during this period come from Düsseldorf. In June he was also working on Op. 30 and the canonic mass.

96. Boetticher does not include the mass in his partial list of the contents of Schumann's library (p. 296). However, since Schumann himself recommended the study of the old Italian masters, "damit man hinter den Gesangsgeist komme" (quoted by Kalbeck I: 185, and many others), it is not unlikely that he owned a copy. See Haberl's edition, p. v, n. 2, for a list of published editions and a comment on the proliferation of manuscript scores.

97. His copy of the Crucifixus in A130, 28-29 is in the original key with unreduced note values, as it appeared in Schlesinger's *Musica Sacra*.

98. The Agnus II was not printed in sixteenth-century editions of the mass, but was obtained from manuscript sources in Rome. See Lockwood's edition, pp. 86, 191.

99. These dynamics are discussed, and photographs of pp. 16 and 17, the central part of the Credo, are given, in Fellinger, *Über die Dynamik,*, pp. 87-88. The solo and tutti indications which Fellinger mentions, except for those at "et incarnatus est" and

"et homo factus est," are in ink in the Abschrift, and presumably come from Brahms's unknown source. Also see Hancock, "Performances."

100. Boetticher, pp. 296, 229. A Crucifixus a 6 by Lotti, in a published version, is also in the Brahms Nachlass, but is not mentioned in the partial list of Schumann's library.

101. *Briefe* I: 207.

102. Schlesinger I: no. 8; Bote & Bock V: no. 13; Rochlitz IIIb. Hohenemser (p. 44) calls this famous work the most important model of a "subjective outpouring" based on chromaticism in the a cappella style.

103. I have not seen a copy of Marx's edition. However, the Crucifixus a 8 appeared as Beilage VI to the *Allgemeine musikalische Zeitung* 21 (1819) to illustrate an article (cols. 850-56) by F. H. A. B. Merx [sic]. The heading is simply "Crucifixus v. Lotti," the tempo is misprinted "Largo assi," and some other details are different; but otherwise it is the same as Brahms's Abschrift. Therefore it seems probable that the later Marx edition, with the mistakes corrected, was owned by Schumann and copied by Brahms.

104. Some but not all of the *Allgemeine musikalische Zeitung* supplements are listed by Eitner. The Lotti Crucifixus a 8 (described in note 103 above) is also missing from his *Verzeichniss*.

105. *Briefe* I: 206; BW V: 191. To Clara he wrote, "I can't tell you much about Rovetta except that he lived about 1640." He also told her that he thought the piece was easy for old church music.

106. The parts, which were preserved until 1979 in the archives of the Singakademie (in 1976 a few samples were moved to the Archiv), appear to have been made from Brahms's altered version, with some additional features from another copy of the score (not in Brahms's hand) also found at the Singakademie in 1976.

107. The Singakademie score, on the other hand (see note 106), is in treble and bass clefs only, and the figured bass does not appear. There is a pencil note at the top of the score, perhaps in Brahms's hand: "Klingt als ob eine füllende Begleitung fehlte (in dieser Form n. möglich)" (sounds as though a filling-out accompaniment is missing [in this form not possible]).

108. Jeppesen, p. 47, says the piece "without doubt owes its origin to a later master." In the 1954 edition of *Chorübungen* it is ascribed to Ingegneri.

109. *Briefe* I: 221-24. See p. 11 above.

110. Boetticher, p. 296. Brahms acquired his own copy after 1868.

111. Brahms also was acquainted with a number of Eccard's works, including "Übers Gebirg," from Winterfeld's *Der evangelische Kirchengesang.*

112. Drinker, pp. 103-4. Brahms's arrangement was published by Henry S. Drinker in the University of Pennsylvania Choral Series, no. 75a.

113. See below, p. 89. The Eccard "Übers Gebirg" in Bote & Bock's *Musica Sacra* XI (ed. Rebling) is a different piece, in four parts.

114. I have not seen original partbooks, and do not know how the various versions of the text arose.

115. Hübbe, p. 18; Kalbeck I: 386. See p. 115 below.

116. J. R. Milne, in *Grove* (5th ed.) 4: 484.

117. For "Velum templi," Eitner's reference to *Musica Sacra* (Bote & Bock) XVI is incorrect; the piece is in volume XIV. A copy of the printed edition of "Tenebrae" which belonged to Kiesewetter is now in the Nationalbibliothek, Vienna.

118. Boetticher, 292. The particular pieces are not specified.

119. Dietrich, *Erinnerungen,* p. 18, quotes a letter written in July, when Brahms reported that he had finished the job, and could now spend all his time sitting and studying.

120. See A130, 15 for a description of this work by Winterfeld. These 1854 Abschriften are the earliest ones Brahms made from this source.

121. The first version may have been copied from Winterfeld for comparison. See the discussion below.

122. For proper names such as "Isaak" (Isaac) and "Insbruck" (Innsbruck), I have chosen to use the spellings at hand in the particular document being discussed.

123. See the further discussion of rhythm in chapter 3 below (p. 160). Brahms used Winterfeld as the source for the complete Abschrift A134, 43-44.

124. Brahms also made an Abschrift of Stoltzer's Tenorlied setting of the secular song (A130, 7-8).

125. Hübbe, p. 66. Drinker includes the Hassler in her list of pieces by composers other than Brahms (pp. 103-4), but gives "Insbruck" only in the list of folk-song arrangements.

126. BW V: 161.

127. When the Abschriften were first examined by the present writer, the two printed sheets which should have been attached were missing. They were later found marking the pages in the Liliencron collection to which Brahms refers, and were returned to A135.

128. V (1892): 45; and VI (bibliography, 1893).

129. On one of his sheets, Brahms corrected the position of a misplaced fermata with blue pencil.

130. The same setting also appears in the 1561 edition of *Psalmodia,* but not in the earliest edition of 1553 (British Library).

131. Liliencron, *Die historischen Volkslieder der Deutschen,* Nachtrag "Die Töne" (1869): p. 25; Meister, *Das katholische deutsche Kirchenlied* I (1862): no. 131; Böhme, *Altdeutsches Liederbuch* (1877), p. 646. All in the Brahms Nachlass.

132. "Brahms als Musikhistoriker," p. 12; "The Brahms Library," pp. 11-12. (In Orel's catalog, an entry added after Brahms's death gives the composer as "Bonnot," a French incarnation.) This artifact of Latin grammar is doubly confusing when one remembers that an Italian/Viennese composer named Giuseppe Bonno was active during the eighteenth century, but is very unlikely to have set such a text in such a manner!

133. Zahn and other authorities; also Geffcken (1857). Johannes Geffcken was the pastor who confirmed Brahms in 1848, according to Niemann (p. 11), who calls him "a distinguished hymnologist" and gives him much of the credit for Brahms's thorough knowledge of the Bible.

134. See Hancock, "Performances," for a history of the different versions. The performance score (catalogued as Q2602, with the earlier Signatur V/25463) and some of the single parts (Stimmen 25463)—those containing Brahms's changes, corrections, and original dynamic markings for the Palestrina—have been moved from the general music collection of the Archiv into the autograph section. One additional piece, Haydn's "Betrachtung des Todes," appears in the parts only.

135. These changes do not appear in the Geiringer transcriptions of the two chorales published with *Zeitschrift für Musik* (1933).

136. Dehn's collection, bound into one volume, is in the Archiv. It once belonged to Mandyczewski, who wrote a pencil note inside the front cover saying that volume 1 appeared in October 1836. Brahms learned the motet before he knew Mandyczewski; the two men first came into contact in 1879.

137. *Music in the Renaissance*, p. 381.

138. See the description of the Brahms catalogs, pp. 9-10 above.

139. According to the Brahms-Levi correspondence (BW VII: 34), the performance took place on 12 May 1869. The plans were changed several times, however, and the commission for the Forster copy was probably made some time in advance of the actual date of the performance.

140. RISM numbers 1560^{25}, 1553^{30}, 1552^{28}, 1556^{28}, and 1556^{29} respectively. Geiringer in "Brahms Library" gives only a publication date of 1549; in "Brahms als Musikhistoriker" he gives 1551.

141. Johann Gottfried Walther's *Lexikon* (1732), in Brahms's library. Walther summarizes Praetorius's description of three types: in the first each part has a different and complete text; in the second each part has its own text, but it is broken up and distorted; and in the third all voices have the same text at the same time, but it is incomplete and truncated, and soon a different text interrupts it.

142. Otto Biba, private comm., June 1983. I am greatly indebted to Dr. Biba for his identification of Nottebohm's hand and for a copy of the collection of melodies. It was missing in 1976 and was later found with the sheets separated, but has now been reassembled, bound, and catalogued.

143. Brahms was with Nottebohm when he died in Graz, and their mutual friend Pohl made the necessary decisions about the disposition of Nottebohm's library (Kalbeck III: 370). Perhaps Brahms requested these items because of the copies he had made years earlier.

144. Nottebohm probably made a substantially larger number of transcriptions of polyphonic Lieder settings than that which is now in the Brahms Nachlass. The collection of tunes has 38 numbers (of these, three include more than one tune for the same text, and five are listed with references to sources but without tunes), whereas the polyphonic collection now contains only 26 settings of different tunes. Presumably

the others were lost at some unknown time, since unfortunately neither Nottebohm nor Brahms had the collection bound.

145. The composer of this setting was not identified when the transcription was made. However, a note has been added, saying that the setting is by Walter and has already been printed as no. 7 in Winterfeld's *Dr. Martin Luther's deutsche geistl. Lieder* (Leipzig, 1840).

146. The changes are described above, pp. 20-22. Although Nottebohm had written the text only in the soprano of Zirler's "Die Sonn' die ist verblichen," he copied the tenor into his collection of melodies.

147. Orel, *Brahms und Allgeyer,* p. 13; my translation.

148. Morik, in his discussion of Schumann's study of Italian polyphony and its influence on Brahms (p. 160), cites a "Facsimileabdruck v. Schumanns Spartierung d. 'Adoramus te Christi' b. H. Abert, R. Schumann, Berlin, 4. Aufl. 1920, S. 90." An earlier edition of Abert's *Schumann* in the Archiv has no such facsimile. It may be that Schumann did indeed prepare his own score of the piece from partbooks somewhere, but it seems much more likely that the work spoken of is, in fact, this Abschrift from Tucher.

149. Actually by Roselli (Reese, p. 469).

150. Also copied by Clara Schumann (A134, 29-34), whose source was Rochlitz's collection. The piece is not by Palestrina.

151. Composer unknown (Reese, p. 601).

152. *Briefe* I: 153-54.

153. Drinker, pp. 103-4. Hübbe (p. 66) includes them in his list of works arranged by Brahms for four-part women's choir; but the pieces, both in this manuscript and in Alfieri, are already for soprano and alto voices only.

154. He provided similar help to the copyist at the Musikverein for the oboe and English horn parts in the Pastoral Symphony from Bach's *Christmas Oratorio.* The original parts are for oboe d'amore and oboe da caccia.

155. In Brahms's copy of the Schütz *Werke*: VI (1887), this piece contains a number of his annotations, including question marks, corrections, and notations about parallels. He also called attention to it by underlining its number.

156. The manuscript has the note "Si conosce fatto due nomi di Giacomo Perti = e di Giuseppe Corsi."

157. BW XVI: 52, 54, 60. Flynn Warmington has found that the errors in this copy correspond to those Brahms mentioned to Spitta in BW XVI: 62 (personal comm., November 1982).

158. Specht (transl. Blom), p. 270. His source is presumably Siegfried Ochs's reminiscences, *Geschehenes, Gesehenes* (Leipzig, 1922), to which he refers in another connection. Also see Fellinger, "Brahms und die Epochen vergangener Musik," pp. 152-53.

159. *Die Bibliothek von Johannes Brahms* (1974).

160. It has already been observed, in connection with the Abschriften not made by Brahms, that not everything he owned was listed in his catalogs. Unfortunately, finding every-

thing he left out is a logically impossible job. When such works were located among the Abschriften, the finds were made through a knowledge of what Brahms had performed, through the helpfulness of Drs. Mitringer and Biba, and through blind luck.

161. Brahms owned collections by Arnold, Loman, and Tappert; one of the two Dutch collections by Loman is missing. See Bozarth, "Liedersammlungen," for comments on the Arnold volumes.

162. Geiringer, "Brahms and Chrysander," p. 131.

163. Friedrich Nicolai published it, under the title *Eyn feyner kleyner Almanach vol schönerr echterr liblicherr Volckslieder,* as a satire on the new folk song movement. Many of the melodies were parodies composed by Reichardt or himself, but some quickly assumed the status of real folk songs. See Harrison, p. 91, and the *New Grove* article on Nicolai.

164. The writings of Morik, Wiora, Friedländer, and others deal exhaustively with this subject. Also see the discussion below, p. 81, in connection with Kretzschmer & Zuccalmaglio's collection.

165. In his introduction (pp. 2-3), Wüllner gives many of his sources and explains his editing procedures. He emphasizes the importance of stressing word accents and disregarding bar lines, and says that many of his dynamic signs are intended to aid in that process. He also says that other performance suggestions are given mainly for pedagogical purposes—to provide practice in sight-reading interpretive material as well as notes—and that most conductors will want to use their own ideas also. He warns especially against trying too hard and thus producing too pretentious renditions—"the worst thing that can happen to these pearls of early composition."

166. Quoted by Kalbeck (II: 76).

167. Appendix 3 contains a list of the entire collection of printed material on early music, arranged alphabetically by composer, author, editor, or title.

168. I am grateful to Dr. A. Hyatt King for calling my attention to this volume. See chap. 2, n. 9; also see May, 1st ed. (1905) I: 188; 2nd ed. (1948), pp. 197-98.

169. *Briefe* I: 156. My translation.

170. Hofmann, *Bibliothek,* pp. xxiii, xxvii.

171. Mandyczewski, p. 7; Geiringer, *Brahms,* pp. 22-23.

172. Brahms-Clara Schumann *Briefe* I: 154.

173. BW V: 123.

174. A copy of Simon Sechter's 1843 edition of Marpurg's *Kunst der Fuge,* given to Brahms by Clara Schumann in Jan. 1856, is also in the Archiv. It is described by Hofmann in the Detroit exhibition catalog, p. 31.

175. Harriss, p. 11.

176. Harriss's book contains, after a brief introduction, an English translation of the entire work.

177. The catalog number shows that this book is not shelved with the other contents of Brahms's library in the Archiv; hence it was overlooked in my investigation. I am grateful to Otto Biba for his answers to questions, and for copies of a number of pages.

178. "Das Buch ist neben die deutschen Sagen von Grimm zu stellen, denn es gehört Johannes." The *Deutsche Sagen* of the Brothers Grimm had been a gift from Joachim to Brahms the previous summer (see Hofmann, *Bibliothek,* p. 39).

179. Harriss, p. 104. Unfortunately, this short passage does not go far toward answering Kross's question (*Chorwerke,* pp. 462, 617) about how far Brahms was acquainted with the Figurenlehre of the Baroque period.

180. Harriss, p. 263; the original (p. 109) is "dass er viel hören, aber wenig nachahmen müsse."

181. Harriss, p. 514; the latter phrase is part of a quotation from Werckmeister.

182. Harriss, p. 865.

183. "Brahms library," p. 13.

184. Morik, pp. 17, 21.

185. BW XVI: 98-99.

186. Böhme, p. lxxii. "Jene mittelalterlichen Tonsätze des 15. und 16. Jahrhunderts, selbst die der sogenannten klassischen periode des Contrapunktes zu Palestrina's, O. Lassos Zeit sind uns modernen Menschen des 19. Jahrhunderts grundlich f r e m d a r t i g und für die Menge wie für den modernen Künstler, der sich nicht gerade in das Historische hineingelebt hat, u n g e n i e s s b a r geworden."

187. See Brahms's correspondence with Spitta, Deiters, and others, cited by Fellinger in "Grundzüge," pp. 114-16, and many other commentators.

188. A quantity of blue pencil comment on the paper cover of the book has unfortunately been obliterated.

189. BW XVI: 97.

190. Wiora shows that most of the tunes appearing in the collection do originally stem from authentic folk music, but that they were altered and "romanticized" by Zuccalmaglio in ways that tended to make them more appealing to Brahms.

191. Wiora examines all the folk song collections published after Nicolai's *Almanach* and ascertains the sources for most of the tunes. Zuccalmaglio composed a few himself also.

192. See p. 159 below. In discussing changes Zuccalmaglio made in the genuine tunes through lack of understanding of early music, Wiora (p. 129) cites his alterations of note values in order to create regular two-bar or four-bar phrases, and his imposition of regular rhythms in the cases of some tunes in free, unmeasured rhythm.

193. BW XVI: 99.

194. See A128, 14-21, the Corner sheets. (See also p. 122 below.) Meister's edition is also discussed by Bozarth ("Liedersammlungen," source C), who points out that it con-

tains "Ach lieber Herre Jesu Christ," obtained from Wackernagel (1860), and also set by Brahms.

195. Perhaps Brahms first learned of Corner's *Gesangbuch* from this introduction. It is one of Meister's sources.

196. See the discussion of A134, 39-40, where Eitner's low opinion of this collection is cited.

197. Kalbeck (I: 382) gives Wackernagel as the source, presumably relying on Ophüls. Kross (p. 78) dismisses Ophüls' attribution on the ground that Wackernagel's collection appeared after Op. 13; but he has reversed the publication dates of Wackernagel's two collections, so that this one could in fact be the source. See the further discussion of this problem in Hancock, "Evidence."

198. "Die Sonn' die ist verblichen." Brahms had copied Zirler's setting into A130, 7-8. The tunes' Stollen are identical, but there are major differences in the Abgesang.

199. Morik (p. 39) also discusses and prints Arnold's tune. He does not mention the Forster model, but takes Wackernagel's word for the attribution, and comments that the tune resembles the nineteenth-century buildings constructed in "echt" Romanesque or Gothic style.

200. BW VII: 120; my translation.

201. This is the original version of the song. Brahms had set the tune by Reichardt. See A128, 5-12 (chap. 2, n. 32).

202. Geiringer, in "Brahms . . . Mandyczewski," p. 378; and in "Brahms als Musikhistoriker," pp. 11-12.

203. BW XVI: 85-86 (letter of 2 Dec. 1888). He may have read it more often in later years; Mandyczewski referred casually in a letter written during the summer of 1890 (ibid., p. 343) to someone whom Brahms would remember from an article in the *Vierteljahrsschrift.*

204. Vol. 9: 304ff. A number of the examples in "Octaven und Quinten" are taken from villanelle, and there is a reference to this article on p. 6 of the manuscript.

205. For the significance of the Bach *Werke* in nineteenth-century music, see Blume, *Two Centuries of Bach,* pp. 59ff.

206. Brahms went back to the volumes that had come out before the biography was published (2 vols., 1873, 1880) to add these notes.

207. During the planning for his first performance of Cantata 21, Brahms wrote to ask Joachim for the same kinds of advice he had given on Cantata 4. Joachim had not looked carefully at Cantata 21 before, and when he did, he wrote to Brahms (BW V: 230; my translation): "The Bach cantata is truly amazing, even when one is so used to astonishment as with this master. Heavens, how powerful, how free in dealing with his resources, how bold, how deep!"

208. See below for Handel's *Samson* (chap. 2, n. 217).

209. Brahms's continuo realizations are described by Geiringer in "Brahms als Musikhistoriker," p. 17. Fellinger discusses the effects of his performance dynamics in *Über die Dynamik,* pp. 86-94, and gives specific examples. Helms, in "Brahms und Bach"

(pp. 71-73), describes the performance markings in Brahms's set of the *Werke* and in the single copy of Cantata 4 without realizing that many were not made by Brahms; he does not mention the Archiv's set. See Hancock, "Performances."

210. Wüllner, in his introduction to the *Werke* edition of the motets (39: xxxii), says that Brahms may have been the first person to point out that the verse is a true chorale variation. Brahms put a light pencil mark in the margin beside this paragraph.

211. Geiringer, in "The Brahms Library," p. 12, cites this copy as an example of music used for Brahms's own performances, as does Helms in "Brahms und Bach," p. 75. However, there is no record that he ever performed "Jesu, meine Freude," and these performance markings are certainly not his.

212. BW XV: 54.

213. See Reese, pp. 355-58.

214. An example of complex rhythm in this piece is described below, p. 164.

215. Archiv catalog number: Stimmen 25206. See Hancock, "Performances."

216. Mandyczewski, p. 9; James, p. 13.

217. Brahms's copy of *Samson* contains a full set of performance markings which resemble his but are not. The volume was probably used by Franz Schalk, who conducted the work at the Musikverein for the first time on 10 January 1912 (Perger & Hirschfeld, p. 319), before the Archiv's other copy of *Samson* was acquired in the 1923 transaction.

218. Fellinger, *Dynamik*, pp. 89-91, has some examples from the Handel works. Also see Hancock, "Performances," and p. 153 below.

219. The third penitential psalm (Ps. 77), verse 4, text "et sicut onus grave gravatae sunt super me."

220. Also from the third psalm, verse 7, text "Quoniam lumbi mei impleti sunt illusionibus, et non est sanitas in carne mea."

221. These volumes have also been used occasionally by other people. Annotations not made by Brahms appear in volumes I, IV, V, VIII, and XI.

222. See the description of Brahms's copy of Winterfeld's *Gabrieli* below, pp. 96-101. He also owned Wüllner's edition (1878) of three of the *Psalmen Davids* (see p. 33). Wüllner's *Chorübungen* III (1880) contains several works by Lasso, but none by any other of these composers.

223. The examples given here are taken from the *Neue Ausgabe*, with its transpositions and bar lines.

224. BW VII: 120.

225. Blume, pp. 42-43; he quotes Rochlitz as calling Bach the Dürer and Handel the Rubens of German music. Blume also says (p. 27) that Rochlitz was one of the choristers of St. Thomas, Leipzig, at the time of the famous occasion when Mozart first encountered the Bach motet "Singet dem Herrn."

226. For a complete list of the contents, see Ebinger, pp. 124-26. The remaining volumes continue to 1760. Besseler, p. 10, characterizes the selection as "often accidental," like most of those made by the enthusiastic amateurs who published the first collections of early music.

227. Rochlitz evidently had no notion of musica ficta at all. One wonders why Brahms wrote no comment when Rochlitz put an asterisk at "memoria," where he had neglected to add an editorial B flat in the soprano where it is needed because of an original E flat in the bass, and then explained in a note (my translation): "These especially intense dissonances just before the end of a piece or a principal section are found in many of the earliest masters, especially the Germans. Our ear can so little accommodate them that—it would have to be tried—one could unhesitatingly discard the flat and therefore have E sung instead of E flat." In the very same chord Brahms corrected an incorrect tenor C to E flat.

228. Kross, *Chorwerke,* p. 560.

229. Moser (transl. Pfatteicher), p. xvi.

230. Quoted almost complete by Moser, pp. 623-24, though in the description of the long tenor notes he leaves out Winterfeld's comparison to the soprano of Handel's Hallelujah chorus. Brahms emphasized this series of notes not only with accents, but by reinforcing the soloist with the chorus tenors, in the parts prepared for his performance with the Singakademie (see Hancock, "Performances").

231. Kenton (pp. 195-96) lists the works by Giovanni Gabrieli published by Winterfeld. He does not include works by other composers.

232. The identifications of Gabrieli fragments given here in square brackets are Kenton's (ibid.). He does not specify which sections of those works were published by Winterfeld.

233. Actually a Ricercar, according to Kenton (p. 195).

234. This fragment is missing from Kenton's list (p. 196).

235. The appearance of this phenomenon in other examples in Brahms's early music library and in his own choral compositions is discussed below, pp. 159-67.

236. In a letter to Joachim in 1860 (BW V: 272), he wrote that he did not like six-four or even six-four-three chords in chorales.

237. See p. 157-58 below for Brahms's elimination of a Dorian sixth.

238. This piece is the only one of the new-style examples that Brahms chose to copy in A130, 1-6.

239. The parts survived until 1979 in the archives of the Singakademie, some with performance dynamics in Brahms's own hand. A few were loaned to the Gesellschaft der Musikfreunde in 1976, and are now nearly all which still exist. See Hancock, "Performances."

Chapter 3

1. This division is based very loosely on the outline by Kross in *Chorwerke* (pp. 50-67). In his long analytical section (pp. 71-524), he gives almost all the historical information available about each of Brahms's choral works. Only for the folk-song settings does he provide just a summary, since they are treated in detail by Morik. In "Volksliedbearbeitungen," Kross combines Morik's list of Brahms's settings and sources with new information obtained from the Hamburg Stimmenhefte; and Bozarth, in "Liedersammlungen," further revises this chronology.

2. A number of the works which were eventually published for mixed or for men's voices also appear in the Hamburg Stimmenhefte, either because they were originally composed for women's voices, or were arranged for them. See Drinker for a complete account, and the list provided by Gotwals and Kepler, pp. 53-58.

3. The only choral works omitted from the list are the folk-song settings from the Stimmenhefte (see the edition by Gotwals and Kepler, and other published versions given in their list, pp. 53-58); and a few small works which appear in the *Werke* XX and XXI (all without opus numbers): the folk-song settings nos. 23-26 for Vorsänger and chorus (all the choral parts are simple refrains), assorted canons, and two occasional pieces.

4. Copies in Grimm's hand of a Kyrie in G minor and of Sanctus, Benedictus, Hosanna, Agnus Dei, and Dona nobis pacem movements from Brahms's planned *Missa canonica* in C major, long thought to be lost, have recently been discovered; they were acquired by the Archiv in 1981, and publication is planned in the near future. See Kross, pp. 514-24, for all previously known information; and Bozarth " 'New' Manuscripts." (A Credo composed in 1861 remains lost.) In the present study, the mass movements are discussed in connection with the motet Op. 74/1 (pp. 133-35).

5. Kalbeck I: 389.

6. There is no actual record of these settings having been composed along with the previous group at Detmold. However, since they all appeared in the Hamburg Stimmenhefte (Kross, "Volksliedbearbeitungen"), and since they are like the Detmold settings in sources and style, it is probable they were set at the same time, even though they were eventually preserved in the archives of the Singakademie.

7. Beuerle (p. 89) suggests a date of 1856; see the discussion below (chap. 3, n. 25). No. 3 was composed for a Vienna group in 1863 and therefore appears as the last item in the list of early works.

8. Kross's assumption that Op. 41/1 must have been composed at about the same time as Op. 62/7 is confirmed by Bozarth ("Lieder 1868-71," p. 45).

9. See chap. 2, n. 36 above, and the discussion below, chap. 3, n. 75.

10. Beuerle (p. 81) points out that Brahms's production of these works coincided with the period when he was most actively seeking a permanent conducting position.

11. Kross classes the Chorlieder Op. 93a with the late works because of the "drive toward motivic concentration" which he says characterizes them (p. 408). Beuerle, on the other hand, prefers to deal with Opp. 62 and 93a together because of their strong similarities (p. 267), and contrasts these two sets with the more serious Op. 42 before and Op. 104 after them. Some of the songs in Op. 62 were actually composed in the early Hamburg years, but in Table 6 they are included with the others for convenience.

12. In correspondence with Dr. Abraham of Peters, Brahms mentioned the possibility that the quartets might be sung by small choirs, but he refused to allow "oder für kleineren Chor" to be printed on the title page of Op. 64 (Kalbeck III: 31).

13. Kamper, "Ein unbekanntes Brahms-Studienblatt."

14. Settings of both these songs are found in the Hamburg Stimmenhefte. There is no information on when the versions for mixed choir were composed, except that "Dort in den Weiden" was sung in a concert at the Gesellschaft der Musikfreunde in March

1873, and both pieces, in parts only, were preserved in the Archiv (Mandyczewski, Revisionsbericht, *Werke* XXI: v).

15. According to Kross (pp. 333-36), the first five may be assigned to 1873-74, but nos. 6 and 7 belong to the works written in Hamburg between 1859 and 1862. No. 6 appears in the Stimmenhefte in nearly identical form (published by Henry Drinker), and no. 7 is so similar to Op. 41/1 that it must surely have been composed at the same time (Bozarth, "Lieder 1868-71," p. 45, says that no. 7 is also in the Stimmenhefte and was composed in 1860). Kalbeck (III:40) thinks that the entire set was written in the early years, but Kross disagrees on stylistic grounds. A setting of the poem of no. 4 also appears in the Stimmenhefte, but it is entirely different from the later Op. 62 version, having only the key of A major and perhaps some harmonic tendencies in common with it. I am grateful to the Music Department of the Free Library of Philadelphia (Drinker Collection) for providing me with copies of this and the other Drinker editions listed in the bibliography.

16. This motet incorporates material from sections of the *Missa canonica* that were composed in 1856. See the discussion below, pp. 133-35.

17. Beuerle, pp. 68-69.

18. BW V: 152-53.

19. I have not seen corroboration of Florence May's statement (2nd ed., p. 351) that Brahms performed a "Madrigal" by John Bennet (1599) and a "Dance Song" by John [sic] Morley (1595), probably from Maier's collection (published with German texts), on 10 May 1864 for the "annual foundation concert of the Singakademie."

20. Geiringer, "Brahms Library," p. 11.

21. Brahms's correspondence is the best source of direct information, although he rarely expressed himself freely on the subject of his own works. He did discuss the folk-song settings with Spitta, Wüllner, Deiters, and others; and in one uncharacteristic letter, in which he was responding to some statements his friend Adolf Schubring had made in an article about the *Requiem,* he gave several examples of situations in which he had deliberately varied musical motives for specific purposes (BW VIII: 215-18; also see the discussion by Frisch, p. 231). Not only his letters, but also the reminiscences of people who knew him, are silent on the subject of "inspiration." See Fellinger, "Grundsätze," and McCorkle, "Obstacles," for further discussion of the problem.

22. *Chorwerke,* pp. 567-70.

23. Boetticher, p. 296.

24. In an often-quoted letter written in April 1856 (BW V: 137), Brahms asked Joachim about one of his canonic exercises, "Is it, not counting the ingenuity in it, good music?"

25. Beuerle (p. 89) suggests that an early date of composition is more reasonable than Kalbeck's suggested 1859 (I: 386), and mentions the involvement with Palestrina beginning at the latest in June 1856 (the date of the *Missa Papae Marcelli* copy).

26. The text is the same as that in Clara Schumann's "Palestrina" Abschrift (A134, 29-34).

27. Kalbeck (I: 386) says that it was inspired by Corsi's setting of the same text, which Brahms had copied. He assumes that Brahms's canon was composed in May 1859, when it was first sung by the Frauenchor, and implies that the Abschrift was made at about the same time; whereas we have seen in A130, 28-29 that it was actually made in early 1853 at the latest. It is difficult to see or hear anything in common between the two settings, which even differ to some extent in their texts.

28. For example, Beuerle (p. 90) points out the similarity of the opening phrase to "Surge illuminare," which is among the Abschriften (A130, 1-6). In his analysis of "Adoramus te" (pp. 89-101), Beuerle discusses motivic development and modal/ tonal ambiguity in the canon, but he never really addresses the issue of stylistic incongruity in the last few bars.

29. See, for example, the final cadence of the Sinfonia, the part writing in verse 1, m. 88, and the two Adagio bars in verse 3.

30. With the Bach precedent, the first chord in m. 25 of the Brahms version sounds like V_5^6 of V in D minor. Beuerle (p. 98) also finds Brahms's progression unexpected: his suggested alternatives are cadences on either A minor (from the E seventh) or G minor (from the D seventh passing chord); but he does not mention D minor as a possibility.

31. The tone is rather reminiscent of Mozart, and one cannot help wondering whether Brahms had recently heard his "Regina coeli" (K. 276), with its Handelian Hallelujahs, sung in Vienna.

32. BW VI: 277. The "Leiermann" is no. 13, based on the last song in Schubert's *Winterreise,* and the last of the Op. 113 canons to be composed. Geiringer (*Brahms,* p. 295) and others mention the similarity of its structure to that of the Reading rota, "Sumer is icumen in."

33. BW V: 191.

34. Kross, "Volksliedbearbeitungen." Also see A128, 5-12 and A129.

35. For the most part, the unpublished settings fall into Morik's category of those having the simplest possible relation to the tune (pp. 126-34); whereas those composed early but published in 1864 tend to appear in his middle category (pp. 135-48), where harmonic color and counterpoint assume greater importance. Morik did not have complete information about the contents of the Hamburg Stimmenhefte, so he assumes that all of the settings published in 1864 were composed for the Singakademie, and says that the style categories of the settings have no chronological significance (p. 132). See above, chap. 3, n. 1.

36. Beuerle, p. 101, discusses this aim with particular reference to Op. 12.

37. Beuerle (p. 213) says that this set of songs, along with Op. 42, represents the first important step in Brahms's development of the true Chorlied as a fusion of art song and folk song.

38. These two bars of canon with the text "allimmer dein" are not unlike the phrase "immerdar" which occurs in the *Requiem,* no. 4. Brahms appears to be text painting in both cases.

39. Kross (p. 187) fails to see the reason for these octave leaps and calls the whole piece one of Brahms's weaker works. I agree with many of his judgments on quality, but not with this one.

40. It is generally assumed that in most cases the women's chorus settings came first. Kross (p. 163) points out, however, that the six-voice, mixed chorus version of "Vineta" (Op. 42/2) may well have been written first. Henry Drinker has published the four-voice version for women's chorus.

41. Catalog number MH 12100/C. The sheet on which they appear is part of the collection given to the Stadtbibliothek by the son of Brahms's housekeeper, Celestine Truxa; it had been torn in half (presumably by Brahms) and thrown away, and then salvaged and taped back together (presumably by Frau Truxa).

42. This movement of the *Requiem* was largely composed in 1857-59, in the same period as Op. 13. It was originally part of a projected symphony which Brahms then transformed into his first piano concerto (Op. 15), leaving out this movement. See Geiringer, *Brahms,* p. 310, and others.

43. Kross (p. 79) says the error began with Heinrich Reimann, one of the earliest Brahms biographers.

44. The presumed source, Wackernagel's *Das deutsche Kirchenlied,* has been discussed above.

45. BW IV: 79. Also see the more detailed discussion of Op. 13 in Hancock, "Evidence."

46. BW IV: 83.

47. Clara Schumann (*Briefe* I: 285) did compare it to the Pastorale from Bach's *Christmas Oratorio*; a more apt comparison might be made with the Pastoral Symphony from Handel's *Messiah.* Beuerle notes the "Tristan'scher Harmonik" of mm. 82ff. (p. 107).

48. Kross (p. 83) says that the text misaccentuation is due to the work's conscious historicism; and Beuerle (p. 118), in connection with "Magdalena" (Op. 22/6), calls such a text-music relation one of the most striking characteristics of German church and folk songs of the fourteenth and fifteenth centuries.

49. Quoted by Beuerle (p. 109), Kross (p. 112), and others from BW IX: 23. The versions published by Henry Drinker for women's voices are transpositions of the mixed chorus edition, not actual transcriptions from the Stimmenhefte (no. 3 does not appear).

50. I: 386.

51. Hohenemser, pp. 70-71, also makes this point.

52. The equivalent secular text appears in Greitter's Tenorlied, "Es wollt ein Jäger jagen" (A130, 7-8), and a different sacred version is in Corner.

53. Kross, p. 149; Hofmann, *Bibliothek,* p. 69.

54. Kross (pp. 160-61) makes the point that these songs are unacceptable nowadays, but that their nationalistic fervor was nothing out of the ordinary when they were written. He also suggests (p. 141) that Brahms may have composed so few works for men's voices not only because he lacked opportunities to perform them, but because he did not care to contribute to a genre in which such a large amount of very bad music had been written.

55. Kross, pp. 153, 350. It is interesting to note that many examples of triads *not* in root position are found in the sixteenth-century settings among the Abschriften.

56. Friedländer (p. 60) says that in 1884 Brahms told him that he wished he had used quarter-note units instead of half notes in Op. 43/3. The only one of the folk-song settings in this notation is "Ach lieber Herre Jesu Christ," which in its simple chordal style is like this earlier pair of settings, except that many first-inversion triads are used. See the discussion on p. 123.

57. Helms (p. 107) places both in his category "whole melodies or melodic framework are taken over with the text and in part newly formed." However, Friedländer (p. 60) prints the 1519 tune of "Ich schell mein Horn" by Arnt von Aich, and it is similar in outline but by no means in detail. Harrison (p. 4) also gives the early and Brahms tunes for "Ich schell mein Horn." Likewise, Forster's "Vergangen ist mir Glück und Heil" (1539; the setting is published in *Antiqua Chorbuch* II/1: p. 60) has a tenor which bears only the faintest resemblance in outline to Brahms's tune; Forster's tenor is not even in one of the church modes, but uses the major scale.

58. II: 16.

59. Geiringer (*Brahms,* p. 299) refers to the influence of Mendelssohn.

60. Gál, p. 124.

61. Harrison, p. 34; Gál, p. 124.

62. Kross, pp. 164-68. He uses the same image (p. 141) to describe Brahms's command of the canon form in the first section of Op. 29/2.

63. Beuerle, pp. 80, 243, 267. He analyzes "Abendständchen" at length, pp. 257-68.

64. The harmonic motion is faster than Bach's tends to be, however. Beuerle (pp. 127-29) compares Brahms's setting with one of Bach's of the same chorale (*371 Chorales,* no. 4). Bach's other two settings, nos. 290 and 335, are more elaborate.

65. According to the *Harvard Dictionary,* 2nd ed. (ed. Apel), in a chorale motet "a chorale melody is treated in motet style, i.e., as a succession of fugal sections, each based on one of the successive lines of the chorale." Kross (pp. 124-29) has a detailed description of Brahms's contrapuntal practices in this motet. Clara Schumann (*Briefe* I: 325) criticized the form because it has no motive which unifies the whole.

66. Beuerle (p. 126) cites both Scheidt and Mendelssohn.

67. BW IV: 57. Grimm asked for "Dein Kanon aus dem 51. Psalm 'Schaffe in mir Gott ein rein Herz.' "

68. BW V: 230.

69. Hohenemser (p. 77) compares Brahms's fugue with the B minor fugue in Book I of the *Well-Tempered Clavier.* The Bach fugue is much more strikingly chromatic than anything in either the cantata or the motet, however.

70. See A130, 1-6 and 27-29 for information on these collections. The piece was later published in Wüllner's *Chorübungen,* Neue Folge (1894), and a recent edition by Hänssler Verlag of Stuttgart (HE 1.004) is also available.

71. Christfriede Caesar-Larson, private comm. Schütz also set the text (SWV 291), but there is no evidence that Brahms knew of it before the *Werke* appeared. (A setting by an anonymous composer, ca. 1620, is published in *Motetten alter Meister.*)

72. The tight contrapuntal structure of all the movements tends to support this idea. We need not give up Cantata 21 as a possible model if we make the not unlikely assumption that Brahms studied it as soon as volume V of the *Werke* appeared (probably in 1856), rather than waiting until he worked on the piece in Detmold. Of course, it is also possible that he wrote only the first section of the motet in 1857, and then decided to finish setting the text some years later, choosing an equally elaborate style for the remainder because he thought it would suit his beginning.

73. Another work Brahms certainly knew where this arrangement is used is the six-voice "Es ist genug" setting by Ahle (A130, 15-16).

74. Brahms uses this modern spelling and syntax. The versions of Hammerschmidt's piece I have seen all use the spelling "Hülfe." Two other versions of the final phrase appear: "der freudige Geist enthalte mich" (in Brahms's Luther Bible, published in 1833), and "den freudigen Geist erhalte mir." (Also see p. 83 above.)

75. For this discussion, I am accepting the dating of Kalbeck and Bozarth (see chap. 2, n. 36 above). One must regret the loss of the "neue Motette" sent by Brahms to Clara Schumann at Christmas 1860 and described by her as a "Choral" when she criticized it in her response, cited by Kross (pp. 360-61) when he assigned a date of 1860 to Op. 74/2.

    A further intriguing possibility is that Brahms might not have composed his setting soon after he copied the text, since he is known to have noted some texts years before he finally set them. The first mention of "O Heiland, reiss" in the *Briefwechsel* is in a letter Brahms wrote to Max Bruch in February 1870 commenting on Bruch's new work "Rorate coeli" (BW III: 98): "Do you know the wonderful old melody to Rorate coeli? I happen to have set an older (and one I like better) German translation in motet and variation form." We can only wonder when before 1870 Brahms "happened" to write the motet.

76. His friend Theodor Billroth, in a letter to another friend, called it "verdammt herbe Musik" (quoted by Kalbeck, II: 418).

77. Hohenemser (p. 74) mentions Pachelbel.

78. This overall plan is suggested by Beuerle, pp. 130-31. It seems a good explanation for the satisfactory development of the piece, in spite of its outwardly fragmented strophic structure.

79. Brahms also uses this figure in its Baroque sense in other works. An obvious example is its appearance in the song "Dein blaues Auge" (Op. 59/8) with the text "noch schmerzt."

80. See the anecdote cited above, p. 69.

81. Brahms marked this passage in his own copy of the *Werke*, Vol. 30, which was not published until 1884 (the chaconne bass mentioned above comes from this cantata). He used a similar device, but without a clear connection with the text, in the *Requiem*, no. 6 (mm. 331-35), where there is a series of eight tightly spaced entrances on an ascending scale.

82. Wüllner wrote to Brahms about this section (BW XV: 80): "No one else can write the double canon in contrary motion at the end as you do. Writing a double canon isn't so hard; what is hard is to write one that sounds as if it weren't."

83. A similar idea is expressed in the "Gottes Hand" pedal in the concluding fugue of the *Requiem*, no. 3, which every writer cites as an instance of text illustration.

84. Each writer on Brahms's choral music has his own favorite works, with reasons for his choices. Judging from the relative lack of attention which Op. 74/2 has received (apart from descriptions of the succession of verses, together sometimes with recognition of the canonic structures of the last verse), it is on no one's list of favorites but mine. The general reaction, expressed by Kross (p. 376), is that it is inferior to the far more famous "Warum" motet, Op. 74/1. The chorale variation structure also tends to obscure the value of Brahms's own contribution to the work for some: for example, Geiringer (*Brahms,* p. 301) writes, "Obviously this is a work in which Brahms all but effaced his own personality in his reliance on the methods of the earlier masters."

   I certainly do not intend to argue that Op. 74/1 is not a great work; however, it is the product of Brahms's full maturity and his years of success and further experience which began with the *Requiem,* whereas Op. 74/2 was written in the course of the development leading to that very success (we do not know, unfortunately, how much of the present form of Op. 74/2 may be the result of revisions for publication made in 1877; also there remains the previously mentioned possibility that the piece was composed any time before 1870). Still less do I wish to downgrade the importance of early music ideas in Brahms's choral writing, but I must emphatically disagree with Geiringer's judgment on this work. After all, Brahms himself considered it worthy of publication beside the "Warum" motet in Op. 74.

85. Morik, pp. 19, 23, 156.

86. Noted by Mandyczewski in his Revisionsbericht, *Werke* XXI: v.

87. Sturke, p. 53, considers the use of "Nebendreiklänge" to be an important characteristic of Brahms's harmonic style. Also see Kross, pp. 592ff.

88. In "Liedersammlungen," where the process is discussed in detail. The first version was crossed out so thoroughly by Brahms that I was unable to decipher it. In Bozarth's opinion, the version shown as Example 10 came before Example 9.

89. Bozarth, "Liedersammlungen." This manuscript, now in the Library of Congress, contains both this version, crossed out by Brahms, and the final version.

90. Much has been made in the literature of the fact that Brahms, in letters of 1879 and 1880 to the Herzogenbergs and Hermann Deiters (BW I: 106; III: 126), regretted the elaboration of many of the settings published in 1864 and was glad that he had not published any more of them. These later opinions do not, however, affect the fact that when he set these old melodies earlier in his career he tended to think in terms of sixteenth-century polyphony.

91. Morik, pp. 149-64. The two settings which were found at the Gesellschaft der Musikfreunde and published after Brahms's death are also in this group. They are discussed briefly on p. 131, with the middle-period works.

92. Morik, p. 151, points out the delay in establishing the tonic. All these attempts are transcribed and discussed by Bozarth in "Liedersammlungen."

93. One might speculate that Brahms's study of the content of the secular part of this collection, containing in particular a number of pieces by Hassler, could have affected his Chorlieder. Not surprisingly, however, no discernible differences between Op. 62 and Op. 93a which might be traceable to this source are to be found.

94. Descriptions and evaluations of the *Requiem* alone would fill several volumes.

95. Evans, p. 25.

96. Kross (pp. 572-73) seems to say that the texts of nos. 3, 4, 6, and 7 of the *Requiem* had all been set by Schütz in the *Cantiones Sacrae* (1625) or the *Geistliche Chormusik* (1648), because he excepts from his sweeping statement about previous settings only the movements Brahms wrote during the Detmold years (nos. 1 and 2, according to his own account on p. 208) and no. 5, composed later than the other movements. However, the *Cantiones Sacrae* all have Latin texts, and none is the equivalent of any of the *Requiem* texts; part of the text of no. 1 does appear in settings by Schütz; and there is no Schütz setting of any part of the texts of either no. 3 or no. 6 of the *Requiem*.
    Musgrave (pp. 3-4) also discusses the Schütz texts and Winterfeld, but his main emphasis is on a possible relationship with Bach's Cantata 27 and its chorale.

97. Moser (p. 609) says, however, that the textual sequence in this case stemmed from theological tradition, and was not originated by Schütz.

98. Schütz also set many more verses of the psalm text in the *Psalmen Davids, SWV 29*.

99. The chronology of composition of the *Requiem* is thoroughly described by Kalbeck (II: 215-59), and revised in some particulars by Kross (pp. 208-22). Blum also makes revisions (summarized in a table on p. 103), but continues to make Kalbeck's error about the dates when Brahms might have used Köster paper (see above, chap. 2, n. 24). Blum also mentions the existence of some measures from Cherubini's D minor Requiem among the Brahms Abschriften, citing A130 (although A134 seems a more likely location from his description); no such copy appears in either collection, however.

100. In *Über das Dirigieren*; quoted by Kross, p. 331.

101. For example, see Geiringer, *Brahms*, pp. 317-18.

102. BW III: 30.

103. *Chorwerke*, p. 331. He refers to the last section of the second movement as "eine Monstrosität" (p. 328).

104. Dietrich, *Erinnerungen*, p. 70.

105. See McCorkle, *Haydn Variations*, p. 11, for an account of Brahms's affinity with Feuerbach.

106. *Brahms and Billroth*, p. 105.

107. Kalbeck (II: 363) was probably the first.

108. Kross, "Volksliedbearbeitungen," pp. 18-20.

109. Mandyczewski, Revisionsbericht, *Werke* XXI: v.

110. Friedländer, *Neue Volkslieder von Brahms,* p. 17.

111. Morik, p. 150. Kalbeck (II: 184) suggests that the similarity of the tune to the Canzonetta of Mendelssohn's E flat major quartet may be the reason why Brahms did not publish the setting. However, since he was not himself the originator of the tune, such a resemblance is not likely to have troubled him; it seems more probable that he simply composed the setting to oblige the choir and did not think it worth publishing, perhaps because he was already having second thoughts about the merit of such settings (see chap. 3, n. 90 above).

112. "Dort in den Weiden" was performed by the Singverein, but there is no record of a performance of "Wach auf, meins Herzens Schöne."

113. The last two songs in Op. 62 were composed around 1860 (chap. 3, n. 15 above) and will therefore not be included in this discussion. "Vergangen ist mir Glück und Heil" has already been mentioned in connection with Op. 41/1 (see pp. 116 above). "Es geht ein Wehen," from the period of the Op. 44 songs, shares many of their best qualities; it has a particular wealth of contrapuntal detail in a highly romantic context.

114. Geiringer, *Brahms,* p. 232; cited by McCorkle, *Haydn Variations,* p. 12.

115. Opinions vary widely on this piece. Kross, in *Chorwerke* (pp. 416-17), grants it many virtues but says it is stiff; and Geiringer (*Brahms,* p. 304) lauds it: "Who but Brahms, in the nineteenth century, could have created in a canon form a work of art so concise, so expressive, and yet so absolutely faithful to the poem! The piece is genuine Goethe, genuine Brahms, and incidentally a genuine canon." My feeling is that the "incidental" canon has stifled the possibilities of the text, much in the way that the Op. 37 pieces are constrained by their canonic straitjackets.

116. Kross, *Chorwerke,* p. 414.

117. A second bass part is added at the end of "O süsser Mai" to hold a long tonic pedal.

118. Kross, throughout *Chorwerke,* implies that this division is characteristic of Brahms's early choral writing; but in fact it occurs frequently in the middle and late works as well, though not for such long stretches as it does in earlier ones.

119. Kross (pp. 367-73) describes it at length; and Beuerle (pp. 136-67) analyzes it in minute detail, as well as reaching what seem to me unjustified conclusions about Brahms's conscious or unconscious intentions.

120. Spitta (p. 411) felt that there could be no other reason for the presence of the chorale, since it could serve no liturgical function. Brahms's dedication of the Op. 74 motets to Spitta has been taken as another piece of evidence to support this idea; but in fact Brahms had second thoughts about the dedication and wanted to withdraw it. He left it in (though he removed a reference to Spitta's Bach biography) only because Joachim had let the secret out to Spitta already. See Kalbeck (III: 162) and the Joachim correspondence (BW VI: 145-46). Kalbeck says that Brahms wanted to avoid the Bach-related dedication for reasons of modesty—the fear that he might be thought to be comparing himself with Bach. Also, Spitta's strongly expressed views on the subject of what was proper in religious music (Blume, pp. 64ff., discusses the effect of his religious beliefs on his scholarly work) may have alienated Brahms. It is perhaps significant that a ten-year gap in their correspondence occurred after Spitta wrote to Brahms thanking him for the dedication, and in the same letter discussed the subject of church music at some length (BW XVI:77).

121. BW XVI: 184; quoted by Kross, p. 364. Brahms wrote, "Ich lege eine Kleinigkeit bei, an der vielleicht—meine Bibelkenntnis zu loben ist. Zudem aber predigt es wohl besser als m. Worte. Ich bin viel spazieren gegangen damit!"

122. Geiringer, p. 301, says that the choice of texts for the motet expresses Brahms's personality, "true Christian that he was." I cannot agree.

123. Kross, p. 367, and others. Kross also mentions Schütz in connection with this motet.

124. *Geschichte der Motette,* pp. 415-16. The resemblance is with a recurring "Siehe," which is present in one voice or another throughout the first section of Schein's motet. Geiringer (*Brahms,* p. 301) repeats the comparison.

125. *Briefe* I: 178. I am indebted to Robert Pascall for the information that other sections of the *Missa canonica* (see above, chap. 3, n. 4) also contain musical material which Brahms incorporated into the motet (private comm., March 1982). Specifically, the Agnus Dei appears in section 1, and the Dona nobis pacem in section 3.

126. BW IV: 97. The surviving copy in Brahms's hand (Waters provides a facsimile) is in SSAT clefs; it was therefore probably made after Grimm's suggestion (Grimm's two copies are also both in SSAT clefs). This canon was a favorite with Brahms's friends; see also the Joachim correspondence, BW V: 141.

127. Beuerle, p. 156; he mentions especially the *Missa Brevis.*

128. Beuerle also says (p. 153) that Brahms's choice of this style for the second movement in contrast to the subjective character of the first shows how exactly he had grasped not only the compositional techniques and principles of the historical styles, but also their ideological implications. I cannot go along with such a far-ranging conclusion on the basis of the available evidence.

129. See Bach, *371 Chorales,* nos. 49 and 325. Beuerle (pp. 162-63) makes a comparison of Brahms's version with both these settings.

130. Most so, perhaps, is Beuerle (pp. 162-67), who feels that Brahms was caught in an ambivalent position between the archaic and modern styles, and that the chorale symbolizes that ambivalence. He argues that certain contradictory turns in the text setting in the chorale and also in earlier sections of the motet indicate that Brahms had at last accomplished the next logical step in the history of the motet, the "emancipation of music from speech." Beuerle concludes that Brahms's turning again in Opp. 109 and 110 to the composition of motets, in which he actually lost ground in this respect and returned to a closer connection with the text, shows that he was not fully conscious of the difficulties arising from the compositional and social tradition of the genre.

   My own feeling is that the apparent contradictions mentioned by Beuerle, such as the use of the sighing figure in the alto voice of the chorale where the text speaks of comfort, probably arise as a result of Brahms's well-known tendency to disregard the text occasionally on musical grounds. I am also certain that Brahms himself was totally unaware of and would have resented the sociological implications which Beuerle finds in his choral compositions and in his entire musical career.

131. *Zur Musik,* p. 411. My translation.

132. This is the volume which Spitta (BW XVI: 81) was sure Brahms would like. He promised publication of the "grossen Conzerte," about which Brahms had specifi-

cally inquired (*Symphoniae Sacrae* III), in volumes IX through XI; they actually appeared in X and XI (IX was the Italian madrigals).

133. *Zur Musik*, p. 409. He clearly refers to the passage "O nimmer kommt dir die Sonne."

134. Beuerle, p. 318. He has a long and extremely detailed analysis of this piece (pp. 314-46), the only work from Op. 104 that he discusses. Most other commentators have neglected it in favor of the two "Nachtwache" settings.

135. *Correspondence* (transl. Bryant), p. 352.

136. Hohenemser, p. 72, makes this comparison.

137. Hohenemser points out the cadential hemiolas as a technique taken directly from early music (p. 72). In this case, they actually occur as a 3/2 cross rhythm in soprano and alto against the 6/4 maintained by the tenor and bass.

138. Kross (*Chorwerke*, p. 462) also points out the correspondence, and says that the possibility of a direct influence of the Bach setting on Brahms is not excluded. My opinion is that Brahms almost certainly intended the reference.

139. Beuerle, p. 203.

140. See, for example, his letter to Wüllner, in BW XV: 164, where he calls the Op. 110 motets "better," and says that Wüllner will have "much more fun" with them. Also see the Brahms-Clara Schumann *Briefe* II: 407.

141. Brahms was well aware that his choice of text for no. 2, which is taken out of context in a manner which severely distorts the original meaning, would cause difficulties— as indeed it has—for later students of his music. He wrote to Widmann in 1890 (Dietrich & Widmann, *Recollections,* transl. Hecht, p. 193), "Have you noticed the theological, even jesuitical subtlety of the second of the sentences? I really wanted to ask you before now, whether such a thing is permissible. Do look it up some time as it will interest you."

142. Beuerle (pp. 189-200, esp. p. 200) concludes that Op. 110 nos. 1 and 3 cannot be successful relative to Op. 109 because the eight-voice medium implies a collective experience which is not suited to the more personal texts of Op. 110.

143. Kross (*Chorwerke*, pp. 464-68) emphasizes the remarkable motivic unity of the piece, even between apparently unlike sections.

144. Kalbeck (IV: 200-202) suggests that the first and third verses resemble a chorale fantasy, and reconstructs Brahms's chorale melody in what I think is a convincing fashion. Kalbeck's analyses have been rated quite low by most later writers, however, and I have not seen this suggestion repeated elsewhere.

145. Beuerle (p. 199) feels that the constant repetition does not convey affirmative emphasis, but more likely connotes an insistence which stems from uncertainty.

146. Beuerle (p. 198) suggests a comparison with Schein.

147. *Neue Ausgabe* 11: 17-18, mm. 49-60. Moser (p. 519) says that Schütz did not use the chorale melody associated with this hymn text because "he apparently wished to abandon himself freely to his affectual study."

148. Kalbeck (IV: 203) may have been the first to mention this resemblance.

149. Beuerle (p. 190) also makes this comparison, and cites two other examples.

150. See Table 1. His reason for copying it may have been its value as an example of methods for avoiding parallel fifths.

151. See pp. 162-64, for other examples in Brahms's music. Further Schütz examples relevant to Op. 110/1 are given in Hancock, "Evidence."

152. In the Schütz *Neue Ausgabe* (23: 73) there is no rest in the soprano line in the middle of this phrase. The square brackets which point out imitative entries in Example 22 are Brahms's, and appear in his Abschrift.

153. Hohenemser (p. 78) makes the same point about this motet, but does not make a comparison with Schütz. This command of the medium and its relation to the text distinguish Brahms's late works from the early "eclectic" works.

154. Kross, in his section "Brahms' Chorstil" (*Chorwerke*, pp. 579-628), also bases a good deal of his discussion on the examination of techniques derived from early music, and the citation of examples from Brahms's compositions. However, he did not have access to Brahms's library, and his conclusions are therefore based on a general knowledge of early music together with the information available from the correspondence and from secondary sources such as Kalbeck.

155. Proske, for example. Brahms did not own the collection; but see above, p. 72. Also see the discussion of Wüllner's *Chorübungen* III, p. 71 above.

156. See A130, 18-19 and A136; also see Hancock, "Performances."

157. Mattheson, p. 19: "Alles Spielen ist eine Nachahmung und Gesellschaft des Singens, ja, ein Spieler, oder der für Instrumente was setzet, muss alles, was zu einer guter Melodie und Harmonie erfordert wird, viel fleissiger beobachten, als ein Sänger, oder der für Singe-Stimmen etwas setzet: dieweil man, bey dem Singen, die deutlichsten Worte zum Beystande hat; woran es hergegen bei Instrumenten allemahl fehlet." A similar passage is marked in *Der vollkommene Capellmeister* (p. 8; Harriss, p. 93).

158. See Dadelsen, pp. 110-15, for a discussion of this aspect of Brahms's instrumental writing.

159. The only complete choral fugue outside the *Requiem* is in Op. 29/2. That in "Es ist das Heil" (Op. 29/1) actually consists of a series of short expositions, one per line of the chorale melody, and thus is not a thoroughly worked-out fugue. See Kross, p. 604, for the incomplete nature of the choral fugues, and Dadelsen, pp. 108-9, for the instrumental fugues. Also see Harrison, p. 37, and Fellinger, "Brahms und die Musik vergangener Epochen," p. 154.

160. Jenner, p. 40; Kalbeck III: 85.

161. *Zur Musik*, p. 402.

162. Geiringer, *Brahms*, p. 267.

163. Wüllner, in a funeral oration delivered after Brahms's death (quoted in BW XV: 188) said, "No one knew better than Brahms how to write middle parts that were at once interesting and unforced." See also Kross, p. 602, on the equal worth of all the voices.

164. BW V: 147-48.

165. "Dein Ohr ist so an rauhe Harmonie gewöhnt, von so polyphoner Textur, dass Du selten die Stimmen, in gegenseitigen Zusammenstoss allein, erwägst—weil sich eben bei Dir gleich das Gehörige, Ergänzende dazu gesellt."

166. Quoted by Kalbeck, III: 85.

167. Hancock, "Performances."

168. May, 2nd ed., p. 17.

169. Kross (*Chorwerke,* pp. 614-22) has a section on this topic. Beuerle (p. 260) feels that Brahms sometimes allowed madrigalisms to endanger the balance of a composition; he cites the word "rauschen" in Op. 42/1 as a specific example. Jenner, on the other hand (p. 41), says that Brahms himself felt that too close adherence to the meaning of individual words in the construction of melodies showed a lack of resource. Beuerle also considers (see, for example, p. 100, n. 15 [p. 363]) that Brahms may have deliberately used "reverse madrigalism" ("negativer Madrigalismus") on occasion—that is, musical ideas which seem to contradict the meaning of the text.

170. Hohenemser's description of Lotti's chromaticism as a "subjective outpouring" has been mentioned above, chap. 2, n. 102.

171. He apparently became reconciled to the expressive use of the interval of the diminished fourth (or augmented fifth) in early music after studying the works of Schütz, although he had objected to it thirty years earlier in the Italian composers he had studied in Winterfeld's *Gabrieli* (see pp. 32, 101, 145 above).

172. Sturke (p. 29) overstates the case when he says that in middle-period works (his dates for Brahms's middle period are 1867-82, thus including Op. 62), "chromaticism with Brahms is always the expression of bitter, tragic pain." The statement is probably more true for early composers than for Brahms. (See note 175 below for an example of dissonance resulting from imitation in one of these chromatic subjects, in Op. 104/1.)

173. Spitta, in *Zur Musik,* p. 393, mentions an example in an early song, Op. 7/5, and says he could write a treatise on the subject. Another early example, which Morik cites (p. 143), occurs in the folk song setting for mixed voices, "Es pocht ein Knabe."

174. BW XV: 164, 170. Another cross relation over a phrase ending, in Op. 110/2, has already been mentioned (p. 138 above).

175. The equally pungent dissonance earlier in the same work (Op. 104/1, m. 7, beat 4) results from imitation of a tightly confined chromatic figure.

176. See A130, 7-9, and the handwritten collection "Deutsche vierstimmige Volkslieder," pp. 62-63, above.

177. Dadelsen, p. 106, suggests that modal writing represented a Romantic idea of the archaic. The best-known example from Brahms's instrumental music is surely the second movement of the Fourth Symphony.

178. Radcliffe (*Grove,* 4th ed., 1: 885) says, "its final bars seem to demand a Phrygian cadence." A recently discovered manuscript, dated 1852, proves that this is Brahms's earliest surviving duet (Bozarth, " 'New' manuscripts").

179. Brahms's other setting of this tune, Op. 122/9, also lacks a Phrygian cadence, but its ending (on an A major chord) is not unsatisfactory.

180. *Zur Musik,* p. 392.

181. Various writers have stated that "Ach, arme Welt" (Op. 110/2) has a Dorian melody; for example, see Hohenemser, p. 72. I agree with Kross (p. 462) that it is not modal.

182. *Zur Musik,* pp. 392-93. He cites the *Marienlieder* as an example, presumably referring to nos. 4 and 7. Also see Kross (pp. 592ff.) on Brahms's harmony, especially his preference for the subdominant side.

183. An often-cited example of musical pictorialism occurs in this dance, where the singers sound the tuning fifths of a violin on "Der Geiger strich." Brahms marked a similarly explicit illustration in the Bach *Werke* (see p. 85 above), the tolling bell in Cantata 53, "Schlage doch, gewünschte Stunde." Also compare the ringing bells in Brahms's Op. 22/2.

184. See, for example, Dadelsen, pp. 97ff.; Kross, pp. 585ff.; Spitta (who makes a comparison with Schütz), pp. 393-94; James, pp. 168-69; Sturke, pp. 5, 38, 51, 72, and elsewhere; and Harrison, pp. 98ff.

185. Brahms was, of course, particularly fond of just this sort of rhythmic complexity and used it frequently from his earliest works in all media. It does not have the same early music connotations as hemiola, notwithstanding its appearance here in Forster's collection.

186. There are no annotations in the other voices. It would be interesting to know whether Brahms also noticed the short triple-meter cross rhythms in the alto and tenor parts.

187. Brahms's relative indifference to the niceties of accentuation has been a matter for much comment and criticism by writers on his songs especially. Harrison feels (p. 101) that there is a historical precedent: that German composers in general had ". . . proved themselves slow in acknowledging correct principles of declamation, as may be seen by comparing, for example, Schütz and J. S. Bach with Byrd and Purcell." He goes on (p. 111): "As already noted, there was a long tradition of bad word-setting before Brahms; examples from Marschner, Weber and even Mendelssohn—all of them educated men—would prove this. The trouble sprang, especially in Germany, from the common practice dating back to Luther's time of setting new words to old melodies without anyone bothering whether the two fitted sensibly. Also, the singing of different verses of a poem to the same melody led to incongruities, whether in the ballads of Zelter and Zumsteeg or in the *Strophenlieder* of Brahms." While Harrison is undoubtedly right in some respects, it also seems clear that many examples of supposedly faulty declamation, both in Brahms and earlier composers, actually arise from this independence of bar lines.

188. Alto, mm. 55-58; tenor, mm. 70-72; alto, mm. 75-77. Note that Brahms does not use these potentially confusing displacements in the soprano or bass lines in this early work.

189. The falling thirds outlined in Op. 74/1 are another instance of Brahms's tendency, cited by Harrison (p. 123), to associate thirds with the idea of death; they are ". . . sometimes ascending . . . but more usually descending."

190. In Brahms's source, the editorial F sharp is written above the staff. He at first copied it in front of the note, and then changed his mind, crossed it out, and rewrote it above.

Bibliography

Items in the Brahms Nachlass are not listed except for a few works which were used extensively for secondary investigation. Page references italicized in Appendices 2 and 3 show where in the text complete bibliographic information on the works in Brahms's library may be found.

Correspondence

Briefwechsel (BW). Berlin: Deutsche Brahms-Gesellschaft. Reprint edition, Tutzing: Hans Schneider, 1974.
 III. Johannes Brahms im Briefwechsel mit Karl Reinthaler, Max Bruch, Hermann Deiters, Friedr. Heimsoeth, Karl Reinecke, Ernst Rudorff, Bernhard und Luise Scholz. Edited by Wilhelm Altmann. 2nd ed., 1912.
 IV. Johannes Brahms im Briefwechsel mit J.O. Grimm. Edited by Richard Barth. 1912.
 V.VI. Johannes Brahms im Briefwechsel mit Joseph Joachim. Edited by Andreas Moser. V: 3rd ed., 1921. VI: 2nd ed., 1912.
 VII. Johannes Brahms im Briefwechsel mit Hermann Levi, Friedrich Gernsheim, sowie den Familien Hecht und Fellinger. Edited by Leopold Schmidt. 1910.
 VIII. Johannes Brahms Briefe an Joseph Viktor Widmann, Ellen und Ferdinand Vetter, Adolf Schubring. Edited by Max Kalbeck. 1915.
 XV. Johannes Brahms im Briefwechsel mit Franz Wüllner. Edited by Ernst Wolff. 1922.
 XVI. Johannes Brahms im Briefwechsel mit Philipp Spitta und Otto Dessoff. Edited by Carl Krebs. 1920.
Orel, Alfred. *Johannes Brahms und Julius Allgeyer: eine Künstlerfreundschaft in Briefen.* Tutzing: Hans Schneider, 1964.
Johannes Brahms and Theodor Billroth: Letters from a Musical Friendship. Translated and edited by Hans Barkan. Norman: Univ. of Oklahoma Press, 1957.
Geiringer, Karl. "Brahms and Chrysander." *Monthly Musical Record* 67 (1937): 97ff., 131ff., 178ff.; 68 (1938): 77ff.
Kalbeck, Max, ed. *Johannes Brahms: The Herzogenberg Correspondence.* Translated by Hannah Bryant. London: John Murray, 1909; reprint ed., New York: Vienna House, 1971.
Geiringer, Karl. "Johannes Brahms im Briefwechsel mit Eusebius Mandyczewski." *Zeitschrift für Musikwissenschaft* 15 (1933): 337-70.
Clara Schumann—Johannes Brahms: Briefe aus den Jahren 1853-1896. Edited by Berthold Litzmann. 2 vols. Leipzig: Breitkopf & Härtel, 1927. (An English version, *The Letters of Clara Schumann and Johannes Brahms, 1853-1896* [no translator identified] [New York:

Longmans, Green, 1927; reprint ed., New York: Vienna House, 1971)], also in two volumes, is much abridged; much of the material relevant to this study is omitted.)
Johannes Brahms an Julius Spengel: Unveröffentliche Briefe aus den Jahren 1882-1897. Edited by Annemarie Spengel. Hamburg: Gesellschaft der Bücherfreunde, 1959.

Books, Articles, and Dissertations

Adler, Guido. "Johannes Brahms: His Achievement, His Personality, and His Position." *Musical Quarterly* 19 (1933): 113-42.
Besseler, Heinrich. *Die Musik des Mittelalters und der Renaissance.* Handbuch der Musikwissenschaft, edited by Ernst Bücken, Lieferung 44. Potsdam: Akademische Verlagsgesellschaft Athenaion, 1931. Chapter 1, pp. 1-24, is "Alte Musik und Gegenwart."
Beuerle, Hans Michael. "Untersuchungen zum historischen Stellenwert der A-cappella-Kompositionen von Johannes Brahms." Ph.D. dissertation, Johann Wolfgang Goethe Universität, Frankfurt am Main, 1975.
Blum, Klaus. *Hundert Jahre ein deutsches Requiem von Johannes Brahms.* Tutzing: Hans Schneider, 1971.
Blume, Friedrich. *Two Centuries of Bach.* Translated by Stanley Godman. London: Oxford University Press, 1950; reprint ed., New York: Da Capo, 1978. Originally published as *Johann Sebastian Bach im Wandel der Geschichte* (Kassel: Bärenreiter, 1947).
Boetticher, Wolfgang. *Robert Schumann: Einführung in Persönlichkeit und Werk.* Berlin: Bernhard Hahnefeld, 1941.
Bozarth, George S. "Brahms's *Duets for Soprano and Alto,* op. 61: A Study in Chronology and Compositional Process," forthcoming.
————. "Johannes Brahms und die Liedersammlungen D.G. Corners, K.S. Meisters, und F.W. Arnolds," forthcoming in *Die Musikforschung* 36 (1983).
————. "The *Lieder* of Johannes Brahms—1868-1871." Ph.D. dissertation, Princeton University, 1978.
————. " 'New' Brahms Manuscripts." *American Brahms Society Newsletter,* spring 1983.
Dadelsen, Georg von. "Alter Stil und alte Techniken in der Musik des 19. Jahrhunderts." Ph.D. dissertation, Freie Universität, Berlin, 1951. (Xerox copy loaned by the Musikwissenschaftliches Institut der Universität Tübingen, through the kind assistance of Dr. Liselotte Bihl.)
Deutsch, Otto Erich. "The First Editions of Brahms." *Music Review* 1 (1940): 123-43, 255-78.
Dietrich, Albert. *Erinnerungen an Johannes Brahms.* Leipzig: Otto Wigand, 1898.
Dietrich, Albert, and Widmann, J.V. *Recollections of Johannes Brahms.* Translated by Dora E. Hecht. London: Seeley, 1899.
Drinker, Sophie. *Brahms and His Women's Choruses.* Merion, Pa.: privately published, 1952.
Ebinger, Hans. *Friedrich Rochlitz als Musikschriftsteller.* Leipzig: Breitkopf & Härtel, 1929.
Eitner, Robert. *Verzeichniss neuer Ausgaben alter Musikwerke aus der frühesten Zeit bis zum Jahre 1800.* Berlin: Trautwein, 1871. First published as a supplement to *Monatshefte für Musikgeschichte* 3(1871), 3-206; reprint ed., Scarsdale, N.Y.: Annemarie Schnase, 1960.
Evans, Edwin, Sr. *Historical, Descriptive and Analytical Account of the Entire Works of Johannes Brahms.* Vol. 1: The Vocal Works. London: Wm. Reeves, 1912.
Fellinger, Imogen. "Brahms und die Musik vergangener Epochen." In *Die Ausbreitung des Historismus über die Musik,* pp. 147-63. Edited by Walter Wiora. Regensburg: Gustav Bosse, 1969.

——————. "Grundzüge Brahmsscher Musikauffassung." In *Beiträge zur Geschichte der Musikanschauung im 19. Jahrhundert*, pp. 113-26. Edited by Walter Salmen. Regensburg: Gustav Bosse, 1965.

——————. *Über die Dynamik in der Musik von Johannes Brahms.* Berlin-Halensee: Max Hesse, 1961.

Friedländer, Max. *Brahms's Lieder.* Translated by C. Leonard Leese. London: Oxford University Press, 1929.

Frisch, Walter. "Brahms, Developing Variation, and the Schoenberg Critical Tradition." *19th Century Music* 5 (1982): 215-32.

Gál, Hans. *Johannes Brahms: His Work and Personality.* Translated by Joseph Stein. New York: Knopf, 1963.

Geffcken, Johannes. *Die Hamburgischen Niedersächsischen Gesangbücher.* Hamburg: Meissner, 1857.

Geiringer, Karl. "Brahms als Musikhistoriker." In *Johannes Brahms Festschrift*, pp. 11-18. Berlin: Max Hesse, 1933.

——————. "Brahms as a Reader and Collector." *Musical Quarterly* 19 (1933): 158-68.

——————. *Brahms: His Life and Work.* 2nd ed. New York: Oxford University Press, 1947. A third edition, with Irene Geiringer (New York: Da Capo, 1981), includes "Brahms as a Reader and Collector" as an appendix.

Geiringer, Karl, and Geiringer, Irene. "The Brahms Library in the 'Gesellschaft der Musikfreunde,' Wien." *M.L.A. Notes* 30 (1973): 7-14.

Gerber, Rudolf. "Brahms und das Volkslied." *Die Sammlung* 3 (1948): 652-62.

Hancock, Virginia. "Brahms and Early Music: Evidence from His Library and His Choral Compositions." *Proceedings of the International Brahms Conference, Library of Congress, May 1983.* Brahms Studies 1, edited by George S. Bozarth, forthcoming.

——————. "Brahms's early music studies and his sacred choral music." *The American Organist* 17 (May 1983): 40-43.

——————. "Brahms's performances of early choral music," forthcoming in *19th Century Music,* July 1984.

——————. "The growth of Brahms's interest in early choral music, and its effect on his own choral compositions." In *Brahms: Biographical, Documentary and Analytical Studies,* pp. 27-40. Edited by Robert Pascall. Cambridge: Cambridge University Press, 1983.

——————. "Sources of Brahms's manuscript copies of early music in the Archiv of the Gesellschaft der Musikfreunde in Wien." *Fontes Artis Musicae* 24 (1977): 113-21.

Hanslick, Eduard. *Vienna's Golden Years of Music, 1850-1900.* Translated and edited by Henry Pleasants III. London: Gollancz, 1951.

Harrison, Max. *The Lieder of Brahms.* New York: Praeger, 1972.

Harriss, Ernest. *Johann Mattheson's "Der vollkommene Capellmeister."* Ann Arbor: UMI Research Press, 1981.

Helms, Siegmund. "Johannes Brahms und Johann Sebastian Bach." *Bach-Jahrbuch* 57(1971): 13-81.

——————. "Die Melodiebildung in den Liedern von Johannes Brahms und ihr Verhältnis zu Volksliedern und Volkstümlichen Weisen." Ph.D. dissertation, Freie Universität, Berlin, 1967. (Printed by Rudolf Rodenbusch, Bamberg.)

Heuberger, Richard. *Erinnerungen an Johannes Brahms.* Edited by Kurt Hofmann. Tutzing: Hans Schneider, 1971.

Hofmann, Kurt. *Die Bibliothek von Johannes Brahms: Bücher- und Musikalienverzeichnis.* Schriftenreihe zur Musik. Hamburg: Karl Dieter Wagner, 1974. Contains a reprint of Orel, "Johannes Brahms' Musikbibliothek."

Hofmann, Kurt, and Fürst, Jutta. *Johannes Brahms: the Man and his Work*. Exhibition catalog (Detroit: Detroit Symphony Orchestra, 1980).

Hohenemser, Richard. *Welche Einflüsse hatte die Wiederbelebung der älteren Musik im 19. Jahrhundert auf die deutschen Komponisten?* Sammlung musikwissenschaftler Arbeiter von deutschen Hochschulen, IV. Leipzig: Breitkopf & Härtel, 1900.

Hübbe, Walter. *Brahms in Hamburg*. Hamburg: Lütcke & Wolff, 1902.

Huschke, Konrad. *Johannes Brahms als Pianist, Dirigent und Lehrer*. Karlsruhe: Gutsch, 1935.

Jacobsen, Christiane, ed. *Johannes Brahms*. 8 vols. Essays included with recordings of the complete works of Brahms. Hamburg: Polydor International, 1983.

James, Burnett. *Brahms: A Critical Study*. New York: Praeger, 1972.

Jenner, Gustav. *Johannes Brahms als Mensch, Lehrer und Künstler*. 2nd ed. Marburg: Elwert, 1930.

Jeppesen, Knud. *The Style of Palestrina and the Dissonance*. 2nd ed., 1946; reprint ed., New York: Dover, 1970.

Kalbeck, Max. *Johannes Brahms*. 4 vols. Berlin: Deutsche Brahms-Gesellschaft. I (1833-62): 3rd ed., 1912. II (1862-73): 2nd ed., 1908. III (1874-85): 2nd ed., 1912-13. IV (1886-97), 1914.

Kamper, Dietrich. "Ein unbekanntes Brahms-Studienblatt aus dem Briefwechsel mit F. Wüllner." *Die Musikforschung* 17 (1964): 57-60, facsimile.

Kenton, Egon. *Life and Works of Giovanni Gabrieli*. Musicological Studies and Documents, no. 16. Rome: American Institute of Musicology, 1967.

Komorn, Maria. *Johannes Brahms als Chordirigent in Wien und seine Nachfolger*. Vienna: Universal-Edition, 1928.

Kretzschmar, Hermann. *Führer durch den Concertsaal*. II. Abtheilung: "Kirchliche Werke" (1888); "Oratorien und weltliche Chorwerke" (1890). Leipzig: A.G. Liebeskind.

Kross, Siegfried. *Die Chorwerke von Johannes Brahms*. 2nd ed. Berlin-Halensee: Max Hesse, 1963.

————. "Zur Frage der Brahmsschen Volksliedbearbeitungen." *Die Musikforschung* 11 (1958), 15-21.

Leichtentritt, Hugo. *Geschichte der Motette*. Leipzig: Breitkopf & Härtel, 1908; reprint ed., Hildesheim: Georg Olms, 1967.

Mandyczewski, Eusebius. "Die Bibliothek Brahms." *Musikbuch aus Oesterreich* 1 (1904), 7-17.

Mast, Paul. "Brahms's Study, Octaven u. Quinten u. A., with Schenker's Commentary Translated." *Music Forum* 5 (1980), 1-196.

May, Florence. *The Life of Johannes Brahms*. 2 vols. London: Edward Arnold, 1905. 2nd ed., London: Wm. Reeves, 1948; reprint ed., Neptune City, N.J.: Paganiniana, 1981.

McCorkle, Donald M. "Five fundamental obstacles in Brahms research." *Acta Musicologica* 48 (1976), 253-72.

McCorkle, Margit L. *Brahms Thematisch-Bibliographisches Werkverzeichnis*. Munich: Henle, forthcoming.

Morik, Werner. *Johannes Brahms und sein Verhältnis zum deutschen Volkslied*. Tutzing: Hans Schneider, 1965.

Moser, Hans Joachim. *Heinrich Schütz: His Life and Work*. Translated from the 2nd rev. edition (Kassel: Bärenreiter, 1953) by Carl F. Pfatteicher. St. Louis: Concordia, 1959.

Musgrave, Michael. "Historical Influences in the Growth of Brahms's 'Requiem.'" *Music and Letters* 53 (1972): 3-17.

Niemann, Walter. *Brahms*. Translated by Catherine A. Phillips. New York: Knopf, 1929.

Ophüls, Gustav. *Brahms-Texte*. Berlin: Simrock, 1898.

Orel, Alfred. "Johannes Brahms' Musikbibliothek." *Simrock-Jahrbuch* 3 (Leipzig, 1930-34). Reprinted in Hofmann, *Die Bibliothek von Johannes Brahms*, pp. 139-66.

Pascall, Robert, ed. *Brahms: Biographical, Documentary and Analytical Studies.* Cambridge: Cambridge Univ. Press, 1983.

Perger, Richard von, and Hirschfeld, Robert. *Geschichte der K.K. Gesellschaft der Musik-freunde in Wien.* Vienna, 1912.
A supplement, *Sammlungen und Statuten,* edited by Eusebius Mandyczewski, contains a catalog of the society's library.

Petzoldt, Richard. "Brahms und der Chor." In *Johannes Brahms Festschrift,* pp. 18-22. Berlin: Max Hesse, 1933.

Radcliffe, Philip F. "Johannes Brahms." In *Grove's Dictionary of Music and Musicians* 1:870-903. 5th ed., edited by Eric Blom. New York: St. Martin's Press, 1955.

Reese, Gustave. *Music in the Renaissance.* Revised edition. New York: Norton, 1959.

Schauffler, Robert Haven. *The Unknown Brahms.* New York: Dodd, Mead, 1933; reprint ed., Westport, Conn.: Greenwood, 1972.

Schenker, Heinrich, ed. *Johannes Brahms "Oktaven und Quinten u. A."* Vienna: Universal-Edition, 1933.

Schramm, Willi. *Johannes Brahms in Detmold.* Leipzig: Kistner & Siegel, 1933.

Schmieder, Wolfgang. *Thematisch-systematisches Verzeichnis der Werke Johann Sebastian Bachs.* Leipzig: Breitkopf & Härtel, 1966.

Schütz Werke Verzeichnis. Kleine Ausgabe. Edited by Werner Bittinger. Kassel: Bärenreiter, 1960.

Simrock, N. [firm]. *Thematic Catalog of the Works of Johannes Brahms.* New introduction, including Addenda and Corrigenda, by Donald M. McCorkle. New York: Da Capo, 1973.

[Singakademie.] *Festschrift der Wiener Singakademie zur Feier des fünfzigjährigen Bestandes, 1858-1908.* Vienna, 1908.

Specht, Richard. *Johannes Brahms.* Translated by Eric Blom. London: Dent, 1930.

Spitta, Philipp. "Johannes Brahms." In *Zur Musik,* pp. 387-427. Berlin: Gebrüder Paetel, 1892.

Sturke, August. "Der Stil in Johannes Brahms' Werken." Ph.D. dissertation, Hamburg, 1932. (Printed by Konrad Triltsch, Würzburg.)

[Thibaut, A.F.J.] *Über Reinheit der Tonkunst.* Heidelberg: J. C. B. Mohr, 1825.

Waters, Edward N. "The Music Collection of the Heinemann Foundation." *M.L.A. Notes* 7 (1950):181-216, facsimiles.

Winterfeld, Carl von. *Der evangelische Kirchengesang.* 3 vols. Leipzig: Breitkopf & Härtel, 1843-47.
I (1843). Der evangelische Kirchengesang im ersten Jahrhunderte der Kirchenverbesserung.
II (1845). Der evangelische Kirchengesang im siebzehnten Jahrhunderte.
III (1847). Der evangelische Kirchengesang im achtzehnten Jahrhunderte.

————. *Johannes Gabrieli und sein Zeitalter.* 3 vols. Berlin: Schlesinger, 1834; reprint ed., Hildesheim: Georg Olms, 1965.

Wiora, Walter. *Die rheinisch-bergischen Melodien bei Zuccalmaglio und Brahms: Alte Liedweisen in romantischer Färbung.* Bad Godesberg: Voggenreiter, 1953.

Zahn, Johannes. *Die Melodien der deutschen evangelischen Kirchenlieder.* V (1892) and VI (index, 1893). Gütersloh: Bertelsmann; reprint ed., Hildesheim, Georg Olms, 1963.

Music

Antiqua Chorbuch. Edited by Helmut Mönkemeyer. Mainz: Schott, 1951.
I. Geistliche Chorwerke deutscher Meister. 5 vols.

II. Weltliche Chorwerke deutscher Meister. 5 vols.

Ave Maria, dich lobt Musica. Edited by Walther Lipphardt. Freiburg im Breisgau: Christophorus, 1963.

Johann Sebastian Bachs Werke. 46 vols. Leipzig: Breitkopf & Härtel, 1850ff.; reprint ed., Ann Arbor: J. W. Edwards, 1947.

Bach, J.S. *371 Four-part Chorales.* (Edition Breitkopf.) New York: Associated Music Publishers, n.d.

Brahms, Johannes. *Sämtliche Werke.* Edited by Eusebius Mandyczewski and Hans Gál. Leipzig: Breitkopf & Härtel, 1926-28; reprint ed., Ann Arbor: J.W. Edwards, 1949.

XVII.   Chorwerke mit Orchester I.

XVIII.   Chorwerke mit Orchester II.

XIX.   Chorwerke mit Orchester III.

XX.   Mehrstimmige Gesänge mit Klavier oder Orgel.

XXI.   Mehrstimmige Gesänge ohne Begleitung.

—————. *Brahms Variations on a Theme of Haydn.* Norton Critical Scores. Edited by Donald M. McCorkle. New York: Norton, 1976.

—————. *Folk Songs for Women's Voices, arranged by Johannes Brahms.* Edited by Vernon Gotwals and Philip Keppler. Smith College Music Archives, Vol. 15 (1968).

—————. *Geistliche Chormusik.* Gesamtansgabe der motettischen Werke. Edited by Günter Graulich. Stuttgart: Carus–Verlag (40.179), 1983.

—————. [Works for four-part women's chorus.] "Vineta" (no. 21), "A Sigh Goes Floating Thro' the Wood" (no. 22), "Todtenklage" ("In stiller Nacht," no. 23), "Thou Gentle Heart" (no. 24), Six Marienlieder (no. 75). Edited by Henry S. Drinker. Philadelphia: University of Pennsylvania Choral Series, 1938.

Corner, David Gregor. *Gross' Catolisch Gesangbuch.* 2 vols. Nürnberg: Georg Ender der Jünger, 1631.

Friedländer, Max. *Neue Volkslieder von Brahms: 32 Bearbeitungen nach der Handschrift aus dem Besitz Clara Schumanns.* Berlin: Deutsche Brahms-Gesellschaft, 1926. The choral arrangements were subsequently published as nos. 23-26 in the Brahms *Werke* XXI.

Gabrieli, Giovanni. *Opera Omnia.* Edited by Denis Arnold. Rome: American Institute of Musicology, 1956ff.

Geiringer, Karl, ed. Two settings of the chorale "Es ist genug" with performance instructions by Brahms. *Zeitschrift für Musik* 100 (1933), Notenbeilage Nr. 5. Geiringer's explanation, "Zu unserer Notenbeilage," p. 465.

Geistliches Chorlied. Edited by Gottfried Grote. 2 vols. Berlin: Merseburger, 1967.

Gesellige Zeit: Liederbuch für gemischten Chor. Edited by Walther Lipphardt. 2 vols. Kassel: Bärenreiter, 1961, 1965.

Hammerschmidt, Andreas. "Schaffe in mir, Gott." Stuttgart: Hänssler-Edition 1.004.

Handel, George Frederick. *Werke.* Edited by Friedrich Chrysander. 96 vols. Deutsche Händel-Gesellschaft, 1858-94; reprint ed., Ridgewood, N.J.: Gregg, 1965-66.

Introiten und Motetten zum Kirchenjahr. 2nd ed. Edited by Diethard Hellmann. Stuttgart: Hänssler, 1962.

Motetten alter Meister. 5th ed. Edited by Gottfried Grote. Berlin: Merseburger, 1967.

Musica Sacra. Edited by Franz Commer, A. Neithardt, and others. 14 vols. Berlin: Bote & Bock, 1839ff.

Musica Sacra: Sammlung kirchlicher Musik der berühmtesten Componisten . . . vom Königl. Domchor in Berlin. 2 vols. Berlin: Schlesinger, [1852-53], 1856.

Osthoff, Helmuth, ed. *German Part Song from the 16th Century to the Present Day.* Cologne: Arno Volk, 1955.

Palestrina, Giovanni Pierluigi da. *Le Opere Complete.* 32 vols. Rome: Fratelli Scalera, 1939-72.

—————. *Missa Papae Marcelli.* Edited by Fr. X. Haberl. Leipzig: Breitkopf & Härtel, 1892. Based on Haberl's edition in *Werke* 11 (1881).

—————. *Pope Marcellus Mass.* Norton Critical Scores. Edited by Lewis Lockwood. New York: Norton, 1975.

Proske, Karl. *Musica Divina.* 8 vols. Regensburg: Friedrich Pustet, 1853-ca.1878.

Schütz, Heinrich. *Sämtliche Werke.* Edited by Philipp Spitta. 16 vols. Leipzig: Breitkopf & Härtel, 1884-94.

—————. *Neue Ausgabe sämtlicher Werke.* Kassel: Bärenreiter, 1955ff.

—————. Stuttgarter Schütz-Ausgabe. Edited by Günter Graulich. 1968ff.

—————. *Drei Psalmen für Doppelchor.* Edited by Franz Wüllner, from the *Psalmen Davids,* 1619. Leipzig & Winterthur: Rieter-Biedermann, 1878. (1. Ach Herr, straf mich nicht in deinem Zorn [SWV 24]. 2. Aus der Tiefe ruf' ich Herr zu Dir [SWV 25]. 3. Singet dem Herrn ein neues Lied [SWV 35].)

Der Schulchor. Edited by Egon Kraus. 6 vols. Mainz: Schott, 1963-67.

Wüllner, Franz, ed. *Chorübungen* III (1880). Munich: Ackermann, 1880.

—————. *Chorübungen der Münchener Musikschule.* Neue Folge [works for five to seven voices]. Munich: Ackermann, 1893-94.

—————. *Chorübungen: 131 A-Cappella Settings from the Renaissance to the Present.* Compiled by Eberhard Schwickerath, 1931; newly edited by Martin Stephani and Reinhard Stephani. Hamburg: Hans Sikorski, 1954.

Appendix 1

Performances of Early Vocal Music Conducted by Brahms[1]

Detmold, 1857-59[2]

Rovetta	Salve Regina
Praetorius	[work unknown]
Handel	*Messiah*
Bach	Cantata 4, "Christ lag in Todesbanden"
Bach	Cantata 21, "Ich hatte viel Bekümmernis"

Hamburg Frauenchor, 1859-62[3]

Bach	duets from "Ein feste Burg" and "Gott der Herr ist Sonn' und Schild"
Byrd	Non nobis Domine
Caldara	Peccavi
Eccard	Übers Gebirg Maria geht
Gallus	Ecce quomodo moritur justus
Handel	Angel chorus, from *Messiah*
Hassler	Mein G'müth ist mir verwirret
Isaac	Innsbruck, ich muss dich lassen
Lotti	Vere languores nostros
Palestrina	Princeps gloriosissime
Palestrina	Gaude Barbara beata

Vienna Singakademie, 1863-64[4]

15 November 1863

Isaac	Innsbruck, ich muss dich lassen
Bach	Cantata 21, "Ich hatte viel Bekümmernis"

6 January 1864

Eccard	Der Christen Triumphlied auf's Osterfest

Schütz	Saul, Saul, was verfolgst du mich?
Gabrieli	Benedictus a 12
Rovetta	Salve Regina
Bach	Cantata 8, "Liebster Gott, wann werd' ich sterben?" (first chorus and final chorale[5])

20 March 1864
Bach   *Christmas Oratorio,* parts 1, 2, 6[6]

Gesellschaft der Musikfreunde, Vienna, 1872-75[7]

10 November 1872
Handel	*Dettingen Te Deum*
Eccard	Übers Gebirg Maria geht
Isaac	Innsbruck, ich muss dich lassen

28 February 1873
Handel   *Saul*

23 March 1873
Bach   Cantata 4, "Christ lag in Todesbanden"

6 and 8 April 1873
Bach   Cantata 8, "Liebster Gott, wann werd' ich sterben?"

9 November 1873
Handel   *Alexander's Feast*

7 December 1873
J.R. Anle	Es ist genug
Bach	Est ist genug
Bach	Cantata 50, "Nun ist das Heil und die Kraft"
Gallus	Ecce quomodo moritur justus

31 March 1874
Handel   *Solomon*

10 January 1875
Bach   Cantata 34, "O ewiges Feuer"

23 March 1875
Bach   *St. Matthew Passion*

Notes to Appendix 1

1. A more detailed list, with information about surviving performance materials and works prepared but not actually performed, is given by Hancock in "Performances."

2. Schramm; also see BW V: 191, 214, 221.

3. Hübbe, p. 66, Drinker, pp. 103-4.

4. *Festschrift der Wiener Singakademie,* pp. 43-44.

5. See above, 175 n. 59.

6. BW VI: 23.

7. Perger and Hirschfeld, pp. 304-5.

Appendix 2

The Brahms Abschriften of Early Music

This list describes the Abschriften which contain primarily complete works of polyphonic early music—Archiv catalog numbers A 130, A 134, A 135, A 136, and A 137. Pieces are arranged alphabetically by composer, and all pages where each is mentioned are cited (italicized page numbers refer to the main discussion). Some modern editions are listed; see also the bibliography.

For the list of the other Brahms Abschriften, see p. 12, and for those which he did not make himself, see pp. 59-60; from the latter group only Forster is included in this appendix.

Ahle, J.R., Es ist genug (A 130, 16: A 136), *27*, 58, 138, 140; 192 n.73
Geistliches Chorlied 1: no. 113
Ammerbach, Wer das Töchterlein haben will; Ich sage ade; Ganz sehr betrübt ist mir mein Herz (A 130, 13-14), 25
[Anon.], Nine sacred continuo Lieder (A 134, 37-38), 48
Arcadelt [attr.], Ave Maria (A 137), *59*, 95
Arthophius, Die Brünnlein die da fliessen (A 134, 41-42), 51
Attaignant, Il me suffit (A 134, 39-40), *49*, 108
Bach, J.S., Es ist genug (A 130, 17; A 136), *27*, 58, 126, 138-40
————, Fugues in F major and G major (A 130, 42), *37*, 126
————, Herrscher über Tod und Leben (A 130, 18-19), 28
————, Prelude quasi Fantasia (A 130, 41) *37*, 126
Bach, W.F., *Deutsche Messe* (copy ordered by Joachim: A 134, 47-62), 53
Bertram, O wy arme Sünders (A 135), *53*, 81, 147, 158
Calvisius, Allein Gott in der Höh' sei Ehr (A 134, 45-46), 52
————, Josef, lieber Josef mein (A 130, 11-12), *24*, 126; 175 n.60
Arion 3: 25 Ed. Lionel S. Benson. London: Laudy, n.d.
Hänssler-Edition (Stuttgart), 1.189
Cesti, *Serenata fatta in Firenze* (A 130, 30-37), *35*, 109, 126
Cherubini, Ora pro nobis (A 130, 45), 38

Clemens non Papa, Psalm 65 (A 130, 13-14), *25*, 88
Reese, *Music in the Renaissance,* p. 358
Corsi, Adoramus te (A 130, 28-29), *34*; 189 n.27
Various editions, mostly not very reliable
Demant, Wer wirdet trösten mich (A 130, 10), *23*, 84, 136
Durante, Misericordias Domini (A 130, 27), *34*, 153
G. Schirmer. Ed. Damrosch. 1968
Eccard, Ich dank dir, lieber Herre (A 134, 41-42), 21, *51*
_____, Übers Gebirg Maria geht (copied by Clara Schumann: A 134, 29-34), *46*, 89, 115, 122, 151
Geistliches Chorlied : no. 4
Erythräus, In dich hab' ich gehoffet, Herr (A 134, 39-40), 49
Forster, *Ein aussbund schöner Teutscher Liedlein* (not copied by Brahms), 11, 21, *60*, 79, 83, 147, 157, 159
Frescobaldi, works from *Toccate d'intavolatura* (A 130, 25-26), *33*, 109
Gabrieli, G., Beata es, virgo Maria (A 130, 1-6), *18*, 41, 99, 100
Opera Omnia 1: 57-61
_____, Benedictus a 12 (A 130, 1-6), *19*, 41, 96, 99, 101, 158
Opera Omnia 4: 124-32; Wüllner *Chorübungen* (1954), no. 24
_____, Jubilate Deo (A 130, 1-6), *19*, 99
Opera Omnia 1: 105-13
_____, O quam suavis (A 130, 1-6), *19*, 99, 101
Opera Omnia 3: 57-65
Gallus [Handl], Ecce quomodo moritur justus (A 130, 16; A 130, 18-19; A 136), 27, *28*, 58, 96, 147
Historical Anthology of Music 1: no. 156
Schering, *Geschichte der Musik in Beispielen,* no. 131
Wüllner, *Chorübungen* (1954), no. 25
Gesius, O Welt, ich muss dich lassen (A 134, 39-40), 49
Gregorian chant, Veni creator spiritus (A 130, 20), 29
Liber Usualis (1964), p. 885
Greitter, Es wollt ein Jäger jagen (A 130, 7-8), *20*, 62, 122; 190 n.52
Antiqua Chorbuch II/1: 50
Das Erbe deutscher Musik, 60 (1969), no. 17
Gesellige Zeit 1: no. 70
Handel, Largo from Trio in B minor (A 130, 40), 37
Werke 27: 102
Handl, Jakob. *See* Gallus
Hassler, Ach Schatz, ich sing' und lache (A 130, 10), *23,* 41, 136
Osthoff, German Part Songs, p. 44
_____, Mein G'müth ist mir verwirret/Herzlich thut mich verlangen (A 134, 39-40, 43-44), 14, 15, 50, *51*, 78, 154, 156, 160
Antiqua Chorbuch II/4: 240
Wüllner, *Chorübungen* (1954), no. 70
Haydn, Andante from Symphony no. 16 (A 130, 43-44), 38

————— [attr.], Chorale St. Antoni (A 130, 43-44), 38

—————, excerpt from *Pastorelle de Noele* (A 130, 40), 37

Heintz, Gar hoch auff einem Berge (A 130, 13-14), 25

Ingegneri, Tenebrae factae sunt (A 134, 35-36), *47*, 112
Motetten alter Meister, p. 24
Der Schulchor 6: 36
Palestrina, *Le Opere Complete* 32

—————, Velum templi scissum est (A 134, 35-36), *47*, 112
Palestrina, *Le Opere Complete* 32

Isaac, Innsbruck (A 134, 39-40, 43-44, 45-46), 49, 50, *51*, 52, 78, 116, 122,
    161, 165
Antique Chorbuch II/ 1: 4
Der Schulchor 1:95
Wüllner, *Chorübungen* (1954), no. 64

Judenkönig, Mag ich Unglück nicht widerstan (A 130, 13-14), 25

Krüger, Herzliebster Jesus (A 134, 37-38), 49

Lasso, Aus meiner Sünden Tiefe (A 130, 9; A 136), *22*, 58, 92
Introiten und Motetten zum Kirchenjahr 1: 124

Lotti, Crucifix a 8 (A 134, 17-19), *44, 153*
Annie Bank edition

—————, Crucifixus a 10 (A 134, 20-24), 44
Wüllner, *Chorübungen* (1954), no. 38a

—————, [Terzett Lamento], 70

—————, Vere languores/Alle die tiefen Qualen (A 130, 28-29), 34

Luther, Jesus Christus, unser Heiland (A 134, 45-46), 52

—————, Komm Gott, Schöpfer, heiliger Geist (A 130, 20), 29

Mattheson, Chor der Juden from *Das Lied des Lammes* (A 130, 38-39), 36
Das Lied des Lammes. Ed. Beekman C. Cannon. Collegium Musicum ser. 2, vol. 3. Madison, Wisc.: A-R Editions, 1971

Palestrina, Crucifixus from *Missa Papae Marcelli* (A 130, 28-29), *34*; 177
    n.97

—————, Haec dies a 6 (A 136), *58*, 141
Le Opere Complete 8: 148-50

—————, Missa Papae Marcelli (A 134, 1-16), 42, *43*, 112, 135; 188 n.25
Le Opere Complete 4: 167-201; see also bibliography

—————, Surge illuminare Hierusalem (A 130, 1-6), *18*, 99; 189 n.28
Le Opere Complete 8: 174-79

—————, Gloria, Pleni sunt coeli; O bone Jesu; Improperia (copied by
    Clara Schumann: A 134, 29-34), *46*, 95, 111; 181 n.150; 188 n.26

————— [attr.], Tenebrae factae sunt; Velum templi scissum est. *See*
    Ingegneri

Praetorius, H., Was mein Gott will (A 134, 39-40), 49

Praetorius, M., In dich hab' ich gehoffet, Herr (A 134, 39-40), 49

—————, In dulci jubilo (A 134, 39-40), 50

————, Maria zart von edler Art (A 130, 15), *26*, 115, 122, 156
Ave Maria, dich lobt Musica, p. 137
————, Nun komm der Heiden Heiland (A 134, 45-46), 52
————, Vom Himmel hoch (A 130, 20), 29
Regnart, Wer wirdet trösten mich (A 130, 10), *23*, 41, 84, 136
Rovetta, Salve Regina (A 134, 25-28), *45*, 92, 153
Scandello, Schein uns, du liebe Sonne (A 130, 9), *22*, 122, 165
Der Schulchor 1: 77
Schein, Veni redemptor gentium (A 134, 45-46), 52
Schütz, Der Herr ist mein Hirt [SWV 398] (A 130, 11-12), *24*, 126
Stuttgarter Schütz-Ausgabe (Hänssler), 13
————, fragments from *Werke* I, II, IX (A 130, 21-24), 4, 11, *29*, 41, 109,
    136, 144, 145, 149, 154
Senfl, Ich stund an einem Morgen (A 130, 7-9), *20*, 62, 122, 156
Das Erbe deutscher Musik 15 (1940): 5
Steurlein, Der Gnadenbrunn thut fliessen (A 134, 41-42), 51
Stoltzer, Entlaubet ist [uns] der Walde (A 130, 7-8), *20*, 62, 122, 165
Antiqua Chorbuch II/1: 33
Das Erbe deutscher Musik 20 (1942), no. 61
Der Schulchor 1: 42
Vetter, Liebster Gott, wann werd' ich sterben? (A 130, 18-19), 28
Vreedman, Ich segge adieu (A 130, 13-14), 25
Walther, Mitten wir in Leben sind (A 134, 45-46), 52
Zirler, Die Sonn' die ist verblichen (A 130, 7-8), *20*, 62, 81, 119, 122, 149;
    184 n. 198
Gesellige Zeit 2: no. 14

Appendix 3

Brahms's Printed Library of Early Music

Italicized page references are to the main discussion of each work. Items which are not now in the Nachlass, and a few which Brahms knew and used but did not own, appear in square brackets.

Appendix 4

Brahms's Choral Works

The list is arranged by opus number, and works without opus number appear at the end. Italicized page references are those for the main discussion of each work. For dates of composition, see Tables 5-7 (pp. 103-8); works which appear only in those tables and are not mentioned elsewhere are not included in this index.

Index

For page references to the Abschriften, the printed books and music in Brahms's library, and Brahms's choral compositions, see Appendices 2, 3, and 4 respectively.